REMEMBER NELSON

REMEMBER NELSON

The Life of Captain Sir William Hoste

TOM POCOCK

'I say he will be a second Nelson'
EMMA HAMILTON, 1798

READERS UNION
Group of Book Clubs
Newton Abbot 1978

This edition was produced in 1978 for sale to its members
only by the proprietors, Readers Union Limited,
PO Box 6, Newton Abbot, Devon, TQ12 2DW.
Full details of membership will gladly be sent on request

Reproduced and printed in Great Britain
by A. Wheaton & Co Limited Exeter
for Readers Union

For Laura

NOTE OF STYLE

Where original or published sources have been directly quoted, the spelling and punctuation is that of the source. All quoted speech or comment within quotation marks is either taken directly from original sources or as quoted in published sources.

CONTENTS

MAPS

ILLUSTRATIONS

Between pages 96 and 97

INTRODUCTION

William Hoste belonged to an England not far removed from that into which I was born; its twin pillars still the Church of England and the Royal Navy. His father and my grandfather, Norfolk clergymen separated in time by only a single lifespan, both lived in a county ruled by great landowning families, where a parson could know his social place to be little above the doctor's, or could join the sporting squires if his personality and purse allowed. He himself might have been described as 'the best sort of naval officer' by my father, who taught his successors history and English at the Royal Naval College, Dartmouth, for many years and understood their strengths and limitations.

Indeed, my father, Guy Pocock, often said that among Lord Nelson's greatest achievements was the setting of standards for the naval officers who, for nearly a century and a half, were the most significant group of professional men anywhere in the world. William Hoste, as the pupil most intimately concerned with his master, was the prototype of these.

The foundation of this book was originally to have been *The Memoirs and Letters of Captain Sir William Hoste*, edited by his widow and published in 1833. An intelligent compilation of extracts from letters, comments from contemporaries and a linking narrative, this was, however, a work of piety for the inspiration of their children. 'I could never teach you to attain that elevation of mind which you ought to possess,' she wrote to them in the note of dedication, 'unless I placed before you the conduct and feelings of your Father, throughout his eventful career. Let these be your guide!' So the resulting portrait was something of a silhouette without much light, shade or colour but abounding with tantalizing hints that urged the biographer to enquire more deeply.

Unpublished material that would add depth and colour I found widely spread at the Public Record Office in London; the National

Maritime Museum, Greenwich; the Nelson Collection at Monmouth; the Holkham Estate Archives in Norfolk; the State Archives at Dubrovnik and Kotor in Yugoslavia, and in a variety of privately-owned collections of manuscripts. Among published sources were the memoirs and biographies of Hoste's contemporaries and histories of the period.

In Norfolk, my thanks are due to Lady Margaret Douglas-Home for her suggestion that I write this book; to the late Earl of Leicester for giving me access to the Archives at Holkham Hall and to Dr W. O. Hassall for guiding me through them; to Mr and Mrs John Garner of Godwick Hall Farm for allowing me to explore the site of the Hostes' old home; and to Mr D. P. Mortlock, the County Librarian and his staff.

Also in Norfolk, I am indebted to others for their advice and encouragement including (in alphabetical order) the Dowager Marchioness of Cholmondeley, Mr John Ellis, the Rev. Llewellyn Fawcett, formerly Rector of Tittleshall; Mrs Gillian Ford; the late Lord Walpole; the Rev. Ernest Wilks, Rector of Longham; and Mr Leslie Winter, landlord of The Lord Nelson inn at Burnham Thorpe.

In London and elsewhere in the United Kingdom I received valuable help from the Trustees and staff of the National Maritime Museum, Greenwich, and, in particular, from Dr Roger Knight; from the staff of the Public Record Office and the Royal United Service Institution Library; from Mr Keith Kissask, Administrative Director of the Nelson Museum, Monmouth; Mr H. A. Hanley, the Buckinghamshire County Archivist; and Mrs John G. McCarthy.

I must also thank Mrs Veronica Bamfield; Mr Desmond Fortescue; Commander John Fremantle, RN; Mr and Mrs Roland Gant; Rear-Admiral D. H. F. Hetherington; Mr Theodore Dixon Hoste; the late Colonel Robert Parker, Miss Ann Parry and Mr Hugh Pocock.

On my visits to Yugoslavia I was greatly helped by Mr R. Maksimović, Cultural Attaché of the Yugoslav Embassy in London; Mr Zvonko Jakopović of the Yugoslav National Tourist Office; Mr Gino Sukno of Dubrovnik; Professor Armando Moreno of Split; Dr Mato Jaksić, who showed me the scars of Hoste's cannon-balls in Dubrovnik; Mr John Bezzina of the Royal Malta Library, Valetta, who helped so generously in the Dubrovnik Archives; the Directors and staff of the State Archives and Maritime Museums at Dubrovnik and Kotor, and the Museums at Perast and Vis; Mr Peter Rosling, then of the British Embassy, Belgrade; and to Sir Fitzroy Maclean, MP, for introductions in Yugoslavia.

On my visits to Italy I was shown help and hospitality by Professor Mario Montuori of the Italian Cultural Institute in London; Mr John Greenwood of the Italian National Tourist Office; Baron Rubin de Cervin of the Museo Storico Navale, Venice; Viscount Bridport; and Mr Frank King of the Ducea di Brontë in Sicily.

Historian friends were as kindly as ever; Mr Brian Fothergill, Lieutenant-Commander Peter Kemp and Professor Christopher Lloyd and the late Mr Oliver Warner with generous guidance; Mr Richard Hough bravely joined my scrambles in Hoste's footsteps over a Dalmatian mountain and Mr David Woodward was a sure guide to the wilder shores of the Austrian Empire.

Just as I was about to start writing, Oliver Warner telephoned with the news that a vast collection of Hoste's private papers was about to be sold by auction at Christie's saleroom in London. These proved to be not only the letters from which his widow had selected extracts for the *Memoirs* but many more, written by him from the age of twelve until the end of his life, together with a large number of documents concerned with his career and private life. Without access to this I would have had to abandon the biography.

Thanks to the generosity of the late Sir William Collins, I offered a joint bid with the National Maritime Museum for the collection that was half as much again as the auctioneers' maximum estimate. However, at the sale we were easily outbid by stamp dealers, whose principal interest was in the franking on the backs of the folded letters. Luckily, the successful bidder was Mr J. A. L. Franks of Fleet Street and he and his son, Graham, responded to my request for access to the papers with sympathy and unbounded generosity. They first loaned the entire collection to the National Maritime Museum so that it could be recorded on microfilm and presented the Museum with Hoste's dramatic letter about the siege of Cattaro. They then not only allowed me complete and unrestricted access to the original documents but gave me many of them and allowed me to buy others at peppercorn prices; these are now at the National Maritime Museum. The most important letters concerning Nelson were purchased by our American benefactress Mrs Lily McCarthy for her magnificent collection of Nelsoniana, which she has presented to the Royal Navy, and papers relating to Hoste's command of the Royal yacht are now in the Royal Archives at Windsor Castle.

None of this could have been undertaken without the permission and encouragement of Mr Charles Wintour, then Editor of the *Evening Standard*, and the freedom of movement that I, as the travel editor of that newspaper, enjoyed. I have been lucky in having as my editor at Collins, Mr Richard Ollard, who is not only a wise friend but a brilliant historian. To my wife, Penny, I am again grateful for her pertinent and constructive criticism.

Tom Pocock,
Burnham Overy Staithe,
Norfolk

PROLOGUE

A blue light flaring in the darkness and the thump of two signal guns fired in quick succession was the warning for which Captain William Hoste had longed. It meant that an enemy was nearby, but sometimes this had proved to be only fishing-boats or another British warship. This time, as before, nerve and muscle stiffened in fierce anticipation.

It was three o'clock on a dark and windy morning and, as his frigate beat into the north-westerly breeze, Hoste had ordered the main-sail to be set, his eyes straining for sight of the other ships under his command. Now came the signal for an enemy to windward; this was at once acknowledged with another blue light. Again the warning – the two reports of guns and the flare – was seen and heard and again answered.

Eyes strained into the night but it was not for two hours that the first dim daylight lit what lay ahead. First it was the masts and sails of the British frigate that had made the signals. Then, faintly at first, Hoste could see beyond her the towering shapes of ships. It was the enemy, this time.

The squadron he had long hoped to fight was, Hoste knew, at least as strong as his own. But as the masts, yards and sails of individual ships became gradually more distinct and detached from one another, he could see that the enemy was stronger than any he had ever imagined in these waters. In an evenly-matched fight, the British would have the advantage of more experienced seamanship and more efficient gunnery, whereas the French ships would be more strongly manned so that they would hope a decision by boarding and hand-to-hand combat might go to them. This, he now saw, would not be their only advantage. As he identified each enemy ship, recognizing some, not others, and judged the weight of each broadside, it became apparent that he would not have to fight a squadron that was slightly stronger than his own but one that was more than double his strength.

This was the moment for which eighteen years of Hoste's youth and manhood had been in preparation. The first twelve of those years had been spent under the guidance of Lord Nelson. Even now, William Hoste had not overcome the personal grief and professional frustration that the action off Cape Trafalgar had brought upon him. The ship he now commanded was a constant reminder of his loss because, the finest frigate under Nelson's command and one that had flown his own flag, she had been, as he would put it, 'the last gift of that excellent man'.

The enemy was still standing towards him and it was clear that they, having the advantage of the wind, were ready to fight this time. Hoste had cleared for action and had heard the drums beat to quarters in his other ships. He had had the frigate's port-lids opened, the guns loaded with double shot and run out, their crews closed up. The opposing squadrons were now two miles apart and approaching each other under full sail.

Nelson must have felt as exalted before Trafalgar as he felt now. All his years at sea, Hoste had tried to emulate his hero and now, for the first time, he would be able to do so in a general action even if it were not between great fleets of ships of the line. Before Nelson's last battle he had sent a shock of elation through his ships with the signal that had since become the war-cry of the nation: 'England expects that every man will do his duty.'

How could Hoste hope to inspire his own squadron with an exhortation that would summon up the blood as that had done? Nelson's signal had been a spontaneous impulse from his genius for command, something that could never be imitated. If only some spark of that could ignite his own imagination to find such words for the men whose eyes would be on the signal halyards of his ship.

As the two squadrons closed and would be within extreme range of each other's guns in a matter of minutes, the spark came. Captain Hoste turned to his signal midshipman and ordered him to make an immediate signal to the squadron.

It was: 'REMEMBER NELSON.'

I

FAREWELL TO GODWICK

Britain be awed! the dread alarm is given,
Action's bold shout assails the vault of heaven!
The trembling earth returns the mighty roar,
And boding echoes ring along the shore . . .

Such rhetoric was superfluous during the first week of 1793 because the pages of the *Norwich Mercury*, in which it appeared, had for months past been publishing news more ominous than any in living English memory, that found its echo in a mounting sense of alarm. These echoes rang as far as the shore of Norfolk, the eastern county that had always considered itself, geographically and temperamentally, apart from the rest of England. The newspapers had often printed news of foreign wars and disasters and of political upheaval in London, but now the implications reached every market-town and hamlet, hall and parsonage, farm and ale-house.

News of the revolutionary convulsions in France and the consequent reactions, both in favour and in fear, in London and the county towns was published each Saturday in the *Norwich Mercury* and the *Norfolk Chronicle* and by evening had spread across the county from the heaths of Breckland in the south to the salt-marshes of the north, from the delta of the Wash in the west to the lagoons of the Broads in the east. Nowhere in the county can the news of distant violence have been read with more eagerness than in two village parsonages so remote that for most of the year, as one of the parsons wrote, 'all is Hush at High noon as at Midnight'.

That had been a description of winter at Burnham Thorpe, two miles from the northern coast of Norfolk, by its rector, Edmund Nelson, but it would have been as true of Tittleshall, sixteen miles to the south, where Dixon Hoste was the incumbent. The two clergymen, both Norfolkmen by birth and comparatively near neighbours all their lives, first met at this time and the coming together of their interests and their families was directly due to the news from Paris.

Both men were concerned with the possible effect of this news upon the future of one of their sons and, subsequently, upon the fortunes of their families. If the political crisis boiled over into war, both sons could expect active and perhaps profitable employment at sea with the Royal Navy. For Parson Nelson's son, Horatio, it would be the longed-for return to the profession he loved after five years in temporary retirement on half-pay. For Parson Hoste's son, William, still a child, it might be the beginning of a career that could bring riches to his family. In these hopes, the latter depended upon the former. If the unemployed naval officer, aged thirty-four, took a liking to the schoolboy of twelve, and Captain Nelson returned to sea, he might be persuaded to take the lad with him. In time of war, the naval officer, whatever his age, rank and experience, could dream not only of glory but of fortunes in prize-money from the capture of enemy ships.

This shared interest alone brought together the Nelsons and the Hostes, who otherwise would have had little in common beyond the ecclesiastical calling. Edmund Nelson and Dixon Hoste had both graduated from Cambridge University – the former from Caius College, the latter from Trinity Hall – but each belonged to a class of clergy that enjoyed totally differing tastes. At heart, Edmund Nelson was a gentle, whimsical scholar; Dixon Hoste, the sporting squire.

The Nelsons were of sturdy East Anglian stock in which strains of gentry and tradesmen had come together in the firm, resilient English middle class. Edmund's father had been educated at Eton College and at Cambridge before becoming rector of Hilborough in Norfolk – thirty miles to the south of Burnham Thorpe – where his son succeeded him for a time, while his mother had been the daughter of a prosperous Cambridge baker. Edmund himself had married Catherine Suckling, a clergyman's daughter, whose great-uncle had been Sir Robert Walpole, the dominant British statesman of the first half of the century.

The Nelsons had eleven children and, of the three who died in infancy, one was named Horatio after Lord Walpole of Wolterton, a distant cousin, in whose honour another boy – the third surviving son – was also given the name, although known by his father as Horace. It was this Horatio, born in 1758, who had begun his naval career at the age of twelve, being taken to sea by his maternal uncle, Captain Maurice Suckling, three years after his mother had died. The loss of his adored mother followed by the exchange of a peaceful and loving home for the rough practicalities of a ship of the line was a sequence of experience that left Horatio Nelson with a lifelong vulnerability. His subsequent career had been active – it had included a scientific expedition to the Arctic and amphibious warfare in Nicaragua – but it had ended, temporarily at least, with the command of a frigate in the West Indies. Now, a small, neatly-built man with a winning warmth and vivacity, he was a restless element in the otherwise placid family life at Burnham Thorpe.

As a widower, Edmund Nelson's interests were his family, his ministry, the Classics and his garden. His children's prospects were remote from those of their distant, lordly cousins; the eldest daughter had, for a time, to be apprenticed to a milliner at Bath and the youngest son, after being apprenticed to a Suffolk draper, kept a small grocery shop in the Norfolk village of North Elmham. Hopes of prosperity had to rely upon a successful career at sea for Horace.

The Nelsons lived modestly at the parsonage, built like a Norfolk farmhouse with a steeply-pitched roof of red pantiles and dignified by an added wing from which gabled Venetian windows overlooked the pretty garden and the little river Burn which ran, clear and reedy, for more than half a mile through the straggling village of Burnham Thorpe to the church of All Saints. This garden with its pond and ornamental trees and what he called the 'Spring entertainment of rose and hyacinth' gave the parson much pleasure but, with characteristic unselfishness, he was to hand over both house and garden to his sailor son, his wife, Fanny, and her son by her first marriage, Josiah Nisbet, so that they could have a home of their own during his enforced stay 'on the beach'. Edmund Nelson himself moved to a cottage close to his other church at Burnham Ulph, a mile over the low chalk downs from Burnham Thorpe and part of a cluster of hamlets that together formed the handsome village of Burnham Market.

When the newspapers reached Burnham Market on Saturday afternoons Parson Nelson did not himself read them. One of his religious affectations was the refusal to give his God's gift of eyesight, however failing, the artificial aid of spectacles and so he had to confess, 'I am quite shutt out from politicks, having no news-reading Eyes'. Generally this was no great hardship for he was not a political man and would describe the elections, which could throw the county into a whirl of excited controversy, as a 'noisy nonsense'. But he was eager for news that might affect his son's professional prospects and for this he depended upon Horace and his avid reading of the newspapers.

Captain Nelson, frustrated in his repeated attempts at persuading the Admiralty to give him employment, awaited the arrival of the Norwich coach and its bundles of newspapers with impatience.

He read the news of the imprisonment and trial of King Louis XVI in Paris and, of more immediate importance to him, the preparations for war at the Admiralty. While the snow still lay thick on Norfolk fields he would have read in the *Norwich Mercury*: 'Last night a Board of Admiralty was held at the Admiralty Office, Charing Cross, which did not break up before ten o'clock; when several officers attended and received their commissions . . .'

As more officers were recalled and more ships made ready for service at sea, Captain Nelson, still undeterred by five years of frustra-

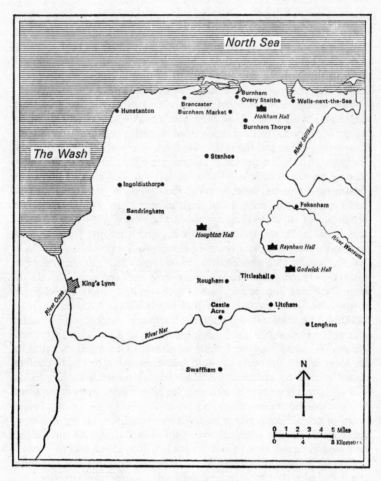

North Sea

The Wash

Hunstanton

Brancaster
Burnham Market

Burnham
Overy Staithe

Wells-next-the-Sea

Holkham Hall

Burnham Thorpe

Stanhoe

River Stiffkey

Ingoldisthorpe

Fakenham

Sandringham

River Wensum

Houghton Hall

Raynham Hall

Godwick Hall

King's Lynn

Rougham

Tittleshall

River Ouse

Castle
Acre

Litcham

River Nar

Longham

Swaffham

N

0 1 2 3 4 5 Miles
0   4   8 Kilometres

WEST NORFOLK

tion, decided upon another visit to London in the hope of being, at last, given a ship – even if she was, as he used to joke, only a cockle-boat.

His journey to London took him south over the rolling farmland of High Norfolk, down into the valley of the river Wensum at Faken-ham and up again on to chalk that would swell to about two hundred feet above the level of the sea and seemed high above the East Anglian levels. Here the London road passed a few miles to the west of Tittleshall, where that other parson's family, the Hostes, followed the news with equal eagerness and as avidly as they followed the hounds.

Parson Hoste, like Edmund Nelson, lived some distance from his church, St Mary's. His parsonage lay half a mile across the fields on the site of the medieval village of Godwick, which had been abandoned during a plague and was now no more than the ruined tower of All Saints' church and the humps and ridges of turf that covered the foundations of its houses. The house itself, Godwick Hall, was a small Tudor manor standing against a background of dark woods, facing west across the uneven fields around the desolate church tower and down a long avenue of wind-stunted oaks to the lower ground where Tittleshall and its little grey church huddled among tall, billowing trees. It was E-shaped and built of red brick patterned with dark brick; its windows were mullioned and its porch stood to the height of the three storeys. Above the front door was inscribed the date of 1586 when the house had been completed by a John Drury of Suffolk, who sold it four years later to Sir Edward Coke, the Lord Chief Justice of England, in whose family it remained and from whom it had now been leased by the Hostes.

Unlike the parsonage at Burnham Thorpe, this was recognizably a gentleman's house with a drawing-room rather than a parlour and the brick piers at the gates of the walled garden surmounted by large stone balls in the manner of elegant country house decoration. Set apart from the house were farm buildings and a massive, red-brick granary, for the glebe-land that went with the living was considerably more than the thirty acres farmed by Parson Nelson.

Both families found pleasure in field sports on their own and their neighbours' land. But while Horatio Nelson enjoyed the occasional coursing of the big wild hares with fast hounds and lurchers across the stubble he never took to the county's principal sport of shooting. He was reputed to carry his gun at full-cock and fire at partridges from the hip and his father wrote that he found 'an Enemye floating Game is a better Mark'. The Hostes, on the other hand, were brought up with horses and gun-dogs and, were never happier than when out shooting or fox-hunting and their presents at Christmas of dozens of brace of game-birds to their friends were considered generous even in comparison with those of the rich landowners.

Just as Edmund Nelson was typical of the scholarly clerics, who contributed much to English literature and education at that time, quietly enjoying a life of good works, pious contemplation and simple bodily comforts, so Dixon Hoste was a strapping example of the sporting parson, impatient to throw off his surplice and spring into the saddle, a robust figure lending itself to caricature by such cynical pencils as Thomas Rowlandson's.

Dixon Hoste seemed, and indeed was, a typical Englishman of his class and time but the roots of his family were Flemish. His ancestors of the sixteenth century and before had prospered as merchants and burghers in Bruges and Middelburg. A Jacques Hoste – or Hoost – had been chief magistrate of the latter city but had had to make his escape when, during the Spanish occupation of the Netherlands, the Duke of Alva began his savage repression of the Protestants. One of his sisters, who remained at home, was burned at the stake for her religion and her sombre portrait in a black dress, starched ruff and cap and holding her Bible, was treasured by her family and eventually came to England – together with the Bible itself – to be revered long after her Christian name had been forgotten.

Escaping across the North Sea by privateer, Jacques Hoste and his wife Barbara, the daughter of a Flemish notable named Theoderick Hendricks, reached London in the year 1569. More fortunate than the many thousands of refugees who arrived with nothing more than their various skills and knowledge of their trades to sustain them, Hoste already had friends and commercial links in London, where he decided to settle. Before long he had taken English nationality, and been granted a pair of wings to decorate his crest and coat of arms to commemorate his flight from danger.

His son, Theoderick, married a Jane Desmastres, the daughter of a rich merchant, and became politically active as a Puritan during the Civil War and Commonwealth. Their son, James, who also married the daughter of a London merchant, Elizabeth Sley, decided towards the end of the seventeenth century to settle his family in Norfolk. Several years after the move he bought a fine country house, Sandringham Hall, to the north-east of King's Lynn and close to the eastern shore of the Wash, and settled down to the life of a country gentleman.

Norfolk has always been suspicious of strangers but for those with Dutch connections it was easier than for most. There had long been trade and passenger traffic between East Anglia and the Low Countries and, at the time Jacques Hoste had fled to London, several thousand other refugees had arrived in Norfolk. Many of these were craftsmen and three particular skills which they practised were of the highest value in their new surroundings. These were weaving, horticulture and the draining and reclamation of land. Much of the trade across the North Sea had been the carrying of Norfolk wool to the looms of Flanders and of Flemish cloth back to Norfolk and it was of obvious value that the wool could now be woven by Flemings working in Norwich. The Dutch were already famous in England as gardeners and, in particular, for their development of the tulip and, on arrival in Norfolk, the bulb-growers found that the flat fen-country in the south-west of the county was ideal for their purposes. These fens had, in fact, been drained by Dutch engineers and their feats of reclamation were continued around the coast, embanking and draining salt-marshes to produce, eventually, rich grazing for sheep and cattle.

Their son, also James, married as successfully in Norfolk as his father and grandfather had in London. His first wife was Elizabeth Walpole, daughter of Sir Edward Walpole of Houghton Hall, a cousin of Sir Robert Walpole, the Whig statesman. This marriage brought him no children but established aristocratic and political connections and, when his wife died young, he married another girl of a well-established English family, Anne Burleigh, who bore him four children.

Of these, one son died young; another, James, married into a Norfolk family, the Hamonds of Swaffham, and inherited the Sandringham estate; William became a Parson; the daughter, Anne, married into the Nelthorpe family of Lynford Hall. The second son, Theodore, who was to father Dixon Hoste, married Mary Dixon Helmore of Clenchwarton, also in Norfolk, and settled at Ingoldisthorpe Hall near Sandringham.

Dixon Hoste's elder brother died in childhood so he became the heir to the fine house on the edge of the low escarpment where the fields of the north Norfolk plateau fall away to the salt-marshes of the Wash. His younger brother, William, followed the family tradition of marrying into prosperity, his choice being Anne Glover of Barwick House at Stanhoe, a few miles to the south-west of Burnham Thorpe.

Dixon himself, on coming down from Cambridge, married Margaret Stanforth, whose family were well established at Salthouse on the coast and she bore him six sons and four daughters. To the maintenance of a large family, a fine house and a taste for field sports was added the expense of social and political ambitions. Dixon Hoste was a gregarious man and his good looks and charm readily made friends among the minor gentry of Norfolk who were his social equals in the stratified society of his time. To move upward into aristocratic society needed not only wealth, which he did not possess in necessary measure, but one of two avenues of approach. One was marriage into a great county family, but his grandfather's marriage to Elizabeth Walpole was too remote to be of much social advantage as was the Nelsons' connection with another branch of the Walpoles.

The other avenue was that of politics, in particular Whig politics. Since the Glorious Revolution of 1688, the powerful county families had, in general, supported Whig policies, which began as a movement to prevent a Roman Catholic monarch from returning to the throne and developed as a political party. In Norfolk the Whigs were led by the county dynasties such as the Walpoles, the Townshends and the Cokes. Their opponents, the Tories, were more conservative and their ambitions were more concerned with trade.

Since the death of Sir Robert Walpole, the dominating figure – politically and socially – that was emerging was that of the forceful Thomas William Coke of Holkham. As one of the two Members of Parliament for the county, who were of more significance than the twelve Members representing the five urban boroughs in Norfolk, Coke was also a power at Westminster. He had opposed the war to suppress the American Revolution and, at first, regarded the French Revolution as the birth agonies of a more just society. He had even confessed, 'Every night during the American War did I drink the health of George Washington as the greatest man on earth.'

His was a rich inheritance. His great-uncle, the Earl of Leicester, had been a man of taste as well as wealth and his life's work had been the construction of a great house, park and agricultural estates which were, however, to become more closely associated with his great-nephew. The Earl had moved the seat of the Coke family from God-wick Hall, which they continued to use as a hunting lodge, to the hamlet of Holkham on the desolate northern coast of Norfolk. Here he determined to build the most magnificent mansion in Norfolk, even more splendid than that being built for the Walpoles at Houghton. As Holkham Hall slowly grew over three decades from 1734, it assumed a strange, uneasy character. Vast as it was, it only stood higher than two storeys where four square turrets rose above the *piano nobile* in the main block and the windows seemed meagre for its bulk so that the house appeared to crouch among the young trees of its parkland, narrowing its eyes against the northerly wind. Bleak as it looked from without, within all was of such opulence that the state apartments seemed to demand a Mediterranean sun to blaze on their marble, gilding and brocades. While much of Holkham was the seat of a landed country gentleman and the headquarters of spreading agricultural estates, within it lay the extravagance and spirit of an Italian *palazzo*.

So it was that when Lord Leicester joined his ancestors in the Cokes' mausoleum at Tittleshall, across the fields from their old home at Godwick Hall, Holkham and all that lay within and around it passed to his sister's son and so to his heir, Thomas William Coke.

When he inherited in 1776, Thomas Coke was aged twenty-four and already a man of wide interests matched by vigour and intelligence. On leaving Eton he had embarked on the Grand Tour and, on these travels had enlarged the Holkham collections (it is a tradition that the evergreen ilex oaks that flourish in the park were grown from the foliage in which statuary was packed in Italy for shipment to Norfolk).

He took his father's place in representing the county at Westminster and was quickly recognized as a politician with prospects by his fellow-Whigs. He made a serious study of agriculture, inviting the advice of neighbouring farmers whom he entertained at Holkham with as much warmth as other great landowners would welc me artists, architects or writers to enjoy their hospitality.

To bask in the sun of Holkham patronage was the ambition of Dixon Hoste of Ingoldisthorpe and with his social connections across the county and his love of sport there can have been no difficulty in making the first approaches. Dixon Hoste was two years older than Coke and, while his knowledge of farming was not enough to earn him a place at one of the agricultural gatherings at Holkham, there were other services that he could offer.

Heavily involved in politics, Coke was not a political man by nature and had originally entered Parliament with reluctance. Hoste, on the other hand, was a natural politician: ambitious, sociable and something of a schemer. He was, above all, an enthusiast and, while this would be superfluous in Coke's social and agricultural lives, it was of use in the political, where enthusiasm combined with a talent for planning, if not plotting, could be of the utmost value in promoting the Whig interest.

But, as Dixon Hoste was to discover, a political life, even on the fringes of a political campaign, was expensive. Coke's electors were all countrymen living outside the five urban boroughs and numbered only about seven thousand, being those freeholders whose property was valued at more than forty shillings a year. Thus many of the most substantial farmers and merchants were, because they were leaseholders from such as himself, without a vote. Those who were enfranchised had to make the journey to Norwich to record their vote which was then published in the Poll Book in which it could be seen how every elector in Norfolk had chosen. Thus it was natural that many, without a passionate interest in party politics and not wishing to offend a powerful Whig or Tory neighbour, might be reluctant to commit themselves publicly, let alone go to the expense of making the journey to Norwich.

So political henchmen, such as Dixon Hoste, had the important and continuing task of recruiting Whig supporters by entertaining, if not actually bribing, neighbouring freeholders and of paying the expenses of the election jaunt to Norwich and entertaining them further while they were there. A man of ambition would consider such expense as an investment.

Dixon Hoste's campaigning for Coke and the Whigs in west Norfolk reached a point of crisis in 1784. The coalition government in which

Coke's friend Charles James Fox had joined with his old opponent Lord North had fallen and a general election had been called. Coke had fought one election – in 1780 – since entering Parliament and his popularity was such that it seemed that the seat must be his for life. But, four years later, the Whigs were divided, Coke found himself widely out of favour as a follower of the fallen Fox and assailed by some of those he counted as friends and political supporters.

The election was as fierce as any within memory both between Whigs and Tories and between Whigs and Whigs. Dixon Hoste remained loyal to Coke and played his part in persuading the electors to accept their hospitality in Norwich on polling-day. The expenses for both parties were enormous. While the Tories rented forty houses in Norwich for the accommodation of their supporters, the Whigs took fifty-five. Coke himself paid £746 to Norwich innkeepers, spent £115 on Whig cockades and another £160 for sedan chairs, watchmen, messengers and tellers at the polls.

Despite all this, the divisions within the Whig party became acrimonious. A malicious rumour was spread that Coke was planning to accept a peerage, the re-created Earldom of Leicester, as a bribe from William Pitt to withdraw his support from Fox. So vicious did the quarrelling become and so potentially disastrous for the Whigs that, two days before polling-day, Coke withdrew from the contest.

For Coke this was only a temporary, if expensive, political set-back but for Dixon Hoste it was ruinous. Extravagant by nature, his unstinting support for Coke in the heady days of the election campaign had brought financial ruin and it was clear that he could no longer afford to maintain his comfortable style of living at Ingoldisthorpe Hall. The house and estate would have to be sold.

For a gentleman without capital or employment there were two principal means of attaining a life of respectable prosperity and these were offered by the twin pillars of English society: the Royal Navy and the Church of England. But to become a naval officer with hopes of promotion and prize-money meant beginning that career as a boy and Dixon Hoste was now aged thirty-four. But he had graduated from Cambridge and there was no reason why he should not take Holy orders, supposing that some patron would nominate him for a living.

The patron that he sought was to be the grateful Thomas Coke. For the past forty-two years his uncle William Hoste had been rector of Tittleshall, where the living was in the gift of the Cokes, for nearby stood Godwick Hall which was still a favourite hunting lodge. Recently, the elderly Parson Hoste had died. Now this living, together with Godwick Hall as a parsonage and its adjoining farm at an annual rent of £112.12s., was offered to Dixon Hoste. There were no difficult formalities in the way of his ordination and, that same year, the Reverend Dixon Hoste moved his family to Godwick Hall and preached his first sermon in the fourteenth-century church of St Mary the Virgin at Tittleshall.

The gift of this living was a particular honour because, standing against the north wall of the chancel, was the large red-brick mausoleum wherein lay the coffins of the Cokes, and the church itself, while much like many another Norfolk parish church in appearance, was ornamented within by their elegant and grandiose monuments. Dixon Hoste can only have felt that this was a church worthy of a gentleman-parson of his standing.

The Hoste family settled happily at Godwick Hall, loving its ancient cosiness and massive oak beams. The woods and fields that surrounded the house were full of game and now that Holkham was less than two hours' ride away, instead of being distant and awe-inspiring, the aspirations of Dixon Hoste seemed to have found fulfilment. As a parson he could still engage in politics and there was another prize to be sought: a bishopric.

But just as politics had been ruinously expensive, so was keeping up appearances in company with those he called familiarly 'the Holk-hamites'. To visit Holkham one had to be well-mounted and it was gratifying to be able to offer the loan of a horse to a fellow-guest. Once, usefully, this was the distinguished Whig politician William Windham, who for many years shared the representation of the county in Parliament, when he wanted to ride over to Raynham Hall to visit the Townshends.

Parson Hoste could also sing for his supper and not only in church. He had the knack of composing jaunty and flattering ballads to meet any occasion and at the boisterous hunt breakfasts at Holkham would lead the singing of his *A Song of Mr Coke's Hunt*, praising his patron as

> *Attentive and civil till Reynard is found,*
> *Then hears nor sees ought but the head leading hound.*

In keeping with his style of life, Hoste sent his eldest son, Theodore Dixon Hoste, to school at Rugby, from which he won a scholarship to Trinity College, Cambridge, with the aim of following his father into the Church. Such education proved too expensive and so the second son, William, born on 26th August, 1780, was sent to boarding school at King's Lynn at the age of seven and later moved to the Paston School at North Walsham, where Horatio Nelson had been educated.

By 1792, the Hoste family's expenditure was such that there was worry about the future prospects of William and his younger brothers

George and James. At the age of twelve, William expressed no interest in any particular calling, his enthusiasm being taken up in the family passion for hunting, shooting, riding and skating on the frozen pond by Tittleshall church. But he was a cheerful, adaptable child and seemed quite ready to accept whatever future was chosen for him by the parents to whom he was devoted.

As Dixon Hoste read the newspapers at the turbulent close of 1792, it seemed likely that one form of employment would soon be available and this was fighting. In time of peace, the naval officer could manage on his modest but regular pay – and even on half-pay when unemployed – and enjoyed a social status that kept his position well up in the middle class and could even help him into the halls of the aristocracy. But in time of war, the chance of making a fortune was always present. As an incentive to zeal, the regulations covering the distribution of prize-money – the proceeds of the sale of enemy ships and cargoes captured on the high seas and sent into British ports under prize crews – were generous. Every member of a ship's company would benefit according to rank, the captain's share being nearly half the total so that, with luck and skill, the captain of a frigate in his early twenties could make his family's fortune within the hour. Occasionally, such a share could amount to tens of thousands of pounds.

Thus, despite its dangers and hardships, a naval career was sought for many a son of an impoverished gentlemen. The procedure for the launching of this was clear and required, above all, 'interest', the patronage of some prominent individual with influence at the Admiralty or in the Fleet. The most usual method of entry was for a boy to be taken to sea by the captain of a warship – as Horatio Nelson had been by his uncle at the age of twelve – and rated as 'captain's servant'. It was then in the captain's power to rate the boy as a midshipman, but he only attained commissioned rank by passing the examination for promotion to lieutenant and this he could only take after six years at sea, two of them as a midshipman. He might spend the remainder of his career as a lieutenant but his aim was that, after becoming a commander and a captain, he would be confirmed as a 'post captain', which would mean that he would rise automatically in seniority so that, if he survived, his progress through the flag ranks would follow and eventually, without further effort on his part, he could become the senior admiral in the Royal Navy.

Although 'interest' was essential there was one way by which the process of promotion could be hastened and it took the form of widely-accepted cheating. A boy destined for a naval career could, through influence or bribery, be entered on a ship's muster-book at an absurdly early age – long before he went to sea – so that the time he was said to have served as a captain's servant could date from that time.

While William was a baby, his parents had discussed the possibility of sending him to sea at the age of twelve and, after taking advice, managed to have his name entered in the books of a ship of the line, the *Europa*, as a captain's servant when he was five years old.

This was the career Dixon Hoste had in mind for his second son. It naturally followed that Coke, as his patron, would be asked to make the necessary introduction to a naval officer of suitable rank. But although Norfolk had produced some notable sea-officers at the turn of the last century, the scope for making useful introductions within the county was now small. Indeed, the name that came to Coke's mind was that of a neighbour he hardly knew, a Captain Nelson.

The Parsonage House at Burnham Thorpe lay only two miles from Holkham Hall but, although Captain Nelson had lived there for the past five years, Coke only recalled one conversation with him. That had been when Nelson had called upon him soon after his return from sea to ask for help, in his capacity as a county magistrate, with the formalities of drawing naval half-pay while unemployed. The young captain had made no lasting impression on that occasion and the acquaintance had not been continued. In any case there was a political division between the Cokes and the Nelsons for the latter were Tories.

While Coke and his Whigs had been admiring George Washington, Nelson had been waging the American War with all his zeal and, shortly before his return to England, had aroused the indignation of his own mercantile countrymen in the West Indies by the vigour with which he tried to ensure that American merchant ships should no longer enjoy their former trading rights in British ports.

Since then, events in the world and in the county had brought them, or, rather, their attitudes closer together. Coke, who had resumed his seat in Parliament at the General Election of 1790, may have deplored the talk of war with Revolutionary France, while Captain Nelson hoped for it, not only because it would give him employment, but because he never forgot that his mother had 'hated the French'. However, when the security of the stable English society they both revered was threatened both men could show a fierce patriotism.

This had now happened and the threat was not only, as hitherto, from without, but from within. The principles that had inspired the political reformists in France had been welcomed not only by Whig intellectuals but by the 'Levellers', who were seen as revolutionary agitators bent upon stirring the peasantry into discontent. No county was more aware of such dangers than Norfolk, with its long history of dissent, where the memory of Kett's peasant revolt against the landlords' enclosures and its savage repression was still fresh after more than two centuries. It seemed appropriate that Thomas Paine, who had spoken so effectively for the American Revolution and now for the French and whose recently-published book *The Rights of Man* was regarded as dangerously subversive, should be a Norfolkman from Thetford.

Then, in the August of 1792, the attack on the Tuileries by the Paris mob, the massacre of the Swiss guards and the imprisonment of the royal family had sent a shock across the Channel. From that time, each sign of political unrest in England seemed an ominous echo of Paris and alarm became extreme when, early in December, news arrived of the trial of King Louis XVI for his life.

Something like panic ensued in England, men of the middle and upper classes forming themselves into Patriotic Associations. At Yarmouth in Norfolk was recruited 'the Association for the Preserving of Liberty and Property against Republicans and Levellers', the *Norwich Mercury* reporting that this had been necessary because 'clubs have been established, pamphlets and papers industriously distributed to inflame the minds of the misguided multitude to excite the phrenzy of revolution and to involve the country in confusion and misery'.

Even Nelson became alarmed. Hearing that the Norfolk magistrates – including Coke, the Marquess Townshend and Lord Walpole – had been summoned to discuss measures to meet what the newspaper described as 'seditious writings and illegal associations and conspiracies for exciting tumult and riot within this county', he felt that even more urgent action was necessary and wrote a long letter of warning to the Duke of Clarence – the future King William IV – whom he had met at New York some years previously.

After urging that strong measures be taken – 'take away the licences from those public-houses who allow of improper Societies meeting at them, and . . . take up those incendiaries who go from ale-house to ale-house advising the poor people to pay no taxes, etc.' – he showed remarkable insight into some of the reasons for unrest.

'That the poor labourer should have been seduced by promises and hopes of better times, your Royal Highness will not wonder at, when I assure you they are really in want of everything to make life comfortable,' he wrote. 'Part of their wants, perhaps, were unavoidable from the dearness of every article of life; but much more have arose from the neglect of the Country Gentlemen . . .'

Stronger action was taken and, a few days later, two-thirds of the militia was mobilized, the *Norwich Mercury* reporting that 'the Norfolk Militia have shown uncommon zeal in the cause of their County, King and Constitution by their readiness in joining their regiments at Lynn and Yarmouth'. For Nelson, the news that even neighbours, who had never heard a shot fired at anything but game-birds, were putting on uniforms added an edge of anguish to his frustration as his own pleas for employment were ignored.

But the tide was set for war and soon enough it was Captain Nelson's turn to be called. During the first week of the new year he was in London again but this time his visit to the waiting-room at the Admiralty was not fruitless and he was summoned by the First Lord of the Admiralty, Lord Chatham, who, after apologies for the delay in offering employment, gave him command of a ship of the line. 'After clouds come sunshine,' he wrote to Fanny. 'The Admiralty so smile upon me that really I am as much surprised as when they frowned.'

His ship was not to be a third-rate mounting seventy-four guns – 'a seventy-four' such as made up most of the Fleet's battle-line – but a slightly smaller ship mounting only sixty-four, the *Agamemnon*, and Chatham had promised that he could shift to a more powerful ship as soon as one became available.

Making a last visit to Burnham Thorpe, Nelson found that news of his command had spread and that country gentlemen – Coke among them – were seeking his favour, hoping that he would take some promising lad to sea as a 'captain's servant'. One of these was to be his own stepson, Josiah Nisbet; another was William Bolton, the son of his sister Susannah's brother-in-law, a parson. Two other Norfolk clergymen sent sons to sea with him. Two were the sons of a Parson Weatherhead; one of them, John, showing immediate promise as a potential officer. The other was to be William Hoste, still more than half a year short of his thirteenth birthday.

The introduction had been arranged by Coke and it seems that the newly-confident Captain Nelson not only took to the boy but found his father, whom he had not hitherto met, an attractive and sophisticated man of the world with whom he would have pleasure in corresponding. But there would be no place for so young a child on board his ship until she was ready for sea so, assuring Dixon Hoste that he would write to him with instructions for his son to join the *Agamemnon* in due course, Nelson left Burnham Thorpe for the last time on 4 February.

After five years in semi-retirement, events now moved fast. Nelson had been given his command on 6th January, his commission was signed by the Lords of the Admiralty on the 11th and he formally commissioned the *Agamemnon*, still laid up in reserve and without masts, on 7th February. Meanwhile, the *Norwich Mercury* published a report from Paris dated 22nd January that, 'The unfortunate LOUIS is no more! He was beheaded yesterday morning in the Place de Louis Quinze. He died with the most heroic fortitude.' Then, on 1st February, Revolutionary France, having already halted the armies of Prussia and

Austria that had attempted to halt the destruction of the royal family, declared war on Britain and Holland.

At Chatham, Nelson, accompanied by his stepson, supervised the stepping of the *Agamemnon*'s masts, her rigging and victualling, ignoring gales and rain squalls, intent only on making his ship ready for sea in the shortest possible time. During the third week in March he took her down-river to Sheerness and then to moorings at Black-stakes, where twenty-two years before, in such rough March weather, he had as a twelve-year-old spent a miserable first day on board a warship. Lastly, the sixty-four guns were swung on board, then the shot and the gunpowder and then, on 24th April, the *Agamemnon* made sail and steered for the Nore and the Downs where she was to join a convoy bound for Spithead.

At last a letter reached Godwick Hall from the *Agamemnon* informing Dixon Hoste that William should join his ship at Portsmouth at the end of April. Accordingly, after much leave-taking of his emotional family, William, accompanied by his father and his elder brother, boarded the coach to go jolting south through Swaffham, Newmarket and Cambridge to London and, from there, down the Portsmouth road to the *Agamemnon*, the sea and Captain Nelson.

II

BELOVED CAPTAIN NELSON

William Hoste officially began his naval career when his name was entered in the books of His Majesty's Ship *Agamemnon* on 15th April, 1793, although he was unable to join her for another fortnight. Nelson's orders were to escort a convoy from the Downs off Deal to Spithead and there join the fleet which Admiral Lord Hood was assembling for service in the Mediterranean. But the seventeen merchant ships were not ready to sail until the 28th and it was not until the following day that the *Agamemnon* arrived at Spithead and moored near the wreck of Admiral Kempenfelt's flagship the *Royal George* – capsized at her moorings with heavy loss of life a decade before – and close to the shingle beach by Southsea Castle.

While awaiting the arrival of his first ship, William Hoste's young eyes had watched from the ramparts of Portsmouth the constantly changing panorama at Spithead as warships and merchantmen of all rates and types came and went, framed by the chalk downs of Hampshire and the wooded hills of the Isle of Wight. Seen at a distance, the scene appeared like an animated canvas by one of the popular marine artists whose work was hung on the walls of great houses in Norfolk and the individual ships, too distant to be seen to have crews, looked as neat as models carved in wood or bone, or displayed in bottles, that were sold by old sailors in East Anglian seaports.

William was an observant and enthusiastic boy, rather than romantic and reflective, but a contemporary, Charles Pemberton, who had been swept up by the press-gang despite his education and begun his naval career on the lower deck, left a vivid impression of his introduction to the sea.

He had joined his ship at Plymouth, not Portsmouth, but the ships would have seemed much the same, from the dainty brigs and corvettes, to the lean frigates, sturdy 'seventy-fours' and the great first-rates of the line. Of one such, Pemberton wrote, 'But here was one which, with her vastness of size, her admeasurement of more than two thousand tons, her three tiers of ports, her hundred and twenty guns . . . and lodging within her bowels one thousand men; with the immense thickness and strength of her lower masts and extended yards and upward-towering topmasts, with her tons on tons of cables and cordage, exhibited all the elegance of form . . . even more perfectly than that wondrous thing of twelve inches length, on which I had looked with so much admiration! A fairy's fingers, working on gossamer and pearl, would not have turned out of hand a thing of more faultless order and delicacy.

'Chequered – but stainless, the mighty gorgeousness sat – motionless – not a sound stirred within her, not a sound or sign of life, save the voiceless sweeping in the breeze of the stately banner, and the fluttering of the high, sky-dancing pendant – there she sat, gazing and musing at the image of her majesty . . . receiving proudly as her due, as if she asked it not, the homage of earth, sea and sky. How invitingly beautiful I thought her then! Reader, she was a hell afloat!'

The ship William Hoste joined that blustery April day looked just as handsome as the boat approached along the length of Southsea beach from the forts at the mouth of Portsmouth harbour, yet of all the ambitions her captain had for her the most immediate was that she should not be 'a hell afloat'. His own first days at sea may not have been that but they had been lonely and frightening and had left their mark so that, many years later, on hearing that one of his officers had first gone to sea at the age of eleven, he had muttered sadly, 'Much too young.'

Now he was determined that the boys he had brought to sea with him – including his twelve-year-old stepson Josiah – should be spared the unhappiness that could destroy their enthusiasm. So when William Hoste scrambled up the swelling tumblehome of the *Agamemnon*'s side, welcoming faces awaited him: Captain Nelson and Josiah, two sons of Thomas Weatherhead, a former vicar of Ingoldisthorpe, and an old family friend, William Bolton and several other Norfolk youths, also rated as captain's servants. Amongst the seamen, there were sing-song Norfolk accents for, although the ship was still some two hundred men short of the five hundred she needed, Nelson's recruiting in East Anglia had been successful.

The scene on the main deck was one of intense activity. The ship was only due to remain at Spithead overnight and there was much to be done, notably the embarkation of two officers and fifty-one soldiers of the 69th Regiment who were to take the place of the detachment of marines, who were in short supply because of the rapid commissioning of ships. The long, low main gun-deck, between its two gently-convex curves of cannon, was cluttered with baggage and bustling with men in apparently aimless haste but each going about an ordered duty.

While bringing his ship round from the Thames Estuary and the Downs, Nelson had been much concerned with navigation in those difficult waters and with the welfare of his merchant ships. But now, before Lord Hood's fleet was assembled and ready to sail in company, he was to take the *Agamemnon* to sea for a short cruise with one aim of 'working up' the ship's company and another of snapping up a French prize. The wind was strengthening and when the ship sailed on 1st May the weather was entered in her log as being 'strong gales with rain.'

After his initial disappointment at being given command of a sixty-four-gun ship instead of a 'seventy-four', Nelson had become increasingly pleased with his ship. She had been built, largely of New Forest oak, at Buckler's Hard on the Beaulieu River twelve years before and her bottom had been sheathed in copper so that she was both strong and fast. But it was the very qualities that had at first seemed limitations which Nelson recognized as being exactly those he needed for the methods of fighting he hoped to employ. For the *Agamemnon* was almost as fast as a frigate but carried double the weight of broadside. She answered nimbly to the helm and so could be expected not only to out-sail but out-manoeuvre more powerful and heavier ships of the line. She was proving to be the ideal command for her new captain.

The qualities of ship and captain were put to a first test when she sailed from Spithead with three reefs in her topsails and steered south-west for the coast of France. Rapt in professional enthusiasm as he was, Nelson did not forget the small boys in his care. The midshipmen's berth, deep down in the cockpit on the orlop deck, was uncomfortable at the best of times, but, in a rough sea, certain to prostrate a boy with sea-sickness. So Nelson appointed William Hoste to be, in effect, his errand-boy – what the Navy called 'the captain's doggie' – and told him to sling his hammock in his own airy and roomy quarters aft, below the poop-deck, joking that he must be looked after as carefully as a rare zoological specimen.

When the *Agamemnon* returned to Spithead after a cruise to the Cherbourg peninsula and the Channel Islands four days later, William wrote his first letter from sea to his father and it was clear that the experience had not damped his enthusiasm. 'I was very sick both Thursday and Friday,' he wrote, 'but like my situation very much. Captain Nelson treats me as he said he would as a specimen. I have lived with him ever since I have been on board. I have been up to the foretop and did not go through the lubber's hole . . .'

Nelson had returned empty-handed and without firing a shot but it was not from want of trying as William wrote in the letter, which reflected something of his captain's fierce zeal.

'We have had a very pleasant cruize,' he wrote airily, 'but it would have been more so if we had taken two French Frigates and two man of war brigs which we found riding at Cape la Hogue. We should in all probability have captured them if we could have got a Pilot to take us in. The cowardly rascals ran their Ships in amongst some rocks. Night coming on, we left them, no doubt rejoicing in their narrow escape.

'From thence we proceeded to Cherbourg, we went so near that we could perceive with glasses the people walking on shore, it is remarkably well fortified . . . All attempts of getting anything here being fruitless, we sailed along the coast till we came to the Island of Alderney belonging to the English, where we made a signal for a Pilot. A boat accordingly came off with two but both being ignorant of the Pilotage of the fore mentioned Cape, we were obliged to desist from any further attack upon those dastardly Frenchmen amongst the Rocks. Our time being stated to return, this morning we were obliged to steer for Old England without a prize and are at this moment entering Spithead.'

Three days later, Lord Hood hoisted his flag on board the *Victory* – even at that time a famous old ship of the first rate – and his fleet, the *Agamemnon* amongst it, sailed soon after for the Mediterranean. The strategy of which this was part had been drawn up by William Pitt, the Prime Minister, in reflection of the successful 'blue water' strategy developed by his father, the Earl of Chatham, during the Seven Years War. On land, France was strong and England weak; at sea, France was weak and England strong; therefore the Royal Navy would take the offensive by attacking French possessions in the West Indies and by blockading their ports, particularly those in the Mediterranean. But this strategy was in conflict with the interests of King George III, who, worried about his Hanoverian commitments and his Continental allies, pressed for direct intervention on land. This had led to the dispatch of a British expeditionary force to join the Austrians, Hanoverians and Hessians in defending the Netherlands against invasion by France.

Hood's force did not sail in company, or make directly for Gibraltar. While the flagship delayed some days at Spithead, a division, including the *Agamemnon*, put to sea under the command of Vice-Admiral William Hotham, exercising and hoping to sweep up prizes. But again Nelson was unlucky, all the ships he chased proving to be friendly or neutral, so that William Hoste, writing to his mother in a letter sent ashore at Falmouth, complained that they were 'a little out of humour'. But, he boasted, he had not been sea-sick since their first cruise and now there was 'scarcely wind enough to give a sickening motion to our vessel.'

Despite such brave words and the manly greetings to his father with the hope 'that the May foxes have given him good sport', the letter showed him still to be a small boy remembering his sisters and brother in their Norfolk nursery: 'I hope Miss Polly and Miss Saucebox are both very well – not forgetting Master Pickle.'

Next day, while the ship cruised in the chops of the Channel, the parsons' sons were, for the first time, required to face one of the cruel realities of naval life when the ship's company was mustered to witness punishment. Two seamen, Beats and Davis, and a soldier, McQuade, had been found guilty of theft and each sentenced by Captain Nelson to a dozen lashes. To most of the ship's company, the spectacle was a regular routine – the gathering of the officers under the break of the poop, the seamen forward of the main-mast, the marines – in this case, the soldiers – drawn up with their muskets on the poop-deck above. Then the rigging of the upright wooden grating to which the wrists of the bare-backed prisoner were tied. The captain reading out the offender's crime from the Articles of War while the boatswain's mate ran his fingers through the knotted thongs of the cat-o'-nine-tails. Then the order, 'Do your duty' and the hiss and cut and cries of ritual flogging.

On this morning, the drill had to be carried out three times but, although twelve lashes would tear the skin off a man's back, the punishment was considered moderate and one that a strong man should be able to bear, although he might be unable to stifle his screams of pain. But, a week later, the ship's company was again mustered to witness a punishment that must have turned even the stronger stomachs. Again the crime was theft but while one seaman was to receive three dozen lashes, the other offender, Walter Holmes, was to have a dozen laid on his back although he was rated as Boy, which means that he was not more than seventeen years old.

Yet Captain Nelson was not known as a particularly 'taut hand' but as a humane commander who, ever since he had sailed on a long voyage in a merchant ship as a young man, had had a particular sympathy with the lower deck, recalling the sailors' definition of distinction between officer and sailor: 'Aft the most honour, forward the better man.' But, for him, as for his contemporaries, flogging was the only swift and effective deterrent to indiscipline for a crew of tough men, most of whom were at sea against their will.

Insight into the attitudes to humanity that were bred into naval officers came during the *Agamemnon*'s visit to Cadiz. After cruising for a month in the hope of falling in with a French convoy from the West Indies, the ship crossed the Bay of Biscay in company with Lord Hood's fleet then joined a squadron of six sail of the line that was to pay a courtesy visit to Cadiz, the principal naval base of their Spanish allies. After parting company with the fleet, which continued to Gibraltar, the squadron took several French prizes, including a brig, a privateer and a merchantman, and four prisoners were brought on board the *Agamemnon*, giving the recruits their first sight of their enemy, face to face.

On 15th June, at anchor off Cadiz, William wrote to his elder sister, Kate, that he hoped to get ashore to see a bull-fight but that it was blowing so hard that it might be impossible to leave the ship. Nelson was determined to get ashore during their short stay, more to see what he could of the dockyard and Spanish warships than a bull-fight. When the weather moderated, he landed, taking, in all probability, his Norfolk protégés and it can be assumed that they reflected his own opinions of bull-fighting. Writing to his wife soon after leaving Cadiz, he described the experience, reflecting the Englishman's attitude to cruelty, despite his own enthusiasm for fighting and his acceptance of brutal corporal punishments. 'A bull feast . . . was exhibited in which we English had certainly to regret the want of humanity in the Dons and Donnas,' he wrote. 'The amphitheatre will hold 16,000 people, about 12,000 were present. 10 bulls were selected and one brought out at a time. 3 cavaliers on horseback and footmen with flags were the combatants. We had what is called a fine feast for 5 horses were killed and 2 men very much hurt. Had they been killed it would have been quite complete. We felt for the bulls and horses and I own it would not have displeased me to have had some of the Dons tossed by the enraged animal. How women can even sit much more applaud such sights is astonishing. It even turned us sick, and we could hardly sit it out. The dead mangled horses with their entrails tore out, the bulls covered with blood, was too much. However we have seen one and agree that nothing shall tempt us to see another.'

Nelson's letters to Fanny usually included reassuring references to Josiah ('Josiah is a very good boy and grown very much') and sometimes to William, asking her to pass a message to his parents. 'Perhaps Hoste may not have had an opportunity of writing a letter,' he wrote in July. 'If he has not, send a note to his father to say he is well and a good boy.' In the Mediterranean, a schoolmaster joined the ship and soon Josiah was 'in fractions, preparing to learn navigation' and William was 'in Chronology'. The rounded, copybook handwriting of William's letters home suggest that they may have been written under supervision and, if so, that he had learned something of his father's use of flattery, for in one letter to his mother he wrote: 'I like the sea very much indeed. Captain Nelson is exceedingly kind to me. We have a schoolmaster on board, who is a very clever man.'

At Gibraltar, where Hood's fleet anchored and took on stores, William watched the almost symbolic routine on entering the Mediterranean when a warship's company was given a change in the one luxury they were allowed and the purser brought on board barrels of wine instead of home-brewed beer. Now, instead of a daily issue of a gallon of beer or half a pint of rum, the sailors would be issued with a pint of wine, preferably white rather than red, strong enough to make their rations of salted meat or fish and hard biscuit edible.

It was symbolic also of the mounting state of urgency that, after two days at anchor, Hood ordered his ships to weigh and make sail with urgency and prepare for battle. He had received a reliable report that the French fleet was at sea and could be intercepted before making an escape to Toulon.

Several times William had heard the drums beat to quarters and taken part in the ordered excitement of clearing a ship for action and closing up at action stations. Now a fleet action seemed probable and on 3rd July, as the drums beat, the long gun-decks cleared from end to end, the port-lids opened and the guns run out and the signal for line of battle made by the flagship, he could see and count the supposed enemy force of thirty sail. But it was a false alarm for the fleet was Spanish and news came that the French – twenty or thirty sail of the line – were still in harbour.

Lord Hood's force in the Mediterranean, which the *Agamemnon* rejoined in the Gulf of Lyons, had two principal strategic tasks. One was to blockade a large French fleet in the naval base of Toulon and the other was to support the Austrian war effort. It seemed likely to be an active station and Nelson was particularly contented for two reasons. One was that Hood, who had ignored his repeated pleas for re-employment during his years on half-pay, now seemed affable and Nelson wrote to Fanny that he had become 'tolerable good friends with me'. Hood was now aged nearly seventy but still energetic and aggressive as a commander so that Nelson was quickly able to establish a relaxed relationship with him. So it was that when his other reason for contentment – his delight in his ship and her company – led him to refuse Hood's offer of the promised 'seventy-four', the admiral understood his feelings and did not change the offer into an order.

If there was cause for disappointment it was the expectation that the French Revolution was about to collapse and so bring about peace before there was a chance of glory or prize-money. The United States of America had, despite its alliance with France, declared its neutrality and, in the field, the Revolutionary armies had been thrown back from Germany and the Low Countries into a country seemingly ready to revolt against the tyranny of Paris in a surge of discontent that was

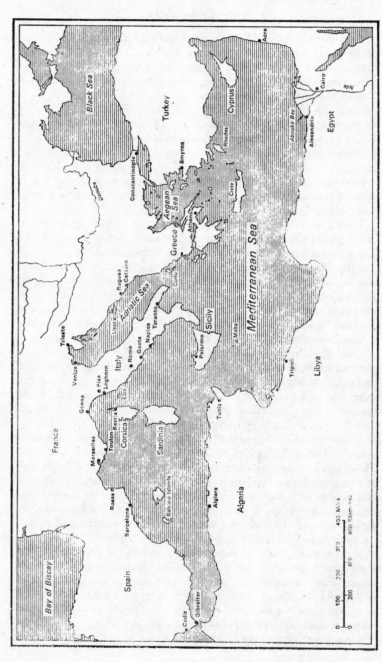

THE MEDITERRANEAN

marked, in July, by the murder of the revolutionary Marat by Charlotte Corday.

Even the savage repression of counter-revolution, wherever it erupted, seemed unlikely to save the dictatorship of the Committee of Public Safety. 'The affairs of France . . . are worse than ever: the guillotine is every day employed,' wrote Nelson to his father in August. 'A Master of a ship, whom we spoke from Marseilles, says there are now only two descriptions of people in France – the one drunk and mad; the other, with horror painted in their faces, are absolutely starving . . . A Peace with England is what they wish for.'

The arrival of the British fleet off Toulon brought about a bloodless victory that took the victors by surprise to such an extent that they were unable to fully grasp its magnitude and possibilities. Horrified by the suppression of moderate Republicans and the massacre of the monarchists throughout France and particularly by the terror at Marseilles, the citizens of Toulon took control of town and dockyard. Then, at the end of August, they invited Hood to join them in defending the base against the Revolutionaries in the name of King Louis XVII, son of the Louis who had died on the scaffold eight months before.

When news that Toulon was in Hood's hands reached London eleven days later, the Government was presented with strategic options of limitless possibilities. Hitherto, they could choose between attempting an advance on Paris from Flanders, or in support of the dissidents in western France, or concentrate on the 'blue water' strategy and use British naval power to strangle the revolution by seizing French overseas possessions – particularly in the West Indies – and blockading their home ports. But now they found themselves in control of a great naval base, together with a fleet of well-built ships, including thirty of the line, from which an offensive could be launched against the enemy from the direction he least expected, the south.

This sudden advantage needed exploiting quickly for the fast and lethal reaction of the Revolutionaries had already been experienced. But before any thought could be given to an offensive based on Toulon, the port and its perimeter defences of fifteen miles must be held against counter-attack and the best professional advice as to numbers of soldiers needed for this purpose was fifty thousand.

But Pitt could not bring himself to give a Toulon strategy the priority it should have had and continued with plans for operations against the French in both Flanders and the West Indies, assuming that the necessary force could be scraped together by the allies: Spain, Austria, little Piedmont and the Kingdom of the Two Sicilies.

Again the particular qualities of the *Agamemnon* proved advantageous to her captain – perhaps with far-reaching consequences in his own life – for Hood chose her as a fast ship of the line with an active and intelligent commanding officer to press the urgency for help at Naples. The bizarre Kingdom of the Two Sicilies was made up of the island of Sicily itself and of Naples and its hinterland. It was ruled by a Spanish Bourbon, King Ferdinand IV, and his wife, Queen Maria Carolina, daughter of the Empress Maria Theresa of Austria and sister of Queen Marie Antoinette, who was about to follow her husband to the guillotine in Paris. The curiosity did not end there for the Prime Minister was an expatriate Englishman from Shropshire, Sir John Acton, and the most effective foreign diplomatist was a vigorous Anglo-Scottish dilettante, an authority on Classical archaeology, painting and volcanoes. This was Sir William Hamilton, who had recently married his mistress, a beautiful *demi-mondaine* he had acquired from his nephew. She, already made notorious by scandal and famous by the painter Romney, was Emma Hamilton, now aged twenty-seven.

Without having had time to enter Toulon with Hood's occupying force, Nelson was bound for Naples, where he arrived on the 11th of September. William Hoste wrote to his father of the famous view. 'Mount Vesuvius . . . we have beheld in all its glory, for now its irruptions are most splendid; the lava spreading from the top at a great distance and rolling down the mountain in great streaks of fire.'

While Nelson hastened ashore to confer with Hamilton before meeting Acton and the King, he did not forget his young charges and William wrote, 'Captain Nelson was so kind as to present me with two orders of admission to the king's museum and the ruins of Herculaneum, which were well worth seeing; but it was a mortifying circumstance to us that our conductors would not speak either English or French; therefore our curiosity was more excited than gratified. To attempt any description is not in my power.'

His attempts to describe Naples itself ('. . . large, but the houses are very irregular; they have some fine buildings, the king's palace and public offices') did not suggest a reflective imagination either, for he was developing into an essentially active, alert youth, modelling himself on his captain. He was again disappointed when King Ferdinand's visit to the ship had to be cancelled because of the swell in the bay and all diplomatic business had to be conducted ashore. But, he noted, 'Sir William Hamilton, our ambassador, came on board with Lady Hamilton, to whom the captain introduced me.'

Nelson had just met the Hamiltons for the first time and the attraction was mutual. Sir William, now aged sixty-two, had had to meet many visiting naval officers during nearly thirty years as ambassador at Naples and most had fitted a conventional pattern, so it was refreshing to meet so stimulating an exception as Captain Nelson. He, on his part, enjoyed Sir William's charm and erudition, perhaps finding in it grander echoes of his own father's whimsical scholarship, and he was impressed by Emma's strong personality, writing to Fanny that 'She is a young woman of amiable manners and who does honour to the station to which she is raised.'

The diplomatic mission was a success but the social niceties were abruptly curtailed when Nelson made his departure in a suitably dramatic manner. Acton had sent word that a French corvette with a British prize had been sighted off Corsica and a breakfast party on board the *Agamemnon*, at which the Hamiltons were guests, was at once broken up and Emma's last sight for five years of her future lover was of his ship standing out to sea to meet the enemy, a spectacle that would have struck a thrilling chord in her romantic imagination.

The quarry turned out to be Genoese but their behaviour was suspicious since they ran under the guns of Cagliari at the approach of the *Agamemnon*. However, they were neutrals and Nelson had to abandon his plan to send his boats into the harbour after dark to cut them out or burn them. Young Hoste had been excited at the prospect, telling his father that he had heard that ashore 'the country people were running up the mountain, crying out, "Mon Dieu!" very much frightened, thinking we should land'.

On 5th October, after a stormy passage, the *Agamemnon* was back at Toulon, which was now under close siege by the Revolutionary armies, amongst whom was a zealous young colonel of artillery, Napoleon Bonaparte. The harbour itself was within range of their guns and Nelson noted phlegmatically, 'shot and shells are throwing about us every hour, but such is the force of habit we seem to feel perfectly safe'. Hood was delighted at the success of the mission to Naples and, in due course, the Neapolitan reinforcements arrived, but Pitt grudgingly added only two battalions and a few guns from the Gibraltar garrison.

The *Agamemnon* lay at Toulon for four days before Hood had another diplomatic mission for Nelson: to join a squadron bound for Tunis to put pressure on the Dey, who had been showing marked partiality for the French cause. The mission was ineffectual and the failure of the senior British officer, Commodore Linzee, to take a stronger line and, indeed, to seize all the French warships in Tunis harbour without more ado, infuriated Nelson, who noted in his journal, 'My spirits are low indeed . . . I should have taken every Frenchman here without negotiating, even had negotiations taken place, I would have had the French men-of-war and believe that the people of England will never blame an officer for taking a French line of battle ship.'

But, for his ship's company, the mission to Tunis was chiefly remarkable for being the first occasion in the commission that the *Agamemnon* lost a man killed in action.

Sailing south down the coast of Sardinia, they had sighted five ships at two o'clock in the morning and immediately given chase, without knowing their nationality or strength, and although the *Agamemnon*, being able to muster only three hundred and fifty men at quarters, was, in effect, no stronger than a ship of fifty guns. In a letter home, William Hoste described the encounter: 'About four o'clock, we got within gun-shot of the hindermost and hailed her in French. On her returning no answer, we fired a gun ahead for her to bring to and shorten sail. We observed her making signals with sky-rockets to her consorts . . . After we had repeatedly hailed to no purpose, we fired one of our eighteen-pounders at her, to oblige her to shorten sail; at the same time opened our lower-deck ports, which frightened her, as she immediately made more sail to get away . . .

'About five a.m. we were within half a gun-shot and found her to be a fine forty-gun frigate. She hoisted national colours and favoured us with a broadside.'

A running fight of three hours ensued with both ships making six knots, while the four other ships, which also proved to be French frigates and had been to windward, attempted to close the *Agamemnon*. Nelson's aim was to cripple the first frigate before he had to engage the other four, or, as William put it, 'we expected to have some warm work therefore were anxious to despatch this gentleman before the others came up'. But, at eight, the wind changed and the damaged frigate was able to escape. 'Our last broadside did her infinite damage,' explained William, 'nor was our's inconsiderable, as our rigging was shot away, and our main-top-mast sprung, which prevented us from going after her. We had one man killed and two wounded.'

Meanwhile, the other four frigates were coming down on the *Agamemnon* with all sail set. 'We expected nothing less than that they would engage us and were prepared for their reception,' William continued, 'but their courage failed them as we had given their friends so complete a drubbing.'

Such nonchalance was expected in a boy of thirteen. The contrast between cosy parsonage and ship of the line was, on the face of it, complete yet there were similarities that made transition easier. In place of the parson and his privileged communion with God, there was the captain with his eye on the almighty admiral's signal halyards. And just as a village had its own social hierarchy, so had the ship; the subtleties including the difference in status between a watchkeeping lieutenant and the master, who would navigate the ship but remain of a lower social order, and between the agile top-men, who handled the highest sails, and the 'idlers', whose work did not involve seamanship in its most direct form. This community, once joined, demanded instant acceptance and along with the harsh environment, from which only the captain in his plain but elegant quarters was partially immune, went the acceptance of violence.

In the *Agamemnon* there were compensations, notably the captain. 'He is acknowledged to be one of the first captains in the service and is universally beloved by his men and officers,' wrote William Hoste after this first blood-letting on board. 'I should be greatly wanting in gratitude were I not to pay this tribute to his merit, and kindness to me.'

This was due largely to Nelson's affection for young people and partly to the presence of his own step-son, to whom he could give no more attention than to the other boys. Yet the time would inevitably come soon when the boys he cosseted would not only have to be exposed to gunfire but would be expected to fight for their lives with grown men, hand to hand. For William Hoste this experience was not long delayed.

Toulon was doomed. The half-hearted strategy dictated by London had failed to provide a viable defending force, let alone an army to strike into Revolutionary France and, in December, the defences broke. An attempt was made by Hood to remove or burn the French warships in the harbour but this had been left too late so that, although eighteen ships were brought out, twenty-seven were left behind, mostly damaged by fire but eleven of them needing little repair.

The work was hampered by thousands of terrified refugees fleeing the inevitable massacre when the city fell and crowding on board the British ships. The *Agamemnon* was away at sea but lurid reports soon reached her; Nelson writing to Fanny, who was staying with his cousins, the Walpoles, at Wolterton, 'Everything that domestic wars produce usually are multiplied at Toulon. Fathers are here without families, families without fathers. In short, all is horror which we hear.' Then, keeping matters in proportion, he added, 'Josiah is very well, as is Hoste and Bolton good boys.'

With the loss of the Toulon base, Hood decided that Corsica and its fine anchorage at San Fiorenzo would be the best alternative. The island was in revolt against the French under its veteran rebel leader, Pasquale de Paoli, who had known Dr Samuel Johnson in London, and support should be given to him in capturing the French garrison towns of San Fiorenzo, Bastia and Calvi. Amongst the ships engaged in these operations was the *Agamemnon*.

The invasion of Corsica was launched early in 1794 in appalling weather. 'Made the ship as snug as possible,' noted Nelson in his journal, 'All night it blew such a gale as is very seldom felt, neither canvas nor rope could stand it. All our sails blew in pieces. Made a great deal of water. A most amazing heavy sea. The ship under bare poles.' When the weather moderated, the ship anchored off Bastia and sent a boat ashore flying a flag of truce with the message that Nelson had come to deliver the town from the French but that even if a musket were fired at him Bastia would be burned. He gave the French five minutes to answer his summons to surrender and this the Governor did, his refusal beginning with the words, '*Nous sommes republicains: ce mot seul doit suffire.*'

Nelson instantly went ashore himself, strode up to the castle and lowered the French colours with his own hands. 'The Governor not choosing to stay with his soldats francais but running off as fast as his legs could carry him,' he noted in his journal. A castle had been captured but the fortified town now had to be besieged.

On 12th February, one of the *Agamemnon*'s boats pulling past a cove near Bastia, where a small vessel was lying, was fired upon from the shore and a man badly wounded. Nelson immediately ordered an assault landing, calling up a cutter with forty soldiers embarked to join his own ship's boats. Leading the little flotilla himself, with William Hoste beside him, he realized that he had set himself an impossible task. Not only were the enemy able to fire on his boats from the cover of rocks but the cliffs were so steep that a direct assault on them was out of the question. The one action he could take was to board and capture the ship lying beneath the cliffs to which she was moored by a rope to her mast-head. So while the soldiers kept up a covering fire on the rocks above, Nelson led his boats to the attack. 'We instantly carried the vessel,' he wrote, 'and killed several of the French, an officer among them. We had six men wounded, round the vessel was a French courier boat from Bastia to Antibes . . .'

Some weeks later, a letter arrived at Godwick Hall from Captain Nelson. 'Dear Sir,' it ran. 'You cannot receive much more pleasure in reading this lettter than I have in writing it, to say that your son is everything which his dearest friends can wish him to be, and is a strong proof that the greatest gallantry may lie under the most gentle behaviour. Two days ago, it was necessary to take a small vessel from a number of people who had got on shore to prevent us; she was carried in high style, and your good son was at my side . . .'

Land warfare now began in earnest but, as the general in command of the troops ashore refused to move against Bastia or Calvi before reinforcements arrived, Nelson began besieging the former with his sailors and marines 'with the few soldiers who were spared to serve in forward areas'.

'The expedition is almost a child of my own,' wrote Nelson to Fanny, but it was his men and boys he regarded with fatherly pride. 'My sea-

men are now what British seamen ought to be . . . almost invincible,'
he boasted. 'They really mind shot no more than peas.' But he was
cautious with the lives of the boys, writing to Dixon Hoste, 'Your dear
boy wishes much to come on shore with me, and if I had not thought
the danger too great, I should have brought him; however, he has been
several times to see me.' On one occasion, he told Fanny, he invited
William ('a charming good boy') to come with Josiah to dine. Yet, in
the same letter, he showed that such affectionate care was balanced by a
necessary ruthlessness; 'It is said a Mid. of mine (a Norfolk lad) is
deserted to the enemy. I do not believe it. If he is, he is certain to be
hanged.'

William not only pleased his captain by his courage and cheerfulness but, as his father was told, 'in his navigation you will find him
equally forward.' Nelson thought that he 'highly deserves everything
I can do to make him happy' and fussed over the frequency with
which he wrote to his family and advised his father not to allow him
too much pocket-money ('Do not spoil him by giving him too much
money; he has all he wishes – sometimes more.')

John Weatherhead, being older and stronger, was allowed ashore
with the captain, working with the landing-parties in hauling up guns
and ammunition to the batteries. Enviously, William told his father of
this, asking that a reassuring message should be passed to Weatherhead's father because he himself was too busy to write but 'has never
forgot the charge he took of me upon your leaving us'.

Bastia was bombarded and many of its stone buildings reduced to
ruins but it was too strong to be stormed, although by now reinforcements had arrived. 'I do not hear we are the nearer taking it,' wrote
William in May, 'only by their being fairly starved out.'

Bombarded by land and blockaded at sea, such an outcome was
inevitable. The town and its garrison of some four thousand, five
hundred soldiers surrendered on 24th May, the besiegers having
been reinforced by strong land forces only five days beforehand, these
arriving just in time to take part in the capitulation ceremonies. Nelson
could now move on to invest the last French garrison in the island at
Calvi.

While he had been absorbed in the intricacies of siege warfare, the
eyes of Europe had been directed to Paris where the Reign of Terror
was reaching its climax. The revolutionary leaders Danton and Camille
Desmoulins had been sent to the guillotine by their rival, Robespierre,
in April and the power of the revolutionary tribunals increased and
blood-letting established as the cure for all suspected political deviation.
In late spring, France received new strength when a huge grain convoy
arrived from America having successfully avoided the Royal Navy at

the acceptable cost of a shattering defeat of its covering fleet by Lord Howe in the Atlantic, his strategic failure being glorified as the Battle of the Glorious First of June.

The siege of Calvi lasted fifty-five days and ran much the same course as that of Bastia with Nelson in command of the naval parties and batteries ashore. But it was later in the summer, the worst season for land fighting. 'It is now what we call the dog-days,' wrote Nelson. 'Here it is called the Lion-Sun; no person can endure it; we have upwards of one thousand sick out of two thousand; and the others not much better than so many phantoms . . . I am here the reed among the oaks; all the prevailing disorders have attacked me but I have not the strength for them to fasten upon; I bow before the storm, while the sturdy oak is laid low.'

Malaria, dysentery, heat exhaustion and probably typhoid put a hundred and fifty of the *Agamemnon's* company on the sick list, among them, as the captain noted, 'Poor little Hoste is also so extremely ill that I have great fears about him.' To be confined to his cot on board was a particular disappointment to William as he had had hopes of being allowed to stay ashore at this siege and had been fascinated by the way his captain had taken to land warfare, supervising the dragging of the ship's guns up rocky hills to be mounted in batteries commanding the defences from above.

But although Nelson's health held out, he was one of the comparative few to suffer from the enemy. While with a forward battery, a French shot struck a breastwork near him, throwing sand and splintered stones into his face and almost blinding his right eye. Although he could never again use the eye for more than distinguishing light from dark, he accepted the disability light-heartedly, writing to Fanny, 'It is no blemish so my *beauty* is saved.'

When Calvi fell, the *Agamemnon* was sent to Leghorn where her sickly company could recuperate and the ship herself refit during the autumn. In October, Hood sailed for England in the *Victory* and was succeeded by his uninspired second-in-command, Hotham. Nelson was ready to rejoin the fleet off Toulon, in which was blockaded a French force of approximately equal strength, including fourteen sail of the line. That they might attempt to break out and even try to re-capture Corsica seemed increasingly likely as news arrived of fresh French successes on land. Although Robespierre had fallen in July and been sent to the guillotine himself, the impetus of the Revolution seemed to gather force. In the east, French armies reached the Rhine and, at the end of the year, invaded Holland. As 1795 began in the gale-swept Mediterranean, it seemed more and more probable that as soon as the weather moderated the well-fitted French ships and their rested crews would sail to try their strength against Hotham's tired, storm-beaten fleet.

William Hoste, who had recovered his health, was inevitably growing up into a worldly, if not sophisticated, youth. In Leghorn, his revered captain showed that he had, like many others, left his marriage vows at Gibraltar and had taken an Italian mistress, Adelaide Correglia, known behind her lover's back as his 'dolly'.

William made no mention of such scandals in his letters home which usually began with news of the war and an account of the ship's activities and complaints at the lack of mail from England: 'I am in doubt whether Old Godwick is still standing.' There were no mentions of the horrors of ship-fighting and references to hardship were generally jocular: 'Two or three brace of Partridges would be very acceptable down in the Cockpit instead of salt beef and pea soup.'

Always he enquired anxiously about the family in Norfolk. He longed to hear more of his baby brother, Edward, born in 1794; sent love to 'dear little George', who was six years his junior, and a message to his elder brother Dick, at school at Rugby, that 'I should like to hear whether the Birch is exercised as often as ever'.

His most tender enquiries were for his elder sister, 'that saucy young Minx Miss Kate', archly hinting that he expects to hear that 'Miss Kitty has followed the example of Mrs Anson' – Thomas Coke's daughter Anne who had married Thomas Anson, great-nephew of the famous admiral – but, if she was only toying with the idea, begged her to wait until he returned home.

Then a letter reached Godwick Hall from the *Agamemnon* dated 20th March, 1795, and it began, 'What we have so long expected and wished for has at last happened. We have engaged the French fleet . . .'

Hotham's fleet was at anchor off Leghorn, resting briefly between bouts of blockading Toulon in winter gales, when on the 9th of that month a frigate 'made a signal for a strange sail in the offing'. The admiral sailed as soon as he could and on the 11th sighted the French line of battle off Genoa. From the British ships, battered by months of rough weather and dangerously undermanned because of sickness, they looked both fresh and formidable, particularly the two giants, the *Sans Culotte* of one hundred and twenty guns and the *Ça Ira* of eighty. In fact, they were fresh but not formidable because, although the ships themselves were magnificent, the Revolution had destroyed French naval professionalism and replaced it with dogmatic fervour.

Of the twelve thousand officers and men manning the fifteen ships of the line, seven thousand five hundred had never before been to sea. On the gun-decks the professional naval gunners, who had been a *corps d'élite* in the pre-Revolutionary fleet, had mostly been replaced by half-trained men, or artillerymen from the former besieging force at Toulon, because to classify a skilled gunner as such smacked of class-distinction. Indeed, the wretched admiral, Martin, estimated that, apart from officers and petty officers – many of *them* promoted for political reasons – he had no more than two thousand seven hundred men in his fleet that could be described as seamen.

So conscious was the French naval command of these shortcomings that the transports that stood ready to carry eighteen thousand soldiers to Corsica were left behind in Toulon so that their presence would not encumber the fighting ships. Only if the British were worsted and driven well away from their intended route, was the invasion force to sail.

But as the *Agamemnon* beat to quarters, the expectation was only of a general fleet action that many of them – from the small boys to the captain himself – would be experiencing for the first time. As the opponents closed it was seen that a large French ship had lost two of her top-masts by carrying too great a press of sail in the squally weather and had become separated from the main force, a frigate trying to take her in tow. She proved to be the *Ça Ira*.

Seeing the lame giant, Captain Thomas Fremantle took his frigate, the *Inconstant*, up to her and fired a broadside only to receive one himself, obliging him to recognize the French ship as a wounded tiger and haul off. But now the *Agamemnon* came into her own. From the first, Nelson had recognized her particular characteristics: speed, manoeuvrability and hitting-power. She might have been designed for just such an encounter as this.

The *Agamemnon* stood some distance to windward of Hotham's main force and she was quickly up with the *Ça Ira*, loosing a broadside through the wide tiers of windows at her stern to rake her gun-decks. Helpless to reply with anything but small stern-chaser guns while her attacker remained astern, the great ship could only take her punishment as, for two hours, the *Agamemnon* plied to and fro beneath the shattered gilding of her stern, throwing in broadside after broadside. Eventually, other French ships of the line came to her relief and her tormentor pulled away.

It had been an exciting day although the expected fleet action had not begun and, in reducing a massive adversary to near ruin, the *Agamemnon* had escaped lightly. 'Extraordinary', wrote Nelson, 'although we were a good deal chipped about the sails and rigging and masts, yet only 7 men were wounded.' The experience had produced some over-confidence; Josiah Nisbet, who together with William Hoste had been their captain's aides-de-camp on the quarterdeck, telling his step-father that he considered there was 'no great danger in French shot'.

Next day, the main forces came near to a full-scale combat and there was a fierce exchange of broadsides between the British and those ships trying to cover the escape of the *Ça Ira*. But the big ship was labouring too heavily and both she and the *Censeur* who had taken her in tow struck their colours. One of Nelson's lieutenants took possession of both dismasted hulks, reporting that one had lost four hundred men killed and wounded and the other three hundred. The French admiral had had enough and, after some shooting at extreme range, hauled away to make his escape and cancel plans to invade Corsica. But to Nelson's amazement and rage, Hotham also felt that enough had been done and decided not to pursue.

The *Agamemnon* had been more badly damaged on the second day but had only had half a dozen men hurt, none killed. They had not experienced a fleet action but their self-confidence was now unbounded. When, three months later, they again fell in with the French in strength and Hotham, who though inactive, was no coward, ordered a general chase, Nelson took the fast *Agamemnon* ahead of the others and was bitterly disappointed when a change of wind prevented him from coming up with his quarry.

Much of the remaining months of 1795 were spent off the Genoese coast in support of the Austrians who were trying without success to throw back the French. At the end of the year, Hotham struck his flag and returned home. Nelson was relieved at this and to hear that an experienced and aggressive admiral, Sir John Jervis, was to come out to the Mediterranean as Commander-in-Chief. He would be needed because, that autumn, Napoleon Bonaparte asserted his authority in Paris with his 'whiff of grapeshot' and even greater impetus was about to be given to French aggression.

For himself, his ship's company and his young protégés, Nelson was well pleased. He flattered himself that news of the actions of the spring would have made the name of the *Agamemnon* as familiar throughout Europe as that of a cockle-boat in the creek at Burnham Overy Staithe, the little seaport near Burnham Thorpe. He wrote to Fanny, only half in jest, that, 'I am so covered in laurels that you will hardly find my little face.' Already he was thinking of himself as one day commanding a fleet.

A cloud of discontent shadowed his relationship with his step-son, Josiah. In her letters to her husband, Fanny Nelson constantly and naturally fussed over the welfare of her son ('Do make him clean his teeth not cross ways but upwards and downwards.') and for the first two years Nelson was dutiful in reassuring her that Josiah was well or was a good boy. Then at about the time of his liaison with the 'dolly' at Leghorn – a scandal that must have become known to the boy – notes of irritation creep in. The boy appears to be lazy and disregards his step-father's instructions to write home; this is usually related with good humour ('Josiah begins to threaten you with a letter and time may produce it') but sometimes the smile fades. 'Josiah will be a good officer I have no doubt,' wrote Nelson in August, 1795, 'but I fear will never be troubled by the graces. He is the same disposition as when an infant. However he has many good points about him.'

Josiah and William Hoste were often together, not only when in their dark, cramped quarters in the cockpit, or at action stations with the captain on the quarterdeck. At Leghorn, Nelson had engaged a tutor to teach French to the two boys and to himself and their names were often linked in their captain's letters home to his wife as both being happy and well. But in these letters, Nelson never wrote of Josiah in such terms as he described William, whom he called 'as amiable a young man as ever lived'.

On 25th August, 1795, William won Nelson's heart by a show of dash in action and a consequent injury cheerfully borne. William described the event in a letter to his brother Dixon. They had been cruising off Vado Bay to the west of Genoa 'when Captain Nelson received intelligence of some vessels lying at Alassio . . . We immediately weighed anchor . . . cleared ship for action and beat to quarters.' At about noon they anchored off a little fort and brought their broadside to bear. There was no need as the crews of the ships fled ashore and what French troops were seen were drawn up behind the town as if expecting a bombardment and a landing. So Nelson ordered his boats away to tow out the abandoned vessels.

One of these boats was commanded by William and he boarded his prize without trouble, expecting to take her round to the British anchorage in Vado Bay. But after getting up cable from below, his men forgot to fit the cover back on the hatch and William, hurrying aft to attend to the working of the ship, tripped and fell into the cable-locker fracturing a leg. He was taken back to the *Agamemnon*, where he wrote, 'Don't you think I was very unlucky to lose the command of my vessel so soon? However, I comfort myself with singing *Dearest Peg* all weathers . . . I assure you, Dick, if I were to go on board of any ship in the British navy, I could not be more happy, nor have more care taken of me, since this accident, than has been taken of me on board the *Agamemnon*.

'I got up yesterday for the first time, and I think if you were to see poor Billy Shanks hopping about on crutches, you would die with laughter. Captain Nelson is very well; he often comes down to see me, and tells me to get every thing I want from him.'

In a letter to Fanny written in the same week as the observation on Josiah's gracelessness, Nelson wrote, 'I am sorry to tell you poor little

Hoste has very near broke his leg but it is in a fair way of being very soon well. He was prize master of a vessel and fell down a scuttle. Josiah is as well as usual.' Three weeks later, he added, 'Hoste quite recovered and none the worse for his accident. He is without exception one of the finest boys I ever met with.'

This affection survived an embarrassing problem with the boy's father, which anyone who had had more than passing acquaintance of the Reverend Dixon Hoste might have expected. Before new regulations came into force during 1794, the boy aspiring to a commission as a 'captain's servant' received no pay and had to rely on an allowance from home, or the generosity of his captain, to pay for more than his rations and working clothes. It was therefore customary for the parent to pay a lump sum to the agent of the captain into whose ship the boy had been accepted. The captain himself then controlled the amount of pocket-money to be allowed, or did so in consultation with the parent. Nelson, as has been seen, clearly took the latter course, suggesting to Dixon Hoste that William's allowance was rather too high.

When the two men first met in Norfolk, Nelson was clearly impressed by Hoste as is shown by the trouble he took to write him long, informative letters from the Mediterranean about the war and the dangers of political subversion in Norfolk. At the time of the commissioning of the *Agamemnon*, he had been so busy and excited that the arrangements for paying a child's pocket-money had been among the least of his concerns. Presumably, therefore, he just gave Dixon Hoste the name and address of his agent in London and perhaps asked what amount should be given to William each month.

And it is probable that Hoste either paid to the agent or gave directly to Nelson an initial sum to cover the cost of fitting out William with the necessities of life at sea not provided by the captain or the Admiralty; this may also have met the demands of pocket-money during the first weeks on board.

From 15th April, 1793, when William's name was entered in the ship's books, Nelson began to give small amounts of money to him, within limits set by his father, whenever he was asked. On 1st February, 1794, when he had been rated midshipman on his captain's authority, William drew naval pay for the first time but as this was only £1.4s. a month, the private allowance was still necessary.

The mail service between England and the fleet was, of course, slow and erratic, being delayed by contrary winds, missing its recipient when his ship was ordered elsewhere, or sometimes captured by the enemy or lost by shipwreck. Occasionally, a letter from home would reach the *Agamemnon* in only one month but it could often be three. Therefore it was some time before Nelson realized that the money he was giving to William was not being supported by a sum paid to his agent by the boy's father. At first, it must have seemed that the mail service was at fault or that the charming parson was preoccupied by some personal disaster and would take the necessary action as soon as he was able. So Nelson continued to draw on his own account to pay William, never mentioning his father's dilatoriness. Eventually he sent a tactful reminder to Godwick Hall.

Then, on 24th April, 1796, Nelson wrote to Fanny, 'Extraordinary, I have not had a line from Mr Hoste since I drew the last bill, although it must be known I advanced the money every day for 14 months before I asked for it, and another is now rising very fast. I am very angry.'

And so it was that Nelson found himself with more than the responsibilities of a commanding officer for the upbringing and welfare of William Hoste.

III
POOR LITTLE HOSTE

The arrival of Admiral Sir John Jervis galvanized the fleet in the Mediterranean and inspired Nelson but it came too late to hold the tide of French victories for, as the latter put it, 'the French fight on shore like our seamen, they never stop and know not the word halt.' But Jervis, aged sixty and a living link with the victories of the Seven Years War – he had been with Wolfe at Quebec – gave his captains the spur of aggressive professionalism that led Nelson to say that where he himself would use a penknife, the admiral would wield a hatchet.

The duties of the fleet were much as they had been under Hotham: blockading Toulon, guarding the anchorage at San Fiorenzo Bay in Corsica and the dockyard and victualling base at Leghorn and hunting enemy merchant ships. Nelson himself commanded the inshore squadron attempting to support the Austrians by hampering the French advance along the Genoese coast. Since his early experience in Nicaragua and, more recently, before Bastia and Calvi, Nelson enjoyed the excitement of amphibious warfare: bringing his ship close inshore to bombard a column on a coastal road, cutting out supply ships from their anchorages and sending raiding-parties ashore to spike guns and demolish forts and signal towers. But this was not enough to halt the French or put fight into the Austrians, who had been swept from the Italian coastline to the west of the neutral port of Genoa.

At sea, despite the weakened state of the British ships and their crews, there was a new spirit. Nelson found that Jervis seemed 'to consider me more as an associate than a subordinate officer' and was soon given tangible evidence of this when Jervis ordered him to fly the broad pendant of a commodore, second-class, which enabled him to exercise the authority of a junior admiral. Writing to his father, William Hoste explained, 'I suppose your curiosity is excited by the word Commodore Nelson. It gives me infinite pleasure to be able to relieve it, by informing you that our good captain has had this additional mark of distinction conferred on him, which I dare say you will agree with me that his merit richly deserves . . . therefore I must beg, my dear father, to draw an additional cork in honour of our gallant country-man.'

William's letters home were usually hearty, only complaining of the lack of replies from his family, and there was no mention of his deteriorating health, which led Nelson to write to Fanny in May, 1796, 'I can only say Josiah is well, indeed he is never sick. I am sorry I cannot say so much of Hoste. He is a very delicate boy. I have not heard from his father this long time.'

After William's letter about Nelson's promotion in April, his family heard nothing until a letter from a Captain Richard Gardiner, written in Pisa on 3rd June, reached Godwick. This was to tell them that William had been so ill that Nelson had had to send him ashore at Leghorn to be nursed by an English family living there. He wrote, 'What with fatigue, and growing at the same time, a slight fever came on, which he neglected and concealed until a very thin face betrayed the secret. Commodore Nelson immediately sent him on shore to a friend of his, Mr Pollard, a merchant of Leghorn, whose family have taken such care of him that nothing remains of his illness but weakness. He now eats with appetite, and to use his own words, sleeps the whole night, middle watch and all.'

Captain Gardiner then spoke of his popularity since the cutting-out expedition when he had hurt his leg. 'Since the affair at Alassio, where he, commanding a small boat only, cut out a vessel loaded with one thousand seven hundred stand of arms and a great quantity of ammunition, he has become such a favourite with the sailors that with a confidence of success, little less than superstitious, they invariably ask that Hoste may command . . . nor can I give you a better proof of the excellence of his disposition than the friendly visit every officer of the ship daily paid him whilst the *Agamemnon* was at Leghorn.'

While William was sick ashore, and later spending a short convalescence with the Gardiners at Pisa, Nelson finally had to give up his worn-out *Agamemnon* and, in June, shifted to the *Captain*, a 'seventy-four', his appointment as commodore being confirmed by having Captain Ralph Miller subordinate to him in command of the ship. Among those whom he planned to take with him into the new ship was William Hoste but there was a report that he had been captured by the French when, sweeping down the west coast of Italy, they took Leghorn at the end of June. But the Pollards had had time to plan their escape, loading all their furniture into one of the *Agamemnon*'s prizes, that was still lying in the harbour, sailing on the morning the French entered the town and arriving safely at San Fiorenzo a few days later.

The excitement of re-union with his friends brought another minor disaster upon William. During horseplay in the midshipmen's mess in the cockpit, he slipped and injured his other leg, this proving to be a double fracture that kept him immobile for six weeks. Nelson felt bound to tell Dixon Hoste of the accident but his letter was cool: 'Our friends in England sometimes accuse us of not writing so frequently as they wish us; on many occasions we can retort the charge; so says your good son William. I can assure you, which will be enough for a letter, that I have never once had cause to wish him anything but what he is; his accidents, I can truly say, have so happily turned out that I hope he is in no way the worse for them, but I have strongly recommended him not to break any more limbs.'

He told Fanny about 'poor little Hoste' and sent reassuring messages about him to his family. But his references to his step-son remained curt: 'I can only say that Josiah is well, indeed he is never sick'. Occasionally he showed irritation, as when answering Fanny's enquiry about the boy's progress in his French lessons: 'You seem to think Josiah is a master of languages. I must say he is the same exactly as when an infant and likes apples and port wine but it will be difficult to make him speak French, much more Italian. However, I hope his heart is good and that is the principal.'

Meanwhile, the news of the war grew more serious. On land, and particularly in Italy, the French seemed invincible and, in October, Spain declared war on Britain. Even the sixteen-year-old William Hoste, for all his natural optimism, could appreciate the scale of the strategic disaster, writing home from Gibraltar, 'I cannot tell what we are going to do in the Mediterranean . . . if I may be allowed to give my opinion, I cannot see what business we have there. The King of Naples has made peace, the ports of Leghorn and Genoa are shut against us, and Corsica is in the hands of the French; so that there is only a small part of the Isle of Elba in our possession, for which it is hardly worth keeping such a large force in the Mediterranean. Indeed, till a reinforcement reaches us, we cannot go up, as the French and Spaniards have such a superiority.'

At one time he had expected to return home in the *Agamemnon* – although had never suggested to Nelson that he wanted to do so – and homesickness now became acute with the news from Norfolk that his brother Dixon was ill. But, for all his anxiety, he wrote jocularly that 'a couple of his Partridges would not be amiss. I could send him in return some fine Beef which has been in Corn these 10 years. It is rather salt but that is a trifle.'

If there was any certainty it was that with Jervis as Commander-in-Chief and Nelson as his most active subordinate commander, and with powerful, combined French and Spanish fleets free to roam the Mediterranean or to surge out into the Atlantic, a major action was probable, sooner or later.

At the end of the year, Jervis charged Nelson with the final removal of the British naval presence east of Gibraltar and he transferred his broad pendant to the handy frigate *Minerve* to evacuate Elba. It was a dangerous mission and involved him in two brushes with the enemy: a sharp and successful little action off Cartagena and a daring rescue of Lieutenant Thomas Hardy, who was in a boat searching for a man lost overboard and was himself nearly lost to two pursuing Spanish ships of the line. Then, on his way to join Jervis, who had now based his fleet on the Tagus, Nelson found himself sailing in fog through a loose formation of great ships. As soon as he made contact with Jervis, and before re-joining the *Captain*, he was able to report that the Spanish fleet, commanded by Admiral Don José de Cordoba, had broken out of the Mediterranean.

Nelson at first supposed the Spaniards to be making for the West Indies to maraud among British islands and shipping but there was a more direct danger. An invasion of the British Isles was being attempted and, late in 1796 and early in the following year, attempts were made to invade Ireland at Bantry Bay and Wales near Fishguard. Now de Cordoba had been ordered to join the French fleet based on Brest and the Dutch fleet from the Texel so to form a combined force strong enough to cover an invasion of England across the Channel. But first de Cordoba had to call at Cadiz for provisions and would have been lying there but for a gale that had blown him off course, so that he was steering south-east before a westerly wind for his base one hundred and fifty miles away.

That night Jervis could hear the enemy's signal guns through the mist and at dawn on St Valentine's Day, 14th February, the weather cleared enough for the signal lieutenant of the *Barfleur* to shout down from his perch on the main-yard, 'I have a glimpse through the fog of their leeward line and they loom like Beachy Head in a fog. By my soul, they are thumpers. I can distinctly make out *four* tiers of ports in one of them, bearing an admiral's flag.'

Jervis's force numbered fifteen sail of the line, including six first-rates of about one hundred guns and four frigates, and through the clearing mist it gradually became apparent that he was out-numbered by almost two to one. De Cordoba had with him twenty-seven of the line, including his flagship the *Santissima Trinidad* of one hundred and thirty-six guns, and ten frigates. But Jervis did not hesitate to give battle.

It had been the fashion in British ships to mock the fighting qualities of the Spanish Navy. Nelson had written four years earlier that 'the Dons make fine ships, they cannot however make men' and, perhaps taking his cue from this, William Hoste had described Spanish sailors as 'a set of dirty, cowardly rascals . . . a *sans culotte* is a prince compared with the best of them'. But Nelson had recently had reason to modify his view, since the frigate action off Cartagena had been particularly hard fought.

The British ships had had since the preceding day to prepare for battle and a midshipman in one of the 'seventy-fours' described the scene. 'Grinding cutlasses, sharpening pikes, flinting pistols, among the boarders; filling powder, and fitting well-oiled gunlocks on our immense artillery by the gunners . . . the men and officers seemed to me to look taller, and the anticipation of victory was legibly written on each brow . . .' Next morning, he continued, 'The day dawned in the east and "Up all hammocks, ahoy!" resounded through the decks . . . Some were sent to barricade the tops, while the remainder were stowed with unusual care as a bulwark around the upper decks.'

As the two unevenly-matched fleets slowly drew together – the British in a tight line of battle, the Spanish in two separate clusters – neither could do more than guess at the qualities of their opponents behind the tiers of open gun-ports. The British could not know that a high proportion of the 'thumpers'' crews was made up of soldiers and recruits.

The Spanish could not know of the superb gun-drill that had become standard in the British ships during their long seasoning in the Mediterranean. This not only involved the handling of the guns themselves – firing, spongeing-out, re-loading, aiming and firing within ninety seconds – but of the coordination of one, two or three tiers of guns amid the din of battle, billowing clouds of choking smoke and the horrors of death and mutilation. It was essential, initially at least, to give and receive the order for the first rippling broadside at exactly the right moment, perhaps to rake an enemy from stern to stem. It was important that the gunlayers should know not only the range of their target but whether, as was customary in British ships, they should aim for the enemy's hull to knock out his fighting ability or, in the French manner, for his masts and rigging to immobilize him. Similarly to avoid an enemy's raking fire down the length of the gun-decks there must be means of warning the gun-crews to throw themselves to the deck between their guns before the enemy's shot came smashing through the stern windows.

While the guns' crews might decide the action, the seamen must be ready in case of battle damage; perhaps to steer the ship manually from below if the wheel were shattered, or to cut away a tangle of fallen spars and rigging that hampered the fighting of the ship. The marines must be ready to pick off snipers in the enemy's tops and repel boarders, as well as help fight the guns. The boarders had to stand by ready to rig nets from bulwark to yard-arm to keep enemy boarders off the weather decks, or to themselves swarm over the bulwarks or leap from the rigging on to the enemy's decks. Such were some of the practised skills in which the British ships' companies excelled.

The Spanish fleet, steering south-east towards Cadiz, was sailing in two loose formations, one of six ships some seven miles ahead of the main force. Jervis, approaching them on a south-westerly course, decided to thrust his line of battle between the two groups, then turn and engage the stronger with the intention of destroying or mauling it before the other six ships could join battle. Seeing Jervis's intention, de Cordoba turned his main body north so that they would pass the British on an opposite course and the smaller division turned south in the hope of avoiding the British van. The two Spanish divisions might then be able to combine.

Passing between the enemy squadrons, Jervis ordered his line to turn back on to a course parallel with de Cordoba. But his signal was for each ship to wear in succession from the van, a slow process which would keep each ship on its present course until the one ahead had put her helm over. To Nelson in the *Captain*, lying third from the rear of the line, the obvious move was to order the fleet to wear simultaneously so that the whole line would be on the course to engage in the time it took one ship to go about. Indeed, it quickly became clear that by the time the whole line had completed the long, slow turn, the two enemy squadrons would be united in one battle-fleet that, despite its deficiencies, might well be too powerful for the out-numbered British to engage.

Therefore, without receiving orders, or making a signal of explanation, and breaking one of the most sacred of tactical laws, Nelson hauled his ship out of the line, putting her helm hard over and steered straight for the leading 'thumpers' of de Cordoba's fleet. Seeing the *Captain* turn to port and reverse her course by more than a hundred and eighty degrees, Jervis instantly understood the purpose of Nelson's brilliant disobedience and made a signal to the rear ship of his line, the *Excellent*, commanded by Captain Cuthbert Collingwood, a gunnery specialist, to wear his ship also and support the lone challenger.

By half-past one in the afternoon, the *Excellent* had sailed into the billowing gun-smoke that already hid all but the top-masts of the *Captain*. Having seen that Nelson had not only engaged the giant *Santissima Trinidad* but the whole van of Spanish first-rates, and now seeing nothing but the smoke stabbed with the flashes of broadsides, the superb gun-crews of Collingwood's ship were amazed to find the *Captain*, as she appeared through the acrid murk, seemed to have inflicted more damage than she had received. Then came the first rippling thunder of a broadside from the *Excellent*, from cannon manned by crews who claimed to be able to fire, re-load and fire again three times faster than any others. Soon other British ships came up and the action became general.

Nelson now followed his stroke of tactical genius with a demonstration of sheer dash that was to become an heroic legend, immediately throughout the embattled fleet, and later across the world. In the close action, where ships' sides were scorched by their opponents' muzzle-flashes as their hulls thudded together and their yards and rigging became interlocked, the *Captain* crashed against the first-rate *San Nicolas*, her spritsail yard running through the Spaniard's rigging like a harpoon and her port cathead – the beam to which a main anchor was made fast – catching the gilded carving of her starboard quarter-gallery.

Nelson, drawing his sword, shouted for boarders to follow him and ran forward from the quarterdeck for hand-to-hand combat. A soldier of the 69th – one of his acting marines – smashed a window in the stern of the *San Nicolas* and, followed by Nelson himself, scrambled through. They were in one of the officers' great cabins but the Spaniards had locked the doors. These were smashed down with musket-butts and the boarders burst on to the quarterdeck to find that others, who had leapt across the bulwarks above, were already hauling down the Spanish ensign and enemy officers were giving up their swords.

At this moment there was a crackle of musket and pistol fire from the admiral's stern gallery of another enemy first-rate, the *San Josef*, that had loomed up alongside the *San Nicolas*. Instantly, Nelson ordered his men to board her, he himself springing into the main-chains that made fast her standing rigging to the hull. Aghast at this onslaught of wild-eyed men, blackened and bloodied and wielding swords and pistols, pikes and cutlasses, a Spanish officer shouted from the quarterdeck rail that the ship surrendered. Then, as Nelson put it afterwards, 'on the quarterdeck of a Spanish first-rate, extravagant as the story may seem, did I receive the swords of vanquished Spaniards, which I gave to one of my bargemen, William Fearney, who put them with the greatest *sang froid*, under his arm.' And he added delightedly, 'There is a saying in the fleet too flattering to omit telling – viz. "Nelson's Patent Bridge for boarding first rates."'

It had been a day of high excitement which reached its climax as Jervis, standing on the quarterdeck of his flagship, the *Victory*, led his men in three cheers for the *Captain* as they sailed past the half-wrecked ship. Nelson had not only been instantly forgiven for his disregard of orders and tactical dogma, but Jervis was congratulating him just as much for that as for boarding and taking two enemy first-rates, one stormed from the deck of the other.

The battle had lasted more than two hours and then, as the smaller Spanish division at last joined the fight, Jervis decided that enough had been achieved and more need not be risked and, taking his four prizes in tow, broke off the action, leaving the battered enemy to escape to Cadiz. The British casualties had been surprisingly light, even the hotly-engaged *Captain* suffering only about seventy-five, a third of them killed, but the Spanish had lost heavily, ten of their escaping ships being heavily damaged.

Nelson had left Josiah with Captain Miller in the *Captain*, helping to muster more boarders to send over his 'Patent Bridge' to the *San Josef* and William Hoste was, despite his protests, also left behind. Two days afterwards, the latter, resting from the labour of repairing battle-damage, found time to send his father a scrawl, justifiably boasting that 'never, I believe, was such an action fought'. Two days later Nelson wrote to Dixon Hoste, 'You will be anxious to hear a line of your good and brave William after the sharp services of the *Captain* on the 14th. I have hitherto said so much of my dear William, that I can only repeat, his gallantry never can be exceeded, and that each day rivets him stronger to my heart.'

The family at Godwick were disappointed at the lack of a stirring description of the battle to read to their friends and Dixon Hoste wrote to his son, asking for 'an accurate account of the action'. But this was not forthcoming, even when he had time to write at length. All he would say on this was, 'Certainly my scrawl of the 16th of February was not the most elegant epistle, but I hope you will excuse it, for at that time we were all hurry and confusion. However, I believe it fully answered the purpose it was written for, in letting you know that poor Billy Shanks was among the living, and ready to lend a hand to thrash those cowardly Dons once more.'

Nelson, in his letter to Fanny, was scant in his praise of Josiah: 'I am most perfectly well and rich in honour as is Josiah and Hoste.' In his next two letters he did not mention his step-son then, on 3rd March, told Fanny that he was sending Josiah to join another ship, a sloop commanded by his friend Captain Edward Berry, another Norfolkman. 'I have sent Josiah with Captain Berry, who wished to have him and he will learn more with him than he could with me and he must be broke of being at my elbow,' he wrote, adding in an attempt to reassure, 'I assure you I love him and I am confident it's reciprocal. His understanding is manly and his heart is as good as we can wish, but the same shyness is still visible and it is his nature and cannot be altered . . . Hoste is with me here, in the action he made me promise never to leave him again.'

The Battle of Cape St Vincent, as it was named after the nearest point of land, was the beginning of Nelson's national and international fame. Although he had not known it, his automatic promotion to rear-admiral had been gazetted twelve days before the battle and now to full flag rank was to be added the first of the honours, the King creating him a Knight of the Bath.

The *Captain* had been so cut about in the battle that she had to stay at Lisbon for repairs while Nelson hoisted his flag in the *Irresistible*, taking Hoste with him. They made a dangerous expedition into the Mediterranean to bring out the last of the forces left at Elba but again withdrew to the west of Gibraltar, although there had been talk of sending Nelson in command of a squadron to support the Austrians in the Adriatic. Nothing came of this bold idea but it was recognized by the Admiralty that there would be only one junior admiral to be considered for such a mission.

On their return to Jervis, who had now been created Earl of St Vincent, the two moved to the *Theseus*, of seventy-four guns. Hoste was disappointed because, although many officers who had served in the *Agamemnon* went with them, most of the *Captain*'s company, many of them old *Agamemnons*, remained where they were, and the crew of the new flagship had not been in action since she had been commissioned. Hoste wrote home that he hoped that the Spaniards would attempt a sortie from Cadiz so that 'our brave admiral will have an opportunity of initiating the *Theseus* crew into his fighting rules'.

One reason for the exchange of officers, including Miller as flag captain, was that the *Theseus* had played a prominent part in the mutiny at Spithead. Discontent with the hardships of life on the lower deck – the lack of shore leave, the cramped living quarters, the disgusting food, the pitiful pay and the rough discipline – had been brought to a head by two principal factors: the forcible impressment of vast numbers of civilians for service at sea and the revolution in France.

At Spithead, mutiny had broken out in mid-May and lasted for a month. The Admiralty, forced to face realities, had met the modest demands of the mutineers, who had behaved throughout with moderation, making it clear that they would at once return to duty should the French try to take advantage of the situation and put to sea. The mutiny at the Nore was a different matter since it began only three days before order was restored at Spithead and lasted for more than a month after these grievances had, in part, been settled. This was seen by the Admiralty as an attempt at social and economic revolution rather than a demonstration to air discontent and it was put down with severity and many hangings at the yard-arm.

Mutinous ripples spread far from home ports with the dispatch of ships to join distant squadrons. That summer, there was trouble in one of St Vincent's ships and four leaders of what was regarded as subversion in the *St George* were hanged at the yard-arm in view of the assembled fleet on a Sunday morning, a day on which executions normally never took place. But the communicated enthusiasm of Nelson and his officers quickly made itself felt and, soon after he had hoisted his flag in the *Theseus*, an unsigned note was found on the quarterdeck. It read, 'Success attend Admiral Nelson. God bless Captain Miller. We thank them for the officers they have placed over us. We are happy and comfortable, and will shed every drop of blood in our veins to support them, and the name of the *Theseus* shall be immortalized as high as the *Captain*.'

There was not long to wait for such an opportunity. In May, Nelson was given command of the inshore squadron off Cadiz and it was clear that he would not be content with the passive work of blockade. By the end of June it was reported that twenty-eight Spanish ships of the line in the harbour were ready for sea and, partly as an attempt to provoke them into doing that and partly to take the British sailors' minds off mutinous thoughts, St Vincent ordered Nelson to bombard the principal naval arsenal of Spain.

The attacks took place on the nights of 3rd and 5th July. In the first, a bomb-vessel anchored about a mile from the walls of the town, covered by gunboats and armed ships' boats under Nelson's personal command. She began to throw her shells but the heavy mortar became unstable on its mounting and the ship had to withdraw, this provoking not the emergence of the enemy's fleet but of a flotilla of Spanish gunboats in an attempt to capture her. There was fierce hand-to-hand fighting, the most savage being between the sixteen officers and men in Nelson's boat and the thirty in the Spanish commander's in what the former described as 'a service hand-to-hand with swords'. Nelson's coxswain, John Sykes, an 'old *Agamemnon*' from Lincolnshire, fought at the admiral's left side, parrying at least two sword-cuts that would have proved fatal to him.

That night, the Spanish were driven back into Cadiz, leaving three prizes in British hands, including their commander's boat which had surrendered to Nelson after all its crew had been killed or wounded. The second bombardment by three bomb-vessels covered by a stronger escort was more successful, forcing some of the Spanish ships of the line to warp up the harbour out of range of the plunging mortar-bombs. There was another clash between boat-flotillas and again, after a fierce flurry of swords and pistols, the Spanish withdrew. In one of these actions Hoste was wounded in the right hand and, for a time, there was fear of lock-jaw. But he recovered without having mentioned either the wound, or the circumstances in which it was received, in letters home.

The ship's company of the *Theseus* had now settled down in the rough contentment and intense loyalty that was characteristic of all Nelson's commands. Most grateful of all for his generosity were the boys he had taken to sea with him four years before, for now the time for their promotion to lieutenant and a regular commission was at hand. Before this could be attained, the candidate had to have served, or rather, been 'borne on the books', of one of His Majesty's ships for four years as 'captain's servant' – or, as they were called after 1794, First Class Volunteer – and for at least two years as a midshipman. By the summer of 1797, none of the boys who had joined the *Agamemnon* with Nelson had served the necessary time to qualify to be 'made' lieutenant. Yet there were ways of cheating the regulations, which were well known and usually tolerated in time of war. One of these was for a boy to have his name entered in a ship's muster book while still a small child – as Dixon Hoste had entered William's – this counting as 'time' on his certificate of service.

Thus, Nelson was able to arrange for Josiah to be given a probationary commission as lieutenant by St Vincent – subject to later confirmation by the Admiralty – in April of that year when he had only been at sea four years. Telling Fanny of this, he added, 'I want Hoste, Bolton and Weatherhead to be made . . . but as yet I cannot cheat for their time.' At the end of June, he wrote again, saying, 'Bolton is a lieutenant of a 74 and will be removed into the first good frigate which may be vacant. Hoste would have been the same but I cannot get his time out. Poor Weatherhead cannot be managed. When peace comes I shall change him into a frigate which will remain out.'

This promise to keep John Weatherhead in employment, whether or not he had been 'made', was in recognition of the boy's professional promise. While still in the Mediterranean, he had been promoted from midshipman to the slightly senior rank of mate and, once the problem of producing an acceptable certificate of service had been overcome, he would make an admirable lieutenant. Hoste had been a midshipman for more than three years but his time was still short of the six years by nearly two. Nelson urged the boy to explain this to his father who must send out confirmation that he had been on the *Europa*'s books in 1785. Dixon Hoste was not slow to act since he had need of a lieutenant's prize-money; his wife was about to give birth again and his son George was about to begin schooling at Rugby which Dick had just left for Cambridge. In April, Fanny wrote to her husband, 'Mr Hoste is gone to London to see if he can get his son's time made out, as he was upon some books.'

By midsummer, Nelson had been able to arrange the provisional promotion of Weatherhead to lieutenant and, his step-son re-joining him in the *Theseus*, he could write home, '. . . Josiah very much improved. I hope he will make a good man.' He himself was in high good spirits, basking in the praise of his brother officers and the newspapers from home for his daring at St Vincent and Cadiz. Later, when writing an autobiographical sketch, he noted of this summer, 'It was during this period that perhaps my personal courage was more conspicuous than at any other part of my life.'

He had been disappointed at not being able to thrust his head into the lion's mouth by taking a squadron through the Mediterranean to the Adriatic, but now an even more exciting mission was being discussed, one that had the added temptation of prize-money, possibly on a dazzling scale. This was a plan to cut out a Spanish treasure-ship from the harbour of Santa Cruz at Tenerife in the Canary Islands.

This inhospitable island – with few anchorages in its deep waters, perpetual surf on rocky shores and sudden squalls howling down from its volcanic mountains – was the scene of a satisfactory little *coup* at the end of May. Two frigates, cruising off Santa Cruz, had sighted a smart brig at anchor and resolved to cut her out. Under Nelson's friend, Lieutenant Hardy, the boats had pulled across to her under fire and their crews had seized the ship after a scuffle. She proved to be the French brig *La Mutine*, of fourteen guns, a beautiful little ship of about three hundred and fifty tons, and was at once put in commission by her captors, her command being given to Hardy himself by St Vincent.

Now there was talk of a far richer prize. The idea had been suggested by Nelson himself before the bombardment of Cadiz and now, in July, the raid was authorized by St Vincent and Nelson given command of three 'seventy-fours', a fifty-gun ship, three frigates and a cutter to put it into execution.

It was to be a surprise attack. The frigates, under Nelson's friend Captain Thomas Troubridge, were to make their final approach after dark, their boats, with muffled oars, putting strong landing-parties ashore to the north-east of Santa Cruz. The assault on the fortifications would be launched before dawn and, at first light, the ships of the line would come up to support the assault with their broadsides. The town was not expected to be strongly defended and its surrender, after the loss of the outer forts, was considered probable and therefore no grand attack on the city walls and the citadel of San Cristobal necessary.

Just before sunset on 20th July, the great volcanic peak of Mount Teide rose out of the western horizon and from that moment tension of dramatic intensity was felt on board the ships sailing towards the island over a tossing sea. Also from that time plans started to go wrong. Troubridge's frigates, their landing-parties armed and standing by the boats, stood in towards Santa Cruz and were within three miles of the beaches by midnight. But a strong, unexpected current scoured the coast and, at dawn, they were still a mile off-shore and all hope of surprise had been lost. Had Nelson been in direct command he would, as he suggested later, have attacked despite this. But the cautious Troubridge hesitated and waited until the main force came up with him to ask the admiral's advice. So by the time his landing-parties finally scrambled ashore over the black lava rocks, the commanding heights were strongly held by Spanish infantry and, unable to make progress, the British withdrew under cover of darkness.

Nor had the ships fared any better, finding themselves unable to get within bombarding range of the forts. Now the weather deteriorated further and a full gale was blowing by the 24th, forcing the squadron to shelter in a bay to the north-east of the town. The frustration and the wild weather had given the island an ominous, Gothic malevolence. The surf broke on black rocks and black sand and black cliffs rose to jagged black peaks rising twelve thousand feet to the cone of the volcano, the greenery and the profusion of flowers around the apricot-tiled farmhouses, the pine woods and, higher still, the white-blossoming broom, only accentuating the funereal black of the lava.

Yet Nelson was not to be thwarted and decided to lead a direct assault on the city himself after dark on the night of the 24th. Confident of success, and having given his orders, he spent the evening at supper with Captain Thomas Fremantle, who commanded the frigate *Seahorse*, and his young bride Betsey, whom he had met in Naples and who had married from the Hamiltons' house. Both men were about to risk their lives in the attack but, as Mrs Fremantle put it, 'the taking of this place seemed an easy and almost sure thing' and it was a light-hearted occasion. Nelson, when changing into clean clothes, as was customary before battle to reduce the risk of infected wounds, could find no white silk stockings so put on a pair decorated with vertical blue stripes, so adding to the air of easy confidence.

Both Josiah and William were to be left in the *Theseus* but the former, eager to demonstrate his courage to his critical step-father, insisted that, as a lieutenant, he was as entitled to a place in the boats as was Lieutenant Weatherhead; Nelson, perhaps feeling that he must not be suspected of sheltering the boy from danger, eventually agreed that he should come in his own boat.

At eleven o'clock, nearly a thousand sailors and marines, embarked in the squadron's boats, in the cutter *Fox* and in a captured Spanish vessel, set out in the stormy darkness for Santa Cruz. It was planned that they should run straight into the harbour, storm the mole, fight their way into the town and concentrate in the main square before summoning the garrison to surrender.

The boats lurched through rough seas in total darkness but were still hundreds of yards from the mole when the alarm was given and the shore batteries opened fire. Most dangerous was a battery of five twenty-four pounder brass cannon mounted in a semi-circular fort to the east of the mole; four of the guns, loaded with round-shot, trained out to sea, the fifth, named El Tigre, loaded with grape-shot and trained up the harbour to fire upon any raiders that escaped the other four. As Nelson's boat ran alongside the mole and he was in the act of drawing his sword and springing ashore, the gun-layer of El Tigre saw his target in the light of gun-flashes and fired. The spread of shot caught the British in their backs, one shot shattering Nelson's right elbow so that he reeled, spouting blood, and fell back into the boat. Josiah, waiting to follow him ashore, caught his step-father, and, tearing off his own neckerchief bound it as a tourniquet above the wound, so saving his step-father's life.

On the mole itself, swept by grape-shot, the survivors were driving the defenders from their batteries and spiking the guns. Knowing that the admiral's life was of the highest importance, Josiah ordered the boat back to the squadron, pulling away close under the walls of the commanding fort so that the guns could not be depressed sufficiently to finish their work. As they reached the open sea, they saw the *Fox*, crowded with seamen and marines, come bouncing through the rough seas when a round-shot caught her below the waterline and she began to sink fast.

Nelson insisted that his boat join the attempts at rescue so it was nearly an hour before they reached the *Theseus* at two in the morning. Hoste was on deck and described the scene in a distraught letter to his father: 'Adml. Nelson returned on board being dreadfully wounded in his right arm with a grape shot. I leave you to judge of my situation Sir when I found that the man whom I may say has been a second father to me. [*sic*] To see his right arm dangling by his side while with his left he jumped up the ship's side and with a spirit that astonished everyone told the Surgeon to get his instruments ready, for that he knew he must lose his arm and that the sooner it was off the better.

'He underwent the amputation with the same firmness and courage that have always marked his character, and I am happy to say is now in a fair way of recovery.'

Meanwhile, the assault had met disaster. The landing-parties on the mole had been almost wiped out by grape-shot and musket-fire; other boats that had missed their landing-places had crashed on to the rocks on the far side of the harbour; those who were not drowned scrambled ashore, their ammunition wet and useless. The survivors tried to rally round their ships' flags – Union Jacks with the ships' names painted on the horizontal red stripe – and fight their way into the town. Under fire from the citadel and ramparts and the over-hanging latticed windows of the houses, they fought their way up the narrow streets, paved with black lava cobbles, to the square. There, three hundred and forty men, led by four captains – including Troubridge and Miller; Fremantle was among the wounded – were surrounded by some eight thousand Spanish troops and forty French guns. Hopeless as it might have seemed, they planned to assault the citadel rather than surrender. When, on reflection, this was recognized as suicidal they still had the nerve to issue an ultimatum that they would burn the town unless they were allowed to re-embark in the squadron unmolested.

Hoste remained on deck all night, hearing increasingly disastrous news as boats, which had not even been able to put their men ashore, returned. Nearly a hundred men had been lost in the *Fox* and it was reported that the remnants of the landing-parties in the town had had to surrender. At nine, Hoste heard the most tragic news of all and wrote of this some days later; 'At 9 a Flag of Truce came off from Santa Cruz with a Spanish officer and the Captain of the *Emerald*, who besides other bad news informed us that Lieutenant Weatherhead was mortally wounded in the belly. This was a stroke which indeed I could hardly stand against. However, convinced that it was not a time to give way, I got everything in my power ready for his reception and about 11 he was conveyed on board in a cradle. The Surgeon examined his wound and said he thought it impossible he could live long. I am sorry to say his words proved too true. And now, Sir, am I come to the worst part of my story. He lingered out to Saturday the 29th of July and then departed seemingly without pain. In losing him I lost a good companion and a true friend and I believe I may say the Nation lost as brave an officer as ever stepped on board a ship. He was the darling of the ship's company and universally beloved by every person who had the pleasure of his acquaintance. His body was committed to the deep on Sunday the 30th and 3 vollies of musquetry fired in honor to his Memory.'

At the end of this long letter, Hoste added, 'I had almost forgot to say that on the death of Weatherhead, Admiral Nelson gave me a commission to act as lieutenant in his vacancy; happy would it have made me had it been in any other as I shall ever regret the loss of him.'

As the squadron, the survivors of its landing-parties embarked, sailed away from Tenerife at the end of July, mourning the deaths of one hundred and forty-six officers, seamen and marines, it was apparent that they were also to lose their admiral, whose wound would necessitate a long convalescence and might even end his naval career.

One of Nelson's first signatures with his left hand was on the certificate of Hoste's provisional promotion but he was careful to point out that this could only be confirmed when his certificate of six years' service was submitted. This dashed Hoste's hope of returning to England with Nelson and he told his father, 'He is going home in the *Seahorse*. I am afraid I shall not be able to accompany him as he tells me if I was to go to England before my time was out the Admiralty would not confirm me . . . He wishes you to send my Time out immediately.'

Despite his new rank, he was saddened by the death of one friend and the departure of another, ending his letter, 'I am afraid, Sir, you will think me rather abrupt. You must suppose that I am rather low-spirited about losing two such friends.'

The urgency in getting Dixon Hoste to send out his 'time' certificate seemed more urgent when St Vincent promoted Josiah Nisbet to the rank of commander, giving him command of the hospital ship *Dolphin*. Hoste had none of the feelings for Josiah that he had had for John Weatherhead and noted tartly, 'Pretty quick promotion, I think.' So he again wrote to his father of the need to end his 'servitude as midshipman', which was still his substantive rank.

Dixon Hoste, realizing that the sooner his son commanded a ship the sooner he could hope for prize-money and support for his own heavy spending, had been to the Admiralty and, on 8th November, acquired a certificate of service declaring that his 'time' amounted to exactly six years. This total was, of course, made up of William's time in the *Agamemnon, Captain* and *Theseus* but there were also two surprising entries that claimed that he had served two spells of, together, one year, two months and eight days in the *Europa*. This service had apparently been in the years 1785 and 1786 when William had been five and six years old.

Disappointed as he was not to be accompanying Nelson to England, Hoste gloried in his new rank. Now he had finally, he hoped, left what he called 'the lower regions' to 'mess in the ward room with a jovial set of officers'. While waiting for his certificate to arrive, he wrote to his father that 'great is the difference I find between the wardroom and the cockpit. I should now be able to receive you in *style* on your coming on board.'

He hoped that his father would meet Nelson in England, asking that he 'present my best respects and tell him I ardently long to serve under his flag'. What he did not know was that Dixon Hoste still owed the admiral money that he had advanced to his son. But for William's sake the Nelsons avoided a confrontation, remaining polite yet cool. Fanny, who met the parson in Bath, wrote to her husband shortly before the action at Tenerife, that 'Mr Hoste drank tea here last night, made many handsome speeches. I fancied he felt a little. I was very polite and took care not to be a bit stiff.' But old Edmund Nelson had remarked sharply when Hoste had left that when the latter had spoken of a brief visit to a country house he had probably 'found that neighbourhood too thin' to be attractive. Nelson himself wrote a magnanimous letter to Dixon Hoste about his efforts on William's behalf.

'I did write a line to Mr Coke, to tell him how I had disposed of his recommendations, both of whom have done him so much honour,' he wrote. 'But one gallant fellow Weatherhead is gone; your dear good son is as gallant, and I hope he will long live to honour Norfolk and England. I grieved to have left him, but it is necessary; and Lord St Vincent will continue to be his kind protector and friend: his worth as a man and as an officer exceeds all which the most sincere friend can say of him. I pray God to bless my dear William; happy father in such a son.

'As to myself, I suppose I was getting well too fast, for I am beset with a physician, surgeon and apothecary, and to say the truth, I am suffering much pain with some fever; but time, I hope, will restore me to tolerable health.

'Captain Ralph Willet Miller is captain of the *Theseus*, one who loves William, and is the only truly virtuous man I ever saw. I beg my best respects to Mrs Hoste . . .'

Despite such courtesies, Dixon Hoste did not pay his debts during Nelson's convalescence. A few days after he had returned to sea, hoisting his flag in the 'seventy-four' *Vanguard* in March of the following year, Fanny wrote to say that the parson had been pleading poverty and that his income was only £60 a year. Soon after she heard from him again and told her husband, 'Mr Hoste is very sorry he did not see you but hopes you will take his son and that it will not be inconvenient to me to wait 10 days longer for the money. What can I say to such shabby people. I will wait ten days and then I will write again . . .'

But, towards the end of June, she was writing of Dixon Hoste and two other defaulting parents of her husband's protégés, 'No money from Bolton, Hoste and Cooper.'

William, meanwhile, was making the best of the routine of blockading Cadiz, enlivened by an occasional 'smart touch' with the Spanish gun-boats. Then, at the beginning of 1798, his service certificate, duly authorized by the Admiralty, arrived and in February he took his examination for the substantive rank of lieutenant. Nelson and Dixon Hoste had brought to bear all possible influence and both Thomas Coke and the Marchioness Townshend had written to St Vincent from Norfolk in William's praise. The old admiral himself took an interest and Hoste wrote home that 'the day before my examination, he sent for me on board the *Ville de Paris* and took me into his own cabin. I could not help laughing when he laid hold of me and turned me round three or four times, saying I was a *smart young fellow*. He asked me if I had not had both my legs broke in the service, which I answered in the affirmative; – whether I had heard from home lately, – and hoped all my friends were well. I assure you, my heart was so full with gratitude to a person whom I had never seen more than once that I could hardly speak.'

Next day, he took the examination and passed.

The blockade was not particularly arduous, since the ships could put into either Lisbon or Gibraltar for provisions and Hoste gratefully noted that, instead of salt beef and pease pudding, there was now fresh fish and vegetables and that 'it is quite common to see green peas and beans at every ward-room table in the fleet.' At Gibraltar there was plenty of shore leave and time to explore the fortifications and ride on the neutral ground, which was safe despite being within gunshot of Spain. Indeed, to Hoste's surprise, 'the Spaniards were very civil, and saluted us as we rode along their works, but I believe more through fear than anything else; for the Governor threatens to open the batteries upon them if the least insult is offered to any English officers.'

The wardroom officers made up a party to explore the caverns of the Rock ('wonderful indeed, and well worth seeing') and marvel at the strength of the fortifications. 'In my opinion,' wrote Hoste, 'it would be a capital place for the French Directory to send an army to attack, as I understand their military begin to be rather troublesome.' They were indeed, for the Army of Italy, commanded by General Bonaparte had, sweeping south, just captured Rome.

But, at Gibraltar, the officers enjoyed their peaceful interlude and there was even a chance to dress up for a ball. 'I was not of the party, though invited,' Hoste wrote to his sister Kate. 'You know I never cut a *figure* in dancing when in England, and I assure you I have not improved much since, for God knows we have something else to do besides dancing. We have often a reel on board, and I am a capital hand at it; but a country dance is quite out of my latitude. I am sure you would laugh most heartily were you to see our ball-room and music. Figure to yourself a poor unfortunate fiddler, stuck up in one corner of the ward-room, striking up some merry tune, whilst we, from the rolling of the ship, or the creaking of her sides, can hardly hear him at the other: however, it is what we are used to and it gives us as much pleasure for the moment as the best band at St James's.'

At the end of April when Nelson arrived in the Tagus, with his friend Berry as flag captain of the *Vanguard*, the blockade of Cadiz had become a more dangerous duty with the Spanish gun-boats becoming increasingly aggressive. Although St Vincent kept twenty sail of the line and some frigates off the port, the gun-boats – armed with a twenty-six pounder gun or a carronade throwing a fifty-two-pound shot – did not hesitate to attack when there was a straggler to be picked off. There were said to be a hundred and sixty of these craft in the harbour and more than a third of them might swarm out to sea if a single British ship became becalmed and reinforcements were unable to reach her. Nelson's immediate reaction on assessing this situation was that he should have brought some bomb-vessels with him from England to mount a major bombardment of the port, where, in any case, there were thought to be thirty-three of the line and many frigates ready for sea.

At Lisbon, Josiah Nisbet and his step-father were reunited but relations between the two seemed to have deteriorated. On the day after his arrival, Nelson wrote a letter to Fanny that was hurtfully critical of her son. He had not cultivated diplomatic acquaintance ashore as he ought and there was the tart observation that 'I hope he will make a good man, when we shall be happy'.

A few days later, the *Vanguard* joined St Vincent's ships off Cadiz, Nelson expecting to be given command of the inshore squadron that was now so closely engaged. But the Commander-in-Chief had other, even more exciting, plans for the young admiral – still some months short of forty – whose return, the old man said, 'has given me new life'. Nelson was to re-enter the Mediterranean.

Since the British had been forced to retire west of Gibraltar, the previous year, disturbing reports had been arriving from Toulon. Merchant captains and travellers had heard that the French were not only preparing a major fleet for sea but that a formidable expeditionary force was being assembled under General Bonaparte. Nelson was therefore to undertake a dangerous armed reconnaissance with only three 'seventy-fours' and some frigates to assess the enemy's intentions.

The most likely objective of the French was thought to be Naples. The Kingdom of the Two Sicilies had been forced into neutrality by the advance of Bonaparte's Army of Italy on Rome and the destruction of the Venetian Republic. In the autumn of 1797 the Austrians, who had been defeated by Bonaparte at Rivoli early in the year, made peace with France with the Treaty of Campo Formio, ceding Belgium and Lombardy in return for a shaky hold on Venice, Istria and Dalmatia.

But the subsequent occupation of Switzerland and Rome by the French had alarmed the Empress Maria Theresa of Austria as this pointed to Naples as the next victim and her daughter, Queen Maria Carolina, was the active consort of King Ferdinand IV, King of the Two Sicilies. There was, therefore, a possibility that Austria and the Two Sicilies would unite against the French, a move that the French might try to forestall and the British would have to support.

Both St Vincent and the Cabinet in London had come to the conclusion that naval action must be taken in the Mediterranean and the Admiralty sent reinforcements to the fleet off Cadiz so that a powerful squadron could be spared to sail east of Gibraltar. Knowing that Nelson, who had already departed on his mission, would make contact with the French and take as much offensive action as his strength allowed, St Vincent immediately sent after him a strong squadron of ten 'seventy-fours' with his most experienced captains, 'choice fellows from the inshore squadron'. Among them was the *Theseus*.

Nelson's need for them was more urgent than St Vincent, or the commander of the reinforcement, Troubridge, could have known. While keeping watch off Toulon, his little squadron was struck by a sudden squall of freakish violence and the *Vanguard* dismasted and almost lost. A midshipman named Meek, another of Thomas Coke's recommendations from Norfolk, had been swept overboard but the ship was saved and, four days later, had been re-rigged and was ready for action. But in the storm his two frigates and the twenty-gun *Bonne Citoyenne* were damaged and blown off course, parting company with the three big ships. When the weather moderated, their captains wrongly assumed that Nelson would return to Gibraltar for repairs and so did that themselves. Thus when Troubridge's squadron came up with the *Vanguard*, Nelson found that, although he had a fine fleet of thirteen 'seventy-fours', he had no frigates for scouting, as St Vincent had assumed that the three light ships were still with his squadron. The only ships available for reconnaissance were the *Leander*, of fifty guns, which could well take her place in his line of battle, and the little *Mutine* that had been cut out from Santa Cruz and was still commanded by Hardy. But neither was an effective substitute for a fast, powerful frigate.

What Nelson could not know as he strove to ride out the storm was that the north-westerly gale that had dismasted his flagship had carried Bonaparte out of Toulon with his own fleet and his expeditionary force. While the *Vanguard* had been struggling for survival, she had been passed by an armada of seventy-two warships – including fifteen of the line and fourteen frigates – and some four hundred transports in which were embarked an army of thirty-six thousand men. By the time Troubridge arrived he knew that the French had sailed but he had no idea what their destination might be, only orders to hunt them down to the farthest corner of the Mediterranean, or, if necessary, through the Dardanelles and into the Black Sea.

So he steered first for Naples, sending the *Mutine* and the *Leander* to make enquiries on the coast and from merchant ships. Then, on 17th May, the fleet stood into the Bay of Naples, both Nelson and William Hoste seeing the magnificent sweep of city and volcano for the first time for five years. There was no time for social pleasantries, so Troubridge was sent in the *Mutine* to visit Hamilton and ask his advice. But the ambassador was no wiser than the admiral and could only suggest that Bonaparte had gone to Malta. Nelson himself was convinced that while the French might attempt to seize Malta or sail farther east to Corfu, which had already fallen into their hands on the collapse of the Venetian Republic, there could only be one of two major ambitions worthy of so strong an expedition. One of these was Sicily, the other Egypt. 'If they pass Sicily,' he wrote, 'I shall believe they are going on their scheme of possessing Alexandria and getting troops to India.'

The only way to discover the truth was to follow his strategic instinct for he still had no means of carrying out wide reconnaissance: 'My distress for frigates is extreme.' Sailing south to the Straits of Messina, Nelson received news that the French had, indeed, taken Malta, installed a garrison and departed. This could only mean that the enemy had gone to Corfu or Alexandria and the consensus of his and his captains' opinion was that it was the latter and, crowding sail, the squadron steered for the mouth of the Nile. They arrived off Alexandria on 23rd June to find it empty of French shipping and were aghast at the realization that their strategic theory had been wrong and that Bonaparte must have invaded Sicily after all.

Three weeks later, Nelson was off the Sicilian coast only to hear that there had been no French attack but that their fleet had been sighted sailing south-east a month before. Their destination must have been Alexandria after all and the opposing forces had clearly passed each other on opposite courses in the night.

As the British again put their helms over and made for Alexandria, two further facts were clear. One was that Bonaparte would have been able to put his army ashore in Egypt; the other was that if his fleet could be destroyed his soldiers would be stranded and, in effect, destroyed as a fighting force.

There was no need for frigates now, for it was Nelson's intention to take the enemy by surprise with the full weight of his main force. It was a magnificent squadron, worked up to a pitch of efficiency by the long chase, its captains imbued with their admiral's tigerish zeal. At noon on 1st August, the squadron was again off Alexandria and this time it was crowded with the masts of Bonaparte's transports. There was no point in attempting to destroy empty merchant ships, so the British sailed past the port in search of the warships that could not be far away. They were found fifteen miles to the east, moored in a defensive arc across Aboukir Bay supported by shore batteries and with the great flagship *L'Orient*, of one hundred and twenty guns, anchored in the centre of their line.

The French had thirteen sail of the line and four powerful frigates to oppose thirteen British ships of the line, the *Leander* and the little *Mutine* but their weight of fire was heavier because, in addition to *L'Orient*, there were three ships of eighty guns.

It was already late in the afternoon and, although there was no chance of joining battle until sunset for what would be a night action against a superior force waiting in a strong defensive position, Nelson, remembering the disastrous consequences of delay at Tenerife, decided to attack immediately. The British formed line of battle, the flagship *Vanguard* lying third, with the *Theseus* close astern.

The French admiral, de Brueys, thought himself impregnable with his flanks protected not only by shore batteries and gun-boats but by shoals. So confident was he that the landward side of his gun-decks were cluttered with stores and baggage in the belief that, in the event of a British attack, only the guns on the seaward side would have to be fired. But he had moored his ships some five hundred feet apart and, noting this, Foley of the *Goliath*, acting on his own initiative, steered round the head of the French line, other British ships following his example, and sailed between the enemy ships to batter them from the landward side. Thus, with four British ships within the French position, Nelson's squadron could move down their line at leisure, two ships throwing their broadsides into each one of their opponents. The French fleet was doomed.

In the *Theseus*, Hoste knew that Miller would take his ship into the hottest of the fight. In the hope of attracting the enemy's attention, he had camouflaged his ship to look like a three-decked first-rate by painting black squares on the canvas covering the barricade of hammocks in the nettings around the bulwarks, that acted as protection against flying splinters, to look at a distance like another tier of gun-ports.

As Miller took the *Theseus* along the French line in the wake of the *Goliath* and *Zealous*, he picked his target, the ship alongside which he would anchor for a fight to destruction. Writing after the battle to his wife, he described this final approach to the enemy when he 'observed their shot sweep just over us and knowing well that at such a moment Frenchmen would not have the coolness to change their elevation, I closed them suddenly, and, running under the arch of their shot, reserved my fire, every gun being loaded with two and some with three round shot, until I had the *Guerrier*'s masts in a line, and her jib-boom about six feet clear of our rigging; we then opened with such effect, that a second breath could not be drawn before her main and mizzen mast were also gone. This was precisely at sun-set . . .'

Having raked the *Guerrier*, Miller anchored against the *Spartiate* and had opened with his port broadside when, through the billows of smoke, he saw, lit by gun-flashes, the *Vanguard* engaging the same ship from the far side. So, wrote Miller, 'I desisted firing on her that I might not do mischief to our friends and directed every gun before the main-mast of the *Aquilon* and all abaft it on the *Conquerant*, and giving up my proper bird to the Admiral.'

The battle raged all night in what Miller described as 'all magnificent, awful, horrific grandeur'. The tall, elegant tracery of masts and rigging collapsed on to decks and over ships' sides in tangles of tarred hemp and splintered wood; gun-ports erupted with flame and smoke, then excreted the mangled bodies of dead and dying men, for the hopelessly-wounded were heaved into the sea by their shipmates with the corpses; the sides of ships, painted smartly with horizontal bands of colour, were streaked vertically with blood from the scuppers.

The climax – but not the end – of the battle came when *L'Orient* caught fire. 'She was soon in a blaze,' wrote Miller, 'displaying a most grand and awful spectacle, such as formerly would have drawn tears down the Victor's cheeks, but now pity was stifled as it rose by the remembrance of the numerous and horrid atrocities their unprincipled and blood-thirsty Nation had and were committing; and when she blew up at about 11 o'clock, though I endeavoured to stop the momentary cheer of the Ship's company, my heart scarce felt a single pang for their fate.'

The crew of the *Theseus* were exhausted both by fighting their guns and by throwing buckets of water over their decks and sides to reduce the risk of fire when *L'Orient* blew up. Miller was even able to sleep for half an hour at the height of the battle and was woken by Captain Hood of the *Zealous*, who came on board to propose that, having demolished their immediate opponents, they move farther down the enemy line. 'My people were also so extremely jaded,' Miller recorded, 'that as soon as they had hove our sheet anchor up, they dropped under the capstan-bars and were asleep in a moment in every sort of posture, having been then working at their fullest exertion, or fighting, for near twelve hours, without being able to benefit by the respite that occurred, because while *L'Orient* was on fire, I had the ship completely sluiced, as one of our precautionary measures against fire, or combustibles falling on board us when she blew up.'

The *Theseus* reached her new position before dawn and began to engage comparatively undamaged enemy ships. But by now the French were striking their colours and boarding-parties were being called away to take possession of prizes. One of these was the forty-gun frigate *L'Artemise*, which had been lying within the French line. As the *Theseus*'s broadsides compelled the 'seventy-four' *L'Heureux* to surrender followed by the *Mercure*. At this *L'Artemise* fired her broad-side and promptly hauled down her colours and Miller ordered Hoste to board her. But as his boat came up with the frigate, he saw that her crew had abandoned her, taking to the boats on her landward side, and had set fire to her with a train of gun-powder. The flames had already taken hold so there was nothing for it but to return to the *Theseus* and watch the frigate burn for half an hour before blowing up. Miller was outraged at this breach of etiquette: 'This dishonourable action was not out of character for a modern Frenchman: the devil is beyond blackening.'

The sun rose on a ghastly panorama of shattered ships and a sea bobbing with hundreds of scorched and mangled corpses. Victory had been decisive and almost complete. Two French ships of the line, *Le Généreux* and *Guillaume Tell*, and two frigates had cut their cables and escaped but the victors' masts and rigging had been so cut about by gunfire that they could not pursue. The remainder of Bonaparte's fleet was destroyed or captured, its admiral lost with his flagship. French casualties had been about six times heavier than the British and now their army and its commander were stranded in Egypt.

At daybreak, Miller inspected his ship. Although eighty heavy shot had struck her hull – some passing right through it – only six men had been killed and thirty-one wounded. 'Providence, in its goodness, seemed willing to make up to us for our heavy loss at Santa Cruz', her captain remarked. He mustered the ship's company and thanked them for their efforts, then asked the chaplain to hold a service and the exhausted men 'returned thanks to Almighty God through whose mercy we had been instrumental in obtaining so great and glorious a victory to His Majesty's Arms, and I believe from a body of men more fervent gratitude never mingled in prayer. I had desired the Chaplain to introduce a prayer for the slain, which was attended to with a degree of feeling that could not but delight every good heart.'

Nelson, who had been badly wounded on the forehead, at once set about reaping the political and strategic rewards of his victory. The news had to be carried not only to St Vincent, to Hamilton at Naples and, of course, to the Admiralty in London but to India, where the East India Company knew itself to be threatened by French ambitions. So as soon as he had written his dispatch to St Vincent, through whom the news would be conveyed to the Admiralty, it was entrusted to his flag-captain, Berry, who sailed on the 5th in the *Leander* to find the Commander-in-Chief somewhere west of Gibraltar. And a linguist, a Lieutenant Duval, was sent overland to India to spread the news as widely as possible.

Although the Mediterranean was now dominated by the British fleet, Nelson took the precaution of sending a duplicate of his dispatch to St Vincent direct to London, the courier to go ashore at Naples to proclaim the news before making his way overland to London. It was as well that he did because, on the 18th, the *Leander* fell in with the fugitive *Généreux* and, after a fierce resistance, was captured. Already, on the 13th, the *Mutine* had sailed with the duplicate for Naples. Her captain, Thomas Hardy, had been appointed to take Berry's place in the *Vanguard* so the dispatch was carried by the flagship's signal lieutenant, the Honourable Thomas Capel, who was promoted to the acting rank of captain and given command of the brig until he disembarked at Naples. There he was to hand over the ship to another officer, who would take passage with him for the purpose. This was to be Lieutenant William Hoste, who would thereupon be promoted to the acting rank of captain.

'You may guess my astonishment when I was first told of it,' wrote Hoste to his father. 'I was on board the *Tonnant*, one of the Prizes, when I received a Note from Captain Miller hinting that I should be promoted and desiring me to return on board the *Theseus* immediately. The next day I was received on board the *Vanguard* and the Admiral gave me an acting order for the *Mutine* and said there would be no difficulty in getting me confirmed.'

Nelson also gave him sealed orders, marked 'Most Secret', to be opened when he relieved Capel after their arrival at Naples. When he opened those orders he would, at the age of eighteen, have fulfilled the ambitions of his father and himself, for the first time commanding his own ship.

Hoste's first letter home after the battle had been hastily written between strenuous bouts of work repairing the *Theseus* and the French prizes on 3rd August. It was sent in the *Leander* and so never got to Godwick Hall. At this time it was thought that the *Mutine* would carry the first set of dispatches to St Vincent and then to England, and it was Nelson's decision to send a more powerful ship that deprived Hoste of a happy return to his family or, perhaps, a spell in a French prison.

In his first letter, Hoste had promised his father an account of the battle but when he again sat down to write, a month later, the *Mutine* was standing into Naples Bay and he only found time for a brief sketch of the current situation: 'Buonaparte is at Grand Cairo, in a most horrid condition, surrounded by Arabs and Mamelukes, who massacre every rascal they can catch . . . Our brave admiral says he has got into a pretty scrape and cannot for his life see how he can get out of it.' But he did send a translation of a long letter describing the battle that had been written by Controller-General Poussielgue, the financial administrator of the Army of Egypt, to his wife and intercepted. But the copy that finally reached Godwick was not the one that Hoste had originally been given. In the long and dramatic eyewitness account of the action, there was a short passage about the writer's longing for home and, in it, one sentence that Hoste did not consider suitable for feminine eyes at the parsonage. To his wife, Poussielgue had written, 'I shall be contented with you naked as my hand'. Rather than draw attention to this by trying to cross it out, Hoste copied the letter again himself with the offensive sentence omitted.

On the day that the *Mutine* sailed for Naples, the sloop *Bonne Citoyenne*, commanded by Captain Josiah Nisbet, entered Aboukir Bay. She was one of several light ships St Vincent had sent into the Mediterranean in search of Nelson to give him new orders: to abandon his pursuit of the French, unless he had already made contact, and return to support an assault on Minorca. But Josiah also handed his step-father a sealed letter from St Vincent about himself. Although the Commander-in-Chief had generously met Nelson's requests for the young man's preferment, he now wrote, 'It would be a breach of friendship to conceal from you that he loves drink and low company, is thoroughly ignorant of all forms of service, inattentive, obstinate, and wrong-headed beyond measure, and had he not been your son-in-law [*sic*] must have been annihilated months ago. With all this, he is honest and truth telling, and, I dare say, will, if you ask him, subscribe to every word I have written.'

It was a devastating and humiliating blow to receive at the moment of victory when every thought was of success and glory, and, critical of Josiah as he himself had been, nothing could have prepared Nelson for these brutal words.

On the day that he read this, the little *Mutine* was standing out of Aboukir Bay, carrying among the admiral's dispatches a letter introducing Capel and Hoste to Sir William and Lady Hamilton. In contrast to St Vincent's opinion of Josiah Nisbet, Nelson wrote his of William Hoste, 'who', he said, 'to the gentlest manners joins undaunted courage.'

IV

HALF A NELSON

As the *Mutine*'s anchor plunged into the Bay of Naples on 3rd September and a boat carrying an official from the British Embassy pulled towards her from the shore, William Hoste was finishing a letter to his father. He was concluding his customary messages of affection to the family and could not resist a touch of swagger: 'Pray remember me to my Uncle and Aunt Hoste – tell the former that the sword he gave me in England has not got rusty from want of use.' Then, with characteristic generosity, he remembered a brother officer, Captain Oldfield of the Marines, still sweating on board the *Tonnant* in Aboukir Bay, where he had commanded the prize crew that Hoste had joined. 'P.S.', he now wrote, 'I have to request Dixon as he is so good a shot if he would send to Mrs Oldfield, No. 126 High Street, Portsmouth – a little game.'

That was the last thought of home before he and Capel were swept up in the whirl of excitement that the news they carried brought to Naples. The Kingdom of the Two Sicilies was still nominally neutral but Ferdinand and his Prime Minister, the curious English expatriate, Sir John Acton, feared that the French might suddenly decide to annex Naples as they had Rome, Genoa and Venice. Queen Maria Carolina had more aggressive instincts; avid to avenge her sister, Marie Antoinette, she longed for the return of a British fleet so that the Neapolitans could again take up arms against France.

Capel and Hoste were ashore at three and taken at once to the British Embassy in the great pile of the Palazzo Sessa, standing on a low headland in the northern outskirts of Naples. They at once saw Sir William Hamilton and gave him a letter that Nelson had written to him on 8th August: 'Almighty God has made me the happy instrument in destroying the Enemy's Fleet, which I hope will be a blessing to Europe. You will have the goodness to communicate this happy event to all the Courts in Italy, for my head is so indifferent that I can scarcely scrawl this letter. Captain Capel, who is charged with my Dispatches for England, will give you every information. Pray put him on the quickest mode of getting home.'

When Emma Hamilton heard the news, she reacted – or later imagined she had reacted – in her usual melodramatic style. 'God, what a victory!' she wrote to Nelson. 'Never, never has there been anything half so glorious, so compleat. I fainted when I heard the joyful news and fell on my side and am hurt, but well of that. I should feel it a glory to die in such a cause. No, I wou'd not like to die till I see and embrace the Victor of the Nile.' But William Hoste only recorded in a letter to his mother, 'Lady Hamilton (whom I suppose you have heard of) received us very kindly indeed. I had a letter of introduction from Lord Nelson to her, so that I soon became acquainted.'

Sir William at once took the two young officers to the Palazzo Reale to meet Acton, 'who of course expressed his joy at the laurels we had received.' The Queen's reaction on hearing the news was, according to Emma Hamilton, suitably Neapolitan. 'How shall I describe to you the transports of Maria Carolina, 'tis not possible,' she wrote to Nelson. 'She fainted and kissed her husband, her children, walked about the room, cried, kissed, and embraced every person near her, exclaiming, Oh, Brave Nelson, Nelson what do we not owe to you. Oh Victor, Saviour of Itali, oh, that my swollen heart cou'd now tell him personally what we owe to him!'

As Hoste and Capel left the Palazzo Reale, they saw Lady Hamilton waiting for them at the gates. The former told his mother in a breathless letter how Emma 'made us get into her carriage and parade through the streets till dark; she had a bandeau round her forehead with the words "Nelson and Victory". The populace saw and understood what it meant, and "Viva Nelson!" resounded through the streets. You can have no idea of the rejoicings that were made throughout Naples at the time. Bonfires and illuminations all over the town . . . We went to the Opera and were in the minister's box with him and his lady. Not a French cockade was to be seen; all expressed their joy at seeing us . . .'

Sir William, said Emma, looked ten years younger and, according to her, was as eager as herself to embrace the victor. Meanwhile, Naples was her stage and she described to Nelson some of her theatrical effects: 'I wish you could have seen our house the 3 nights of illumination. 'Tis, 'twas covered with your glorious name. Their were 3 thousand Lamps and their should have been 3 millions if we had had time.'

She also enjoyed the company of Hoste, who in his blue and white uniform with the single gold epaulette of an acting captain, cut a dashing figure among the swarthy Neapolitans. He had grown into a handsome young man with an alert, sensitive face, a strong, straight nose and thick, reddish hair, cut short. To a woman, his most striking features must have been a mouth as sensuous as Nelson's and eyes bright with enthusiasm. When Capel left for London, via Vienna, next day, the Hamiltons continued to entertain the new captain of the *Mutine*. Writing to Nelson of 'dear little Captain Hoste', Emma described how 'he dines with us in the day, for he will not sleep out of his ship, and we Love him dearly. He is a fine, good lad. Sir William is delighted with him, and I say he will be a second Nelson. If he is only half a Nelson, he will be superior to all others.'

The Queen was equally struck by his charm and just before the *Mutine* sailed to rejoin Nelson sent him a present that could only be embarrassing to a parson's son.

To his ship's company, she gave a generous but suitable present of two hundred guineas, six pipes of wine and two calves. Then, as Hoste told his mother, 'I was surprised by an officer arriving from the palace and inquiring for me: on my being presented to him, he gave me a note from the Queen, (but whom I was to consider *incog.*) and a small box with a very handsome diamond ring inclosed in it.' The news caused concern at Godwick and William had to reassure 'such, my dear mother, is the history of the ring, which my father said you were afraid was for private service, but I hope you are convinced now it was out of regard for the English nation.'

Emma Hamilton had the most likely explanation for the secretive presentation of 'a Dymond Ring to Captain Hoste.' She explained, 'Her letter is in English and comes as from an unknown person, but a well-wisher to our country, and an admirer of our gallant Nelson. As war is not yet declared with France, she cou'd not shew herself so openly as she wished . . .' Handsome as it was, the gift was only a foretaste of what was in store for Nelson himself and Hoste was able to express his gratitude in a letter of thanks and, a few days later, by dressing his ship overall with ensigns and signal flags on the Queen's birthday.

Hoste's orders, marked 'Most Secret', which Nelson had written in the *Vanguard* on 13th August and had been opened on the change of the brig's command, were all that he could have hoped for. 'Having at Naples procured such articles of provisions as the *Mutine* may stand in absolute want,' they ran, 'you will receive on board such Dispatches as Sir William Hamilton may send for me, cruize for me eight or ten leagues from the land, between Syracuse and Cape Passaro, frequently sending a boat into Syracuse . . . therefore you will be certain of meeting me.'

With the help of the Hamiltons, the *Mutine* was fully replenished with fresh food and stores and on 12th September was ready to sail to

meet the flagship and some of the squadron that were making their way
to Naples. Before he left, Emma made sure that he would tell the admiral
something of the reception that awaited him, writing to Nelson: 'My
dress from head to foot is alla Nelson. Ask Hoste. Even my shawl is in
blue with gold anchors all over. My earrings are Nelson's anchors;
in short, we are be-Nelsoned all over.'

Hoste was delighted with his ship. Commanding a dispatch vessel
he would again, in effect, be Nelson's 'doggie', running errands under
his direct instructions and in his confidence. The brig, or sloop, as
she was also rated, now mounted two more guns, bringing her
armament to sixteen, and, while carrying dispatches and scouting for
the admiral would be her principal duty, she would be well able to
hunt for prizes among the small merchant ships which carried most of
the trade in the Mediterranean. Then, he, as captain, would be entitled
to three-eighths of any prize-money, although one of the eighths could
be claimed by the commanding admiral.

While the command of the *Mutine* was the most flattering appointment Nelson could have given Hoste, it was also a test of his determination. On his first morning at sea, while standing out from the Bay of
Naples and with the exotic cliffs and pinnacles of Capri on the horizon,
he had to enter in his log, 'Punished William Birkwith with One Dozen
lashes and Patrick Curran (Marine) with Two Dozen for Neglect of
Duty.'

The *Mutine* was not a happy ship. When she had been cut out from
Santa Cruz in May of the preceeding year, Nelson had given her to
her captor, Hardy; she had been commissioned into the Royal Navy,
and her ship's company had been made up of drafts from the squadron
off Tenerife and, later, from St Vincent's fleet. Captains were always
reluctant to lose men from undermanned ships. Sometimes, prime
seamen had to be spared: as when a prize, perhaps suffering from battle-
damage, had to be got into port; but then there was the prospect of
prize-money for all and the prize crew would, in any case, eventually
return to their ship. But when a draft had to be found for the manning
of another ship it was as natural as it was inevitable that this would be
seen as a means of ridding a ship of troublemakers. These were usually
drunkards and thieves but 1797 had been the year of the great naval
mutinies and this had infected St Vincent's fleet as reinforcements
came out from England.

So among the brig's crew was an unusually high proportion of
malcontents and potential mutineers. It was appropriate that the revolutionary name the French had chosen to give her was *La Mutine* – The
Rebel.

Even the experienced Hardy, eleven years older than Hoste, had had a difficult time. Although his ship's complement was only ninety – and the company actually embarked was often less – there were forty-five floggings during his first year in command. Of these, eighteen were for drunkenness or crimes associated with drink, and others for theft and quarrelling but ten were for 'contempt' or 'disobedience'.

A dispatch vessel was particularly vulnerable to mutiny. Often away from the tangible deterrent to indiscipline of her fleet or squadron, sailing alone, she was small enough to be seized and then worked by a small number of determined men. As a carrier of secret dispatches she was potentially of the greatest value to the enemy, who would be likely to reward handsomely the mutineers who delivered her to them. It was perhaps for this reason that in May, 1798, St Vincent sent the *Mutine* a detachment of thirty-one marines, one of whose traditional duties was the protection of officers from mutinous seamen. Even so, during the remaining four months of his command, there were twenty more floggings, the four men punished for contempt or insolence including, ominously, one of the marines.

To have had to order sixty-five floggings in fifteen months was a dangerous sign in so small a ship. In the *Theseus*, which had five times the brig's complement, there had been only twenty-two floggings in the first six months of 1798. Although she had a popular captain and had flown Nelson's flag the year before, she had been rife with mutinous symptoms when she had come out from England. During those same six months there had been thirty-four floggings in the *Mutine*.

Nelson must have heard of the trouble from Hardy, because when he offered him promotion and spoke of sending Capel and Hoste to the brig, he ordered that the most persistent troublemakers be removed. Some were to go into the *Theseus* and the admiral had asked Miller to send some more reliable men to the brig before Hoste took command. 'You were so good as to promise to change six men from the *Mutine*,' he wrote, 'Pray do it, and you will very much oblige me; Hardy will point out the persons to be sent out of the Brig . . . Hoste must come to me, chest and bedding, tomorrow.'

Despite this, she was an uneasy ship to command. Perhaps the crew were testing the determination of their eighteen-year-old captain and he was trying to assert his domination. In any case, Hoste had to order thirteen floggings during his first four months in command. Two of the men he punished were marines, one of them receiving twenty-four lashes for 'contempt and disobedience'.

Gradually the ship's company settled down and the amount of punishment was reduced to the occasional flogging that was part of any warship's routine, the most common time for such ceremonial being the morning after leaving port when, out of sight of land, those who had drunk too much or brawled while ashore were seized up at the gratings and the boatswain's mate did his duty.

Thereafter, Hoste seems to have modelled his enforcement of discipline upon that of Nelson: strict and ready to order a flogging, but fair and, within the limits of circumstances, humane. When, later in the commission, a seaman and a ship's boy were convicted on board for the 'unnatural crime' of a homosexual offence, they 'were both severely punished'. But the boy's flogging was not logged, as it was not obligatory to do so at that time, and the affair went unnoticed by the Commander-in-Chief. 'Had I tried these wretches by a Court Martial,' noted Hoste, 'they must both have been executed.'

As he was more able to relax, Hoste enjoyed playing the part of a ship's captain, living alone in simple, solitary state but entertaining the officers of his tiny command in the day-cabin with its wide and graceful curve of windows at the stern. 'Imagine to yourself a place about 20 foot broad and 10 long with a round table in the middle,' he wrote to his younger brother George. 'I always make it a rule to dine at 2 with 3 of my officers.'

On the 14th, off the volcanic island of Stromboli the *Mutine* came up with the *Vanguard*, which was in company with two others of the line and a frigate, and Hoste went on board the flagship to give Nelson Hamilton's and Emma's letters and tell him of the welcome that awaited him in Naples. Unlike the brig, the *Vanguard* had had little chance of replenishing with fresh food, so Hoste sent a bullock across to her. In return, the admiral sent him a cask of salt beef followed, next day, by another and two of salt pork because he was to send his dispatch vessel on a long voyage. First, Hoste was to take the news of the victory to Gibraltar, from whence it would spread into Spain and along the Barbary Coast of North Africa. Then he was to carry dispatches to St Vincent, who was still expected to be blockading Cadiz, before returning to Naples. Although disappointed to miss the conquering hero's triumphant arrival in the Bay of Naples, Hoste was avid for orders to carry out, writing to his family that 'Lord Nelson behaves like a second father'.

The admiral could guess at the warmth of the coming welcome from a gushing letter from the Queen, who wrote that she had hung his portrait in her room, adding '*Faites un hip hip hip en mon nom chantez God Saeve die King et puis God Saeve Nelson et marine Britannique . . .*' But, still suffering headaches from his wound and exhausted, physically and emotionally, Nelson was more grateful for Hamilton's solicitous promise that 'a pleasant apartment is ready for you in my House, and Emma is looking out for the softest pillows to repose the few wearied limbs you have left.'

Josiah Nisbet in the *Bonne Citoyenne* was the first to arrive off Naples, followed by Troubridge in the *Culloden* and Ball in the *Alexander*. The flagship, towed by a frigate, arrived on the 22nd, to be greeted by a swarm of some five hundred boats and barges and vast crowds lining the mole and waterfront. The Hamiltons came on board, Emma setting herself a new standard of theatricality. 'Up flew her ladyship and exclaiming "*Oh God is it possible*" fell into my arms more dead than alive,' wrote Nelson to Fanny. 'Tears however soon set matters to rights . . .'

The admiral allowed himself to be led ashore to the Palazzo Sessa, where, unlike Hoste, he rested on the softest pillows. On 29th September was Nelson's fortieth birthday and the Hamiltons celebrated it with a dinner party for eighty, followed by a ball for some eighteen hundred and supper for eight hundred. It was 'enough to fill me with vanity,' the subject of the flattery told his wife; '. . . such a style of elegance as I never saw or shall again probably. A rostral column is erected under a magnificent canopy never Lady Hamilton says to come down while they remain in Naples . . . in the front Nelson, on the pedestal "veni vidi vici", anchors . . . were numerous.'

The guests were dressed to match: 'every ribbon every button has "Nelson" etc., the whole service are "H.N. Glorious 1st August". Songs, sonnets are numerous beyond what I ever could deserve.' One of the songs was an additional verse to the National Anthem, beginning, '*Join we great Nelson's name, first on the roll of fame* . . .'

It was a dazzling occasion, marred only by the behaviour of the hero's step-son. Despite his increasing dislike of the young man, Nelson had been doing what he could for his career. He had tried to mollify St Vincent, writing, 'I am glad to think you are a little mistaken in Nisbet. He is young but I find a great knowledge of the service in him . . . He may have laid too long in Lisbon, I hope the best.' On arrival at Naples, he had introduced him to the Hamiltons, writing tactlessly to Fanny: 'Her ladyship if Josiah was to stay would make something of him and with all his bluntness I am sure he likes Lady Hamilton more than any female. She would fashion him in 6 months in spite of himself.'

But at the Hamiltons' ball, Josiah was drunk and truculent, offending Nelson, it was said, by remarking on the attentions his step-father was paying to their hostess, and had to be led from the ballroom by Troubridge and another officer. Later, the Hamiltons were able to effect a reconciliation of sorts, Emma writing to his mother that 'Josiah is much improved in every respect . . . I love him much and although we quarrel sometimes, he loves me and does as I would have him . . . I am sure he will make a very great officer.' So, before the end of the year, Nelson could also tell her, 'The improvement made in Josiah by Lady Hamilton is wonderful. She seems the only person he minds, and his faults are not omitted to be told him but in such a way as pleases him, and his, your and my obligation are infinite on that score . . . But his manners are so rough, but God bless him I love him dearly with all his roughness.'

It did not last. Although early in the following year, Josiah was given command of a handsome frigate, the *Thalia*, Nelson wrote of him to Fanny in words as rough as St Vincent's had been: 'I wish I could say much to your and my satisfaction about Josiah but I am sorry to say and with real grief, that he has nothing good about him, he must sooner or later be broke . . .' and he ended, 'I have done with the subject it is an ungrateful one.'

The incident at the ball and Nelson's erupting infatuation with Emma Hamilton had brought about the final souring of what filial affection there remained between them. Without a son of his own and with abounding fatherly love to lavish on one that fulfilled his expectations, this was now to be devoted wholly to his professional heirs and of these the favourite was undoubtedly the young captain of the *Mutine*.

* * * *

The news of the Battle of the Nile reached Norfolk at the end of the first week in October. Captain Capel had reached London on the 2nd and, after years of bad news, the capital exploded in celebration. Next day, mail coaches raced into East Anglian towns, flying flags and their guards firing blunderbusses in *feux de joie* that were to be echoed by the muskets of the militia. In Norwich, reported the *Norfolk Chronicle*, 'three excellent vollies' were fired to compliment the wife of Captain Berry, happily giving the news that none of the 'many youths from this county . . . among them the son of the Rev. Dixon Hoste' who had been in the battle had received any wound. At the Sessions Ball, ladies wore bandeaux inscribed 'Nelson and Victory', toasts were drunk by the militia over 'a cold collation and wines' at the Maid's Head and, at a Saturday night concert in the city, a Mr Sharp led the singing of new words to the tune of *Rule Britannia*:

> *By Nelson's glorious deeds inspir'd,*
> *Fresh trophies shall thy children bring,*
> *And with his patriot virtues fir'd*
> *Protect their Country, Laws and King.*
> *Rule Britannia . . .*

From Norwich the news spread outwards to the market-towns and the villages where the mail coaches stopped and it was from two of these, Rougham and Burnham Market, that it reached Godwick and Burnham Thorpe.

Norfolk was not to be outdone by Naples with which it had nothing in common but joy. A celebration ball was to be held in the Assembly Room at Swaffham, a handsome market-town near Godwick, where old houses with new Georgian façades stood around a little Italianate temple surmounted by a statue of Ceres in the wide market-place. Nothing could have been farther removed in style from the mingled splendour and squalor, the glittering lamps and tinsel of the Neapolitan festivities than this, but the ebullience was no less and it was described by Nelson's niece, Kitty Bolton, in a letter to Fanny, who was in Suffolk.

'My Father and Mother dined at Mr Wilbraham's to meet Mr and Mrs Hoste, Miss Hoste and young Mr Hoste, who came on purpose for the Ball,' she wrote. 'It was as full as could be expected for the neighbourhood. I went to the Ball and danced five dances: young Mr Hoste danced the first Two dances with me: – They paid Mama the Compliment to ask her to begin the Ball but she danced only one with Mr Hoste it is a dance they brought with them and which they called the *Vanguard* or the *breaking* of the line. We sent to London for all the Songs which are just published and we had them and sung and I am leaving them all to play to your Ladyship . . .

'Mrs Hoste's ribbands which she had from London were half Navy Blue and half red to signify the Knight of the Bath and the Navy: – She gave me a medallion of my Uncle, which I wore round my neck at the Ball. Mrs Micklethwaite had had a very handsome cap from London inscribed in Gold Spangles "The Hero of the Nile".'

This was the jolly, cosy England of which William Hoste dreamed, torn between homesickness and hopes of glory and prize-money. Increasingly, his letters home reflected this. 'I think I could find my way from Tittleshall to Godwick, but no further,' he wrote to his mother after nearly six years' absence. 'I recollect your's and my father's countenance, but the rest of the family would appear quite strangers – I mean in their outward appearance. I often think I see you all sit down to dinner, and the chair on the starboard side of my father left vacant, which once I used to call my place. I suppose George has taken possession of it.'

Sometimes, acute homesickness would bring on bouts of depression made worse by delays in the arrival of mail. 'Excuse me if I begin again upon the old story, your long, long silence,' he wrote to his mother. 'To me it appears an age, and believe me, one line from the old hall

would make me the happiest man alive . . . Often and often I think of
the tender care you have taken of us all, and I am not ashamed to say,
the recollection frequently cost me tears. The idea strikes me now more
forcibly than ever. When in large ships, with so many companions,
my thoughts were more employed . . . At present, the case is altered;
I am in a brig by myself, and having more time, and less hurry and
bustle than formerly . . . I picture to myself the happiness that awaits
me on my return to England; I fancy I see my father, and you, and all
the family round the fireside in the parlour: indeed, I think when I see
it in reality, the old house will hardly hold me.'

William's next letter home was written in St Vincent's cabin in his
flagship, the *Ville de Paris*, which he had boarded with Nelson's
dispatches on 27th September. The Commander-in-Chief had at once
confirmed his appointment to command the *Mutine* and had suggested
that he sit down there and then and write to his family, giving the
news. So this he did, not forgetting to ask his father to tell Mr Coke
of his promotion.

After calling at Gibraltar for provisions, the *Mutine* returned to
Naples, arriving on 13th October to find the *Vanguard* and three
others of the line preparing for sea. During Hoste's absence, Nelson's
attitude towards affairs ashore had polarized. On the one hand he was
disgusted by the tawdriness and unreliability of his Neapolitan allies:
'The miserable conduct of this Court is not likely to cool my irritable
temper. It is a country of fiddlers and poets, whores and scoundrels.'
On the other he had fallen in love with Emma Hamilton, ending a
letter to St Vincent with the words, 'I am writing opposite Lady
Hamilton, therefore, you will not be surprised at the glorious jumble
of this letter . . . Naples is a dangerous place, and we must keep clear
of it.'

Next day the *Mutine* sailed in company with the squadron which was
bound for Malta, still occupied by the French, on an armed reconnaissance in strength. The blockade and capture of this island were part of
the strategic plan to meet the increasing French threat to the Two
Sicilies. Another was to establish liaison with Turkish and Russian naval
forces which, it was expected, would support the British, Neapolitans
and Austrians against the French and dispatches to this end were sent
to the British minister in Constantinople in the *Mutine*. The ambassador
was John Spencer Smith, a former Guards officer, whose brother,
Captain Sir Sidney Smith, a brilliant but eccentric naval officer, was
then on his way to join him and become the senior British representative
in the Levant. The political and military importance of the Ottoman
Empire, which included the Balkans, Asia Minor and the Levant
itself, had been enhanced by the need to prevent Bonaparte's expedi-

tionary force breaking out of its Egyptian confinement and battering its way back to Europe from the east.

Rather than slowly working her way up to Constantinople through the Dardanelles, the *Mutine* was to make for Smyrna and the dispatches were to travel overland while Hoste waited for Smith's reply. The ship arrived on 10th November and was to remain at anchor for five weeks until the courier returned. Hoste, who had heard horrific stories of plague in the city, was agreeably surprised to find that the daily death-rate from such infections was only eight or nine in winter whereas in summer he might not have been able to go ashore without serious risk. He made friends among the Christian population but formed a poor opinion of the Turks: 'I thought them a lazy ignorant people . . . their time is chiefly spent in smoking tobacco and drinking coffee of which they are immoderately fond of . . . Although brave, they are naturally lazy, and as long as a Turk can lie upon his couch and smoke his pipe and eat opium, it matters little whether his neighbours are friends or enemies.' But, he noted, 'since our victory at the Nile, they have altered their tone and pay the English more respect than formerly.'

As soon as Smith's dispatches for Nelson were on board, Hoste sailed and, after a stormy passage, joined the admiral at Palermo at the beginning of January, 1799. When they had parted company, he recalled 'our affairs in Italy were going on as well as possible' but, during his absence, disaster had befallen Naples. Encouraged by Nelson's aggressive instincts and the arrival of the experienced Austrian General Karl von Mack to command his army, King Ferdinand had embarked on a vainglorious attempt to drive the French from Rome and farther from his own frontier. Predictably, the adventure had proved a tragic fiasco. The French, initially taken unawares by the preposterous challenge, reacted quickly and soon the Neapolitans were in headlong retreat. While the unsophisticated poor of Naples had affection for their comical sovereign, a large proportion of the intelligentsia and the middle classes were sick of the Bourbons and more than ready to try republicanism. Thus, as the social structure of his kingdom began to collapse around him, Ferdinand asked Nelson to save him from his subjects and the advancing French.

Shortly before Christmas, the royal family and their retinue, together with the Hamiltons, were smuggled on board the *Vanguard*, at night, escorted by British sailors with drawn cutlasses and, on 23rd December, the flagship sailed for Palermo. Christmas Eve and Christmas Day were spent in the teeth of the most violent gale that Nelson had known, prostrating the royal refugees with fear and sea-sickness, one of the little princes dying of exhaustion following convulsions in the arms of Emma Hamilton. On the 26th, the battered ships reached Palermo, the royal party going at once to the vast palace that had been built by the Saracens and Normans and embellished by the Spanish Bourbons, while the Hamiltons were temporarily housed, shivering, in a noble family's villa that was empty because, built for summer use only, it had no fireplaces or chimneys.

Two days after Hoste arrived, he was sent on a mission to Naples. One purpose of this was to gather intelligence, the other was to salvage some of the Hamiltons' furniture from the embassy and their two summer houses. This he did and, less than a fortnight later, was back at Palermo, the little brig cluttered with gilded furniture, pictures and some of Sir William's collection of Classical antiquities.

While Nelson lay at Palermo, enmeshed in his infatuation, he used Hoste as his eyes on the Bay of Naples. He proved an aggressive scout, always eager to chase a possible prize until she ran under the guns of a French fort or struck her colours, as did a three-masted polacre merchant ship, which the French had seized from the Neapolitans, and was taken by the *Mutine*'s boats in February. But the brig had suffered a bad buffeting in the December gales and, as rough weather continued, became so leaky that she had to be sent for a refit at Port Mahon in Minorca, which had finally been taken from the French in November. He returned to Palermo in April and was sent back to watch Naples, while Nelson prepared his counter-offensive.

When the Bourbons had fled and the French occupied their capital, the Neapolitan liberals had founded what was named the Parthenopean, or Vesuvian, Republic but this, surprisingly perhaps, did not command the loyalty of the mass of the people. So when Ferdinand sent one of his most able and popular supporters, Cardinal Fabrizio Ruffo, to raise his colours in Southern Italy and march on Naples, his success was remarkable. His loyal naval captains joined a small British squadron under Troubridge which soon captured the islands of Ischia and Procida that commanded the Bay of Naples, while a smaller force, including the *Mutine*, stood inshore to support Ruffo's troops as they fought their way along the coast.

Such was the royalists' speed of advance that Ruffo was already in Naples and the rebels defending themselves in its three great castles when Hoste sighted Nelson standing into the bay with eighteen ships of the line. The admiral was in a belligerent mood and at once countermanded the terms of surrender which the rebels had agreed to accept and, instead of allowing them to evacuate the city by sea, held them under his guns until Ferdinand returned. When he did, he showed no mercy and a ghastly sequence of executions began.

Hoste, whose opinions followed his admiral's, showed no regret over such repression, which included the hanging of the rebel naval commander, Admiral Prince Francesco Caracciolo, at the yard-arm of a royalist frigate anchored in the midst of the British fleet. He simply told his father that he was happy to say that his ship had taken part in the operations 'although no pecuniary advantage resulted'.

Naples having been secured, Troubridge's squadron, including the *Mutine*, moved farther up the coast to blockade Civita Vecchia and when he summoned the French garrison to surrender the commander offered to give up not only the port but Rome as well. So, while a landing-party of marines and seamen occupied the forts of Civita Vecchia, royalist troops set out to take possession of the capital. With great satisfaction Hoste told his father, 'Thus was the whole Roman state, with its capital, once mistress of the world, taken by about three hundred Englishmen. How much times are altered since Julius Caesar landed in Britain, and how much have the Romans degenerated from their ancestors!'

The French garrisons of the port and the capital were to be allowed to march out of their fortifications 'with drums beating, colours flying and all the honours of war allowed them' and sail for France in Neapolitan ships and Hoste was left behind, with another brig in support, to superintend this while Troubridge left for Palermo. The Italian peasantry had hated the French occupation and, seeing that the only protection the surrendered garrison now had was Hoste's modest detachment of marines and three hundred Neapolitan troops of poor quality, determined on revenge.

On 12th October, Hoste was dining ashore with two of his officers when they were startled by a burst of musket fire. A moment later, news arrived that a mob, hauling two field-guns loaded with grape-shot, had surrounded the French general's house and were about to murder him and then attack his troops, including those who had just retreated from Rome. The British officers left the table and ran towards the sound of firing to find the report all too clearly true.

'If you have ever been at the quelling of a riot in England, you may imagine a little the confusion and discord that prevailed, but with us it was far worse,' he reported. 'We were strangers to the language . . . everything depended on a moment . . . they had surrounded the French general's house and in another instant would have stormed it.'

Now all the self-confidence that had been instilled by an English upbringing and the strict schooling of the Royal Navy came into its own.

'I will now call your particular attention, to convince you what idea the people of this country entertain of an Englishman,' he boasted. The Neapolitan troops were standing idly by and 'only made things worse' because they 'had not the courage to charge the mob and the mob paid not the smallest attention to the troops'. Seeing Hoste, the crowd assumed that he was about to lead their assault; 'but as our intentions were far otherwise, we, partly by menaces and partly by persuasion, got the two pieces of cannon, and kept them tolerably quiet.'

Then word arrived from the quarters of the French garrison outside the town that, unless their general was immediately allowed to join them, they would attack and, as they numbered between three and four hundred men, they would have had little difficulty in re-capturing Civita Vecchia. So Hoste pushed his way through the crowd to the general's front door and, entering, told him that the only chance of avoiding bloodshed was for him to be escorted through the besiegers by the three British officers to the barracks.

It was a test of nerve. 'We marched through the midst of the mob with him, arm-in-arm, until we arrived at the troops,' said Hoste. 'I confess I expected a ball of some kind or another through me, but luckily we arrived safe.'

At the barracks, the general calmed his troops and, soon after, six hundred Swiss mercenaries in Ferdinand's service arrived and order was restored in the town. Thereupon the French embarked and sailed for France, their general travelling as far as Bastia in the *Mutine*. 'I assure you,' Hoste wrote to his father, 'during the whole course of service I have been in, I have never suffered more anxiety than in this business . . . This was the first service of the kind I ever was employed upon, and most sincerely do I hope that it will be the last.'

Great was the relief to have a deck under his feet again and find salt water between himself and the savage complexities of life and death ashore. His own contempt for his Neapolitan allies now echoed Nelson's, 'their princes (if they deserve the name) seeking redress not by vigour but by complaints. The men seem directed by low, sordid interest alone, and all their thoughts are centred in themselves . . . An Englishman's idea of liberty is never so strong as when he is presented with such prospects as these; and I must confess that in all the hurry and confusion of war, one of my comforts is that I am of that happy country.'

Before sending the captured general and his staff ashore in Corsica under a flag of truce, Hoste had many conversations with his prisoners and was surprised at the frankness of their talk. The ruling Directory in Paris, they thought, were 'an ambitious set of men, who wantonly sacrificed thousands to their private interest' and they forecast that 'unless considerable changes took place at the helm, they would shortly be obliged to make peace on any terms.' It was ominous then that when the general went ashore at Bastia he returned to say farewell to Hoste and give him the news that Bonaparte had escaped from Egypt and had just arrived in Corsica on his way back to France. Hoste recognized something at least of Bonaparte's military genius ('a man of great abilities and it certainly is a pity they are not employed in a better cause') and the French officers had told him that he would remain invincible in the field so long as he was supported by Alexandre Berthier as his Chief of Staff. There were now reports that Bonaparte would return to take command of the disordered Army of Italy and this could only be seen as a storm-warning.

The end of the eighteenth century saw Hoste's career full of promise. His last mission before taking his ship for another refit at Mahon was to ferry the Duke and Duchess of Aosta from Sardinia to Tuscany and on their disembarking the latter presented him with the second diamond ring he had received from a charmed Mediterranean lady. Again he felt it prudent to report this with extreme caution when writing to his parents. While granting the Duchess to be 'a fine woman', he added that 'she speaks little English . . . and was so dreadfully sick on her passage owing to the motion of the vessel that I had very little conversation with her.'

Now promotion to post captain and an assured career, if he survived, to the highest ranks in the Navy seemed probable. 'Lord Nelson still continues as kind as ever; how greatly I am indebted to him!' he wrote home. 'He has been good enough to promise me a post captain's commission and had there been an opportunity of making me, he would have done so ere now.'

The admiral had also, unwittingly, done him an even more valuable service. By removing him from the *Theseus* he had possibly saved his life. Captain Miller had taken the ship to the Levant to support Sir Sidney Smith's attempts to halt the advance of the French from Egypt on Turkey and was heavily engaged in the defence of Acre. But while carrying ammunition from Jaffa for Smith's artillery, a midshipman carelessly hammering fuses into mortar bombs with a mallet and nail set off an explosion that killed forty, including Miller, and wounded many more.

The new century began with dangerous news from France. On his return, Bonaparte had overthrown the Directory and established himself as First Consul. The endemic unrest within the country had been contained, freeing more seasoned soldiers to take part in the offensives that were to throw back the Austrians and re-conquer Italy. In the Mediterranean, Nelson seemed to have been lulled into near-inactivity by his siren and had even ignored orders from Lord Keith, who had taken over from St Vincent, to leave Naples and Palermo for the defence of Minorca.

Reports of his dalliance had reached London and, at the Admiralty, St Vincent felt it time to call him home.

At the beginning of the year, while the *Mutine* was attached to the squadron that was blockading Genoa, the Austrians advanced upon the port along the coast. Hoste was ordered to escort a convoy to Leghorn, where he found Nelson in the *Foudroyant* and the two men dined together in the flagship. The admiral said that because, since the arrival of Keith, he was no longer senior officer in the Mediterranean he had had to recommend Hoste for promotion to the new Commander-in-Chief, who had promised to attend to it.

If Nelson went home, Hoste would be without a patron to steer him towards the most valuable appointments, and all that he owed to his 'second father' welled up in emotion. 'It is exactly seven years since I left Godwick,' he told his mother, 'and, believe me, during the whole time he never has altered his conduct with respect to me. I think every time I see him, he behaves with more kindness than ever.'

Nelson's departure would accentuate his sense of isolation in command of a small ship often sailing alone. He confided in his mother, 'I have a famous cabin on board the *Mutine* but am rather dull from want of society. My officers are not very pleasant men and although we seldom or ever disagree yet still I find it necessary to let them know the distance between the Captain and Officers.

'Next to the duty of the ship, I employ my time chiefly in reading, though my library is so very small that I begin to be almost tired of reading the same thing over again so many times. If you could send me a few books, to make some little addition, I should be very thankful.'

To his brother Dixon, he wrote a long day-dreaming letter planning a cruise for him and his younger brother George in the brig where he had two cabins ready for them. It would not be in January, when he was writing, because it was 'rather uncomfortable . . . as it rains and blows devilish hard' but in summer when they would enjoy it and, 'believe me, it would give me a deal of pleasure'. Then he broke into the rambling reverie, 'But I must clap a stopper on, for I am afraid I am writing about what can never be realized.'

But there were compensations. The ship's company was settling down and a flogging had to be ordered only about once a month. There were enemy merchant ships to be chased and taken and the possibility of prize-money, which was good for morale. It was significant that in one action off Porto Maurizio, in which three small trading ships were boarded under fire and two of the boarders killed, one of the seriously wounded was Marine Robert MacLean, a persistent troublemaker, who had had to be flogged on several occasions. Once twenty-four lashes had been laid on his back for 'contempt and dis-

Nelson the paternal. Rear-Admiral Sir Horatio Nelson receiving a French officer's sword from a midshipman on board the *Vanguard* after the Battle of the Nile in 1798. *Painted by Guy Head.*

The sporting life. The Reverend Theodore Dixon Hoste – William
Hoste's elder brother – grouse-shooting in the Forest of Bowland,
Lancashire, with his friend William Assheton left *Detail of Painting
by James Northcote, R.A.*

Captain Sir William Hoste, Royal Navy. *Attributed to Samuel Lane.*

The blockade of the Spanish Fleet in Cadiz by the Inshore Squadron, commanded by Rear-Admiral Sir Horatio Nelson, in June, 1797. The *Theseus*, Nelson's flagship, is the third ship from the left in the foreground. *Painted by Thomas Buttersworth.*

The Battle of the Nile, 1st. August, 1798. The British squadron, here led by the *Zelous*, engaging the flank of the French line at the beginning of the action. *Painted by Thomas Buttersworth.*

Cattaro. The fort of San Giovanni stands on the peak behind the city.
Engraved by A. Maclure.

Ragusa. The fort of San Lorenzo stands on a crag immediately behind
the city and the lower slopes of Mount Sergius rise from the landward
walls.

Porto San Giorgio at Lissa painted by Dr. Joseph Arnold, surgeon of
H.M.S. *Alcmene,* in 1812. The panorama is a view of one hundred and
eighty degrees seen from the approximate centre of the harbour. From
left to right: the British naval cemetery near the harbour mouth; the
village of Cut; the church of S. Spilice and, behind it, the telegraph
station on Mount Whitby; to the right of the town of Lissa, *trabaccoli*

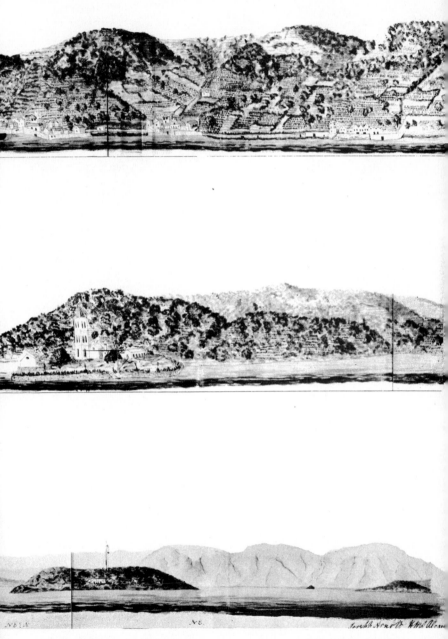

lie at the mouth of English Harbour; the British dockyard on the friary
peninsular with Admiral Fremantle's house to the right of the
campanile; Fort Bentinck on a hilltop and nearer the shore the corner of
Fort George, then building; finally, off the harbour mouth, the signal
station on Hoste Island and the mountains of Brazza and the mainland
beyond.

Rear-Admiral Thomas Fremantle (1765-1819). *Painted by D. Pellegrini.*

The Battle of Lissa: The Franco-Venetian squadron in two columns – the windward division led by Commodore Dubourdieu in the *Favorite* – bears down on the British line, led by Hoste in the *Amphion*. *After a painting by Robert Dodd.*

Commodore Bernard Dubourdieu.

above Lissa: the first broadsides. As the squadrons close, Dubourdieu tries to work forward of the *Amphion,* then attempts to ram her and board. *Painted by John Christian Schetky.*

below Lissa: close action. As the *Favorite*, shattered by the *Amphion's* broadsides, drifts on to the rocks, and the British line goes about on to an opposite course, the *Flore*, now leading the windward division, rakes Hoste's ship. *After a painting by Thomas Whitcombe, from a sketch by Midshipman J. Few.*

above Lissa: trapped between the *Bellona* and the *Flore,* the *Amphion* makes sail, turns across the bows of the latter and, shielded from the fire of the former, batters the enemy until she surrenders. *After a painting by Robert Dodd.*

below Victory: the *Favorite* burns on the rocks; the *Bellona* has surrendered; the surviving Franco-Venetian frigates make for Lesina, pursued by the *Active,* to which the *Corona* surrenders. *After a painting by George Webster.*

Captain Hoste ashore on the Dalmatian Coast. A popular engraving was taken from this drawing.

A cutting-out expedition. Boats from the frigate *Eagle* chase a convoy of *trabaccoli* ashore on the coast of Italy under fire. *Painted by Lieutenant William Innes Pocock.*

The attack on Fiume by the squadron commanded by Admiral Fremantle in July, 1813. The town was stormed by landing-parties from the *Bacchante* and the *Eagle*. *Painted by Lieutenant William Innes Pocock of the Eagle.*

The escaped prisoner-of-war, Donat Henchy O'Brien, who re-joined his old ship, the *Amphion*; wearing the uniform of a post-captain.

Another former prisoner of the French. Captain Sir Jahleel Brenton of the *Spartan*.

After the war: Captain Sir William Hoste, the country gentleman. The coastal scene in the background may be a view of the Hamble estuary.

obedience'; now he had redeemed himself in battle.

Prize-money was a great incentive to Hoste himself, though not only for his own benefit. While escorting two prizes laden with corn and wine that had been intercepted while trying to run the blockade into Genoa, he wrote to his father, boasting that they might sell for £800 to £1000 in Leghorn.

'You see sometimes I reckon for a rainy day either for myself, or some other,' he continued. 'I remitted to my agent, some few months back, £1000, and I intend to do the same with this when I get it. I hope my dear father will excuse me when I say the money is of no use to me, as my pay, with very little addition, serves me; and will take the trouble to put it to any purpose he thinks proper.'

All Hoste's hopes of advancement and prosperity for his family now depended upon Lord Keith, whom he did not know and who was proving himself a very different man from Nelson. A Lowland Scot, of the rich Elphinstone family, he was invariably courteous but he was cautious and there was a cold harshness about him. The war in the Mediterranean could bring out the worst in a commander's character, as Nelson had shown at Naples the year before in countermanding Ruffo's armistice terms. But that had been done in anger and was seen as a military and political necessity, the decision taken by a man in emotional turmoil, at war with his own conscience over Emma Hamilton. But now, off Genoa, Keith was to act somewhat similarly with equally dreadful results but without any such excuses.

The French, under Marshal Masséna, were besieged in the port by the Austrians and known to be near to starvation. In May, while the British ships were bombarding the town they were regularly annoyed by gunfire from a gigantic Genoese galley, part of an aggressive flotilla that would emerge from the harbour to offer combat. With a dash that was worthy of Nelson, a cutting-out party pulled inshore one night and boarded the galley, which was manned by nearly six hundred men, more than half of them galley-slaves. It was a desperate venture but the slaves, sensing freedom, willingly helped the British and pulled their great ship out to sea with its fifty-two long oars, then setting the sails to make their escape.

Pleased as he was with his prize, Keith decided to embarrass the French further by giving them more mouths to feed. So he returned not only members of the galley's fighting crew who had been captured but also the slaves. These wretches, who had been 'jumping about the deck in a delirium of joy' were – all but about fifty who had been embarked in a British ship, which had been blown away from the flagship – sent back into Genoa. There, Masséna, recognizing their part in the capture of the galley, had them all taken to the main square

and shot. A fortnight later, famine forced the French to surrender the
city, evacuating their garrison along the coast to France.

Nelson had hoped to return home in triumph with the Hamiltons
as his guests on board the *Foudroyant* but Keith could not spare the
ship and, in any case, was in no mood to pander to his difficult subordinate. His decision was proved right by news of the crushing defeat
of the Austrians by Bonaparte at Marengo, which again put Italy at
his mercy, on the very day that Nelson arrived in his flagship at Leghorn. So the party set off overland on a grand tour of friendly European
courts which would eventually lead them to London.

Nelson was not the same man that had arrived in these waters in the
Agamemnon seven years earlier. He was now the most celebrated British
commander on sea or land and fully conscious of the fact. His country
had honoured him, but not to the degree he had hoped, with a barony
rather than a viscountcy, prompting a characteristic outburst from
Emma. 'If I was King of England,' she exploded, 'I would make you
the most noble puissant Duke Nelson, Marquis Nile, Earl Alexandria,
Viscount Pyramid, Baron Crocodile and Prince Victory.' But King
Ferdinand had loaded him with tinsel honours and the Dukedom of
Brontë, which carried with it a large estate on the slopes of Etna.
Before battle, it had been a favourite saying of his that soon he would
be crowned with laurel or cypress; as it was, he returned home covered
with glory, sparkling decorations and scandal.

Despite his promise, Lord Keith seemed to have no intention of
promoting Hoste although he treated him 'with uncommon attention,
which must be owing to Lord Nelson'. William himself did not feel
able to write to his patron about this 'for fear he should suppose that
I am not satisfied with what he has done for me'. But his father could
and did and received a reply from London saying, 'Your son deserved
more than I could give him. He ought to have been made Post, and
would long since, had I retained the command. He will do me and all
credit in whatever situation he is placed.'

There was ample opportunity. While the French again crushed
opposition on the Continent – the Austrians were defeated again at
Hohenlinden and a peace settlement imposed upon them, and a neutral
bloc hostile to Britain established in the Baltic in the Armed Neutrality
of the North – the British remained supreme at sea. Malta had been
finally taken in the autumn of 1800 and, early in the new year, a
British army was landed in Aboukir Bay with the aim of administering
the *coup de grâce* to the Army of Egypt. The *Mutine* took part in these
operations, arriving too late for the assault landing, which disappointed
her captain 'as it might have been the means of getting promotion'.

Lying at anchor in the bay where Nelson had destroyed de Brueys' fleet nearly two years before brought to Hoste 'the recollection of the man who (one alone excepted) is the dearest to me on earth', as he tactfully put it to his father. Soon there was more than recollection. He had heard that the admiral had been appointed to command in the North Sea ('if I am not mistaken, he will find the climate too cold for him') but on rejoining Keith in May he was told of the Battle of Copenhagen that broke the Armed Neutrality of the North. He was particularly pleased by a story of his hero identifying himself after the action in a characteristic manner: 'I think I see him making use of the expression, "I am Lord Nelson; look at my fin", and exposing his stump to the Danish officer.'

Now he was to be sent on a mission that once had been considered for Nelson: to put his head in the lion's mouth of the Adriatic. Venice had long been in decline and the Lion of St Mark toothless, but the aura of her great naval and mercantile power still seemed reflected on the sea that led to the Serenissima. Just as the Mediterranean was made a dramatic sea by the contrast between its opposite shores – the old European civilizations to the north, the dangerously unpredictable Barbary Coast to the south – so the Adriatic was a sea of contrast. To the west lay Italy and the remains of the civilizations of Rome and Venice; to the east, the fierce and rugged Balkans with the ancient republic of Ragusa and a few Venetian settlements clinging to its shores like limpets.

When Venice had fallen to the French in 1797, its great Arsenale and what remained of its navy had been largely destroyed. Since then, it was thought, the dockyard had been put back into service and now the French were again in command of the Italian shore. Not only might there eventually be a danger of a new enemy fleet debouching into the Mediterranean through the Straits of Otranto but there lay, through Dalmatia, another route to the Levant which could be severed by sea power in the Adriatic.

The *Mutine* was to join the frigate *Mercury*, which had been watching those waters, and cruise in search of intelligence and prizes. The day after the two ships met, a possible prize was sighted and a chase begun. But the *Mutine* was so short of provisions and water that, after exchanging shots with what proved to be a French privateer off Ancona, she made for Trieste.

Hoste and his ship's company enjoyed Trieste. For the captain there was the opera ('I was there last night for the first time and was highly delighted with the dancing, etc . . . The piece is called *Hannibal*. The house is reckoned the first in this part of the world, and the dresses and scenery beautiful'). For the crew there were the waterfront taverns, if they were allowed ashore, and, in any case, a liberal flow of cheap wine; on the morning of his visit to the opera, Hoste ordered six of his men to be flogged for drunkenness and quarrelling.

Soon after, the *Mutine* escorted a convoy on its way to Malta and, on her way back up the Adriatic to Trieste, sighted two sails off the coast of Italy apparently making for Brindisi. Hoste gave chase and the two ships – an armed brig and a three-masted polacre merchant-man – hoisted Neapolitan colours but continued to run, making for a sandy bay to the north-west of the port which was protected by a little fort.

This presented a dilemma. A Neapolitan ship would be an ally but an ally would not run for French waters at the sight of a British ensign. So they might be enemy ships, using the colours as a *ruse de guerre*, or they might be Neapolitans illegally trading with the French. If this was the case they were legitimate quarry and Hoste, deciding that they were, followed them inshore. Both ships ran themselves aground but the fort appeared to be unmanned and, once the *Mutine* had come within range and fired two shots at them, they struck their colours.

The British ship's boats were called away and pulled across to the prizes, which they found abandoned, their crews wading ashore through the shallows, although both were indeed Neapolitan. But the ships were stuck fast on the sand and it was important to get them out before the French could bring troops along the coast road. This could only be done by lightening them and the boarding-party began by throwing some of the polacre's cargo over the side and preparing to hoist out the brig's guns. Neither action refloated the prizes. The first six of the brig's guns had been lowered into a boat but loaded carelessly so that she capsized, tipping them into the sea where they sank in the soft sand. However, six more guns, two small swivel-guns and some shot were safely removed. Still the ship remained immovable.

Hoste was prepared to work all night to get them away but at three, just before first light, a column of French infantry was sighted marching down the road towards the fort, which was seen to mount a cannon. While some of the soldiers manned the fort, the rest took up firing positions along the shore, half a pistol-shot from the beached brig, and began shooting at the British sailors with their muskets. Hoste at once recalled his boarding-parties, cleared for action and opened his broadside on the Neapolitan ships: if he could not have them nobody else would. The masts of both ships soon went over the side; then the brig caught fire and, after burning for several hours, blew up.

As the *Mutine* stood out to sea, her captain was left wondering what Keith's reaction would be. It would have been one thing to have brought two suspicious Neapolitan ships for the Commander-in-Chief and the Prize Court to consider as legitimate prizes and perhaps make an award to him and his crew; it was quite another to have destroyed two fine ships which, whatever was their business, indubitably belonged to the Kingdom of the Two Sicilies.

On his way back to Trieste, Hoste called for the first time at two remarkable places: the Gulf of Cattaro and Ragusa. The former, one of the great natural harbours of the world, was a deep fjord running in among the grey limestone mountains of Montenegro past Venetian settlements for twenty miles to the fortified city of Cattaro itself. The *Mutine* anchored in the roadstead within the mouth of the Gulf while gales, thunderstorms and squalls showed what the characteristic weather of the region could do to a sailing-ship that attempted to penetrate deeply between the grim walls of rock. A few days later he was off Ragusa; the city, crouched behind its ramparts on crags above the sea, seeming surprisingly small to have been the commercial rival of Venice. Both cities and their satellite settlements stood against the shoulders of mountains that heaved out of the sea to roll, range beyond range, far into the Balkans.

Steering northward again, the brig sailed through the long archipelago of rocky islands, some stripped of their dense forests to furnish the millions of piles upon which Venice stood and to build its ships. This coastline was in complete contrast to the opposite shore of the Adriatic, which Hoste was to see on his next cruise from Trieste, when he ranged down the long flat shore of Italy to the outcrop of high hills that sheltered the port of Ancona. Here the French had three frigates and two brigs ready for sea, a powerful force that, with his usual confidence, he expected to give 'a most complete drubbing'.

But there was to be no action to overshadow the questionable affair of the Neapolitan ships off Brindisi and, as Hoste had feared, he found on reaching Malta that Lord Keith was 'greatly displeased' with him for having 'exceeded the tenour of his orders'. For a time it seemed that a court-martial was likely but opinion in the fleet was on his side and the Commander-in-Chief did no more than send a report on the incident to St Vincent, who was now First Lord of the Admiralty.

But it did seem probable that the controversy would set back hopes of promotion, particularly as peace with France appeared imminent. Hoste finally wrote to ask for another recommendation from Nelson, who advised Dixon Hoste to use his acquaintance with Norfolk landowners to carry the issue over Lord Keith's head. 'Your dear son William has not had justice done him,' he wrote. 'If I was either Commander-in-Chief in the Mediterranean or First Lord of the Admiralty, he should be Post this day, for no man in the Mediterranean has half deserved it so much as he does. Get Lord Cholmondeley to ask Lord St Vincent's for him, as everybody loves William.'

At the beginning of October agreement was reached on the preliminary terms for what was to be signed as the Peace of Amiens early in 1802. By this, Britain was to restore all maritime conquests, except Trinidad and Ceylon to France, Spain and Holland; the French were to pull back from Naples and recognize the integrity of Portugal; both British and French armies were to withdraw from Egypt; finally, Malta was to be restored by Britain to the Knights of St John.

While peace seemed to have blighted Hoste's hopes of promotion, it did at least give him an opportunity of performing a service for his patron. Nelson had never managed to visit his estate at Brontë which lay on the far side of Mount Etna from Catania and was accessible only by the roughest mountain roads. This may have been just as well because the former owners of more than thirty thousand acres that were now his, the monks of the Grande Ospedale of Palermo, had neglected the land, allowed the big house, the Castello di Maniace, to fall into ruin and left a legal tangle with the Commune of Brontë over the ownership of part of the estate.

Although he was now a vice-admiral and a viscount, scandal still made him unacceptable at Court in London so he was immensely proud of having been created *Duca di Bronte*, which suitably translated as 'Duke of Thunder', a title that must have delighted Emma. He looked forward to eventual retirement among his olive groves and vineyards below Etna, so he was anxious to improve the estate and had ordered a quantity of new agricultural equipment to be sent there and it was now at Malta. Hearing of this, Hoste asked the Commander-in-Chief if he could ship 'the packages of ploughs, harrows and garden stuff for my ever-respected patron Lord Nelson' to Sicily in the *Mutine* and 'after a deal of consideration' permission was granted.

Now that the war was over, Hoste was in high expectation of orders for England but disappointments were repeated. Next came a mission to Otranto and, on his return to Malta, he asked Lord Keith if, in view of his long service in the Mediterranean, he might carry his dispatches home. But, he wrote sarcastically, '*my good friend* the Commander-in-Chief . . . sent me to Egypt, being the *pleasantest station* in his command.' From Alexandria, he carried a British diplomat to Constantinople, where he was entertained by the new British Ambassador, Lord Elgin, and his wife, who were 'remarkably attached to a blue coat'.

A dilettante and a friend of Sir William Hamilton's, Elgin's passion was for Classical archeology and he had just received permission from the Turks to set to work on the Parthenon at Athens: 'to fix scaffolding round the ancient Temple of the Idols' and 'to take away any pieces of stone with old inscriptions and figures thereon.' Hoste hoped to see something of this because, after the Elgins took passage in the *Mutine* for a holiday among the Greek islands, they were to stay at Athens to supervise the work.

But first Hoste had to return to Alexandria, 'where I have the pleasant prospect of remaining all the summer under the scorching beams of an Egyptian sun.' While there he contracted malaria and when he did visit Athens with dispatches for Elgin he was too weak to walk. Lady Elgin – 'the most amiable of women' – invited him to their house and nursed him until he felt 'quite stout and hearty' and he was cheered when the frigate *Narcissus* called at Piraeus and her captain congratulated him on his promotion to post captain. Although his father had ceaselessly agitated on his behalf and, as he was to hear later, it was an enquiry from Thomas Coke that had given his family this news, he well knew where the principal credit was due.

'To Lord Nelson I know not what to say,' he wrote. 'He has taken me by the hand from my first entrance into the service and has never ceased his good offices till he has got me a post-captain's commission. O that I may ever have it in my power to show my gratitude! Next to my dearest father and family, who is there who has half so much claim to my gratitude and respect as Lord Nelson? Him I look upon as almost a second father, a sheet anchor, whom I shall always have to trust to.'

The convalescence at Athens was a pleasant interlude, Hoste finding himself 'highly gratified with the beautiful remains of antiquity'. He attempted to describe the temples in a letter to his sister Kate but soon gave up, writing that 'it must require a much abler pen than mine to give you an adequate idea' but that the ruins were 'well worth observing'. He was more at ease remarking with customary satisfaction that 'I never saw such a set of knaves as the Athenians of the present day . . . Smoking is their daily amusement and they seem as if born for nothing else.'

More good news awaited him at Malta when he returned there in June. Not only were the formalities of his promotion completed but he was given command of the frigate *Greyhound*: 'instead of that little *brig* I now have command of a fine thirty-two gun frigate; and, in short, I cannot describe how happy I feel at this very moment.' This was a true warship, able to take part in a fleet action, to cruise for rich prizes or fight one of the duels with an enemy frigate that caused such a stir in the newspapers at home. Twice the size with twice the complement of the *Mutine*, a frigate could accommodate a post captain in elegance, his day-cabin, lit by the curve of windows across her stern, fit for the entertaining of distinguished guests, such as his new friends, Lord and Lady Elgin.

'I like the *Greyhound* more than any ship I have ever been in,' he wrote home. 'We have a very good set of young men for officers, so that we are quite comfortable and happy amongst ourselves. In so confined a space as a ship, it is the greatest comfort to have a set of gentlemen about you, whom you can associate with. I wish you could pay a visit on board the *Greyhound*; I have just got my cabin fitted up in great style.'

He was also able to cut something of a dash ashore. He had bought an Arab horse at Alexandria for twelve guineas – being offered fifty for it by envious officers at Malta – and he planned to take the animal to Norfolk because 'he leaps uncommonly well and the knowing ones say he will make an excellent hunter'. His reticence in expressing himself to Nelson disappeared with the new self-confidence and he sent him a present of a Mameluke sword that he had brought from Egypt because 'though I am now independent of his services, I shall never forget that it was through him that I am so'.

The frigate's first mission was to Naples, where she formed part of the escort to King Ferdinand who was making his triumphal return from refuge in Palermo and now Hoste was able to discard what he had once held in obligatory awe. 'I could not help laughing most heartily at the triumphal arches erected in the place for his reception,' he wrote. 'It must appear truly ridiculous to every one to see the honours of a triumph given to a man who, in the hour of danger, had basely deserted them . . . I do not think he was well received by any means. About two or three hundred old fishermen welcomed him on shore . . . and the Russian grenadiers were his guards, which is very strange, and shows the little confidence he places in his own troops, and not without reason.'

Hoste found himself 'rather in disgrace' with the Neapolitans and Sicilians for destroying their brig during the summer but remarked, 'I don't care much for their good opinion.' However Naples, with 'the gaieties of this dissolute city', was preferable to Malta, in comparison with which it was 'a paradise'. But the latter was the principal British base and it was from there that the *Greyhound* would be sent on her next mission: a reconnaissance of Toulon.

His new command had, at first, taken the edge off her captain's homesickness, but by the autumn it had returned. Without the excitement of war, Mediterranean voyages varied only with the weather and Hoste became 'heartily tired of the old *jog trot* . . . in this old wooden box'. He longed for 'dear old Godwick and its inhabitants' but had not heard from any of them for seven months.

He wrote regularly to all his family. To his brother Dixon at Cambridge he chaffed about 'the Pretty Girls of Old England', to his younger brother George, who was destined for the Army, he joked, 'If you think a cat of nine tails will be of any use in the house be sure you mention it in your next and I'll send one in miniature. You know very well it's necessary to keep youngsters in order by the old rule of spare the birch, spoil the child' and of the youngest he remarked affectionately, 'You say Master Edward is a great Pickle and very much like I was at his age.'

He was particularly attentive to his sister Kate, whose matrimonial opportunities he advised upon, although an exchange of letters could take months. 'You tell me Miss Kate has declared war with the Male part of the Creation,' he wrote to his father. 'I don't wonder at her refusing so many landlubbers as you have got at home – I mean in England – and shall certainly bring her home a good honest Jack who I'll be bound will grapple with her fast enough.'

He did, in fact, make contact with home in this way but none of the visitors grappled with Miss Kate. Norfolk officers on leave would visit Godwick Hall and those who had met the Hostes would seek out their son when they returned to sea. Hoste himself would ask his father to look out for his returning shipmates, particularly the young officers of the *Mutine*, for whom he had come to feel some affection. It was not only officers that were to be welcomed and he wrote to his father after the brig had returned to England, 'The sailor you were good enough to take care of did belong to the *Mutine*, but did not come with me from the *Theseus*. Poor fellow! he lost his arm, as he told you, in cutting out some vessels on the Italian coast. Should you see him again, give him a good dinner on my account; for though he did not bear the best character with me, yet he was as brave as a lion and behaved very well in the fighting way.'

Then, just as the Elgins had come to his aid during the first bout of malaria, another British family appeared to relieve his homesickness. This was the British minister to Genoa, Sir Francis Drake, a descendant of the Elizabethan navigator and a friend of Nelson's. The Drake family took passage in the *Greyhound* to Leghorn and there invited Hoste to accompany them on a visit to Florence and 'the happiest time I have spent since I left England'. Still unable to convey aesthetic thoughts on paper, he was clearly able to appreciate what he was shown, writing home, 'The gallery at Florence has universally been reckoned, and very justly, the seat of the arts . . . I have been looking today over the most beautiful paintings I ever saw in my life.' He even began to consider himself something of a dilettante: 'I was at the famous Sculptor's yesterday and I purchased some beautiful figures in Alabaster which I intend for the dear old House in Norfolk.'

He also found himself lionized by the rich and usually intelligent

British families who were taking advantage of peace by touring Europe: 'It seems to be quite the rage for travelling as we have met a great many English families who intend passing through Italy and are continually on the move.' He even grandly suggested that, were he not due home before long, his family should make 'a trip through France and Italy'.

With the Drakes, there was the opera or a dance every night and fascinating introductions. One of these was to 'Lady Esther Stanhope' who was 'on her travels'. Although Lady Hester Stanhope was the niece of the Hostes' political arch-villain William Pitt, Hoste was clearly impressed by her – although she was yet to achieve fame and notoriety as an eccentric traveller in the Levant – and he offered to give her brother, who was with her, passage to Gibraltar in his frigate.

Now it was back to the Rock ('I would almost prefer Botany Bay to it') and a new and disturbing prospect. While the coming of peace had half-promised a happy return to England, now renewed war threatened – the French continued to interfere in Italy and Switzerland and the British to hold Malta – and this, while welcome from a professional point of view, could well keep all available warships in the Mediterranean. Making the best of this, Hoste optimistically hoped that Nelson might take command again in those waters: 'I hope most truly, if ever war takes place, I may belong to the squadron he commands.' But he was reluctant to ask a favour of his greatest Norfolk patron directly, although he hinted that his father might mention at Holkham that a word to St Vincent might be all that was required: 'I am ashamed to ask Mr Coke for anything but if he spoke to the *Man at the Helm*, I might be ordered home directly.'

Then on 8th March, 1803, just after he had resigned himself to almost permanent banishment east of Gibraltar ('I have not the smallest prospect of leaving'), the *Greyhound* was ordered home. On 4th April, he anchored in the Thames off Woolwich and a few days later entered the long drive from Tittleshall and could see the gables of Godwick Hall above the trees. It was almost exactly ten years since he had left.

The welcome was everything Hoste had dreamed about. His parents were as generous and jolly as ever. His elder brother, Dixon, had proved a brilliant Classical scholar at Trinity College, of which he was being elected a Fellow, and, although suffering from a worryingly persistent cough, took his brother out duck-shooting, showing off the discipline of his favourite gun-dog, Gull. Young George had just been commissioned in the Corps of Engineers and, while this was unlikely to result in sudden gain through prize-money, it could well lead to social advancement. Little Edward, whom William had never seen, was aged only nine, but there were already suggestions that in two or three years he might go to sea with his elder brother in the new and official rank of Volunteer (First Class) that would lead directly to a commission.

The girls – Kate, Jane and little Anne – all flourished. Miss Kate, despite many suitors, had not married and, to the family's delight, Jane, who was intelligent and witty, had become a close friend of Thomas Coke's unmarried daughter, Elizabeth.

For the coming months, there was a round of visits to the great houses – Holkham, Houghton, Raynham, Wolterton and the rest – and, in autumn, invitations to shoot and hunt with the great land-owners. There was one disappointment: Nelson was no longer at Burnham Thorpe; indeed he had never returned to the village of his birth since he, Josiah, William and the others had joined the *Agamemnon*. He had been created a viscount after his victory at Copenhagen – his subsequent bloody failure at Boulogne had been overlooked – and was now installed in his elegant house at Merton with 'his amiable consort', as Hoste described Emma.

War broke out again in May but it was not until the end of the follow-ing year – in November, 1804 – that Hoste again went to sea. He was appointed to the command of the frigate *Eurydice* and took his brother Dixon down to Portsmouth with him for the commissioning. The ship he found in a poor state ('I have been on board the *Eurydice* and in a little time hope to make a man-of-war of her, for she is anything but that at present') although he noted that his quarters were more spacious than those in the *Greyhound*. Yet, once at sea, he was delighted with 'this jolly old hooker', boasting that she was 'as good a sea boat as ever I sailed in, and one of the *true old build*; the harder it blows the faster she goes'. He also liked his officers and found his First Lieutenant 'particularly gentlemanly'.

He had new hope of joining Nelson, who was again commanding in the Mediterranean, but this was to be deferred. There was a stormy passage to Gibraltar, where he arrived early in January to hear from one of Nelson's officers that, as he told his father, the admiral was 'very anxious that I should be with him again'. But first there was an un-expected mission to the Cape Verde Islands, off the west coast of Africa, taken by the British the year before as a base to protect shipping and subsequently to harass the trade of Spain, which had just declared war on Britain at the instigation of France.

The principal port, Goree, a slaving station, was, Hoste decided, a 'miserable hole', much hotter than Egypt, even in the supposedly cool season and he sweltered all night in his cabin despite keeping all the doors and windows open. The inhabitants were mostly 'black as your hat and the plainest most ill-proportioned set of people I ever met with', a somewhat churlish description since they were 'partial to the English to a fault'.

Despite the excitement of renewed war and the prospects of prize-money – the *Eurydice* had taken a Spanish timber ship bound from Havana to Barcelona with a cargo worth some £800 on passage to Gibraltar – Hoste was homesick. The pleasures of Godwick were still fresh in his memory and his friendship with his brother Dixon, now a young sporting parson, was between equals rather than, as it had been, between child and adolescent. This was accentuated by meeting an old schoolfriend of Dixon's, a Captain Langford, commanding the sloop *Lark*, which had been on the African station for some months but had only succeeded in taking one small prize since the outbreak of war.

Hoste had a poor opinion of the embittered Langford, whom he considered 'a seedy kind'. He had married a black wife, since 'it has been the custom of the English when at Goree to look out for the best-looking black lady and after about three weeks you take possession *in due form*. I think it is a cruel custom though so frequently practiced.' Langford had been at school at King's Lynn so the two men had 'a good deal of talk or *gab* together' including, naturally, 'a good deal of old Norfolk'. But Langford had lacked the social assurance of Hoste, who, to his amazement, found that the former 'abominates the very *mention* of the County, he says everybody is so cursed proud and *unsociable* that he was heartily glad to cut and run'.

'I stuck out most sturdily for the *honour* of Norfolk,' Hoste wrote to Dixon, 'gave it the preference to any other county in England and rather too boldly asserted that the *fine flat varigated* scenery, particularly around Swaffham and Brandon, was equal to the so-much-boasted garden of Kent, or the *beautiful romantic* hill and dale of Westmoreland and Lancashire, and frequently interlarded it with "I've heard my brother say so".'

Dixon he regarded as an authority on field sports; not only hunting and shooting in Norfolk but also such lordly pastimes as grouse-shooting in Lancashire, where he had been invited by a land-owning friend with whom he had been painted after a shoot in the Forest of Bowland by the artist James Northcote. Now, sweating in the tropics, his younger brother wrote to him enviously, 'Perhaps at this moment you are skating on Tittleshall pond, or freezing with cold over one of your favourite duck ponds.' William went on to describe his own rough shoots at Goree, when he and his officers and his old dog Brontë – named after Nelson's Sicilian title – shot 'wild turkeys and guinea fowls by dozens!' The day before he had killed eleven wild turkeys but the sport had to be stopped because of the intense heat and the birds taken back to where 'an old black lady prepared a *dinner*, if I may call turkey and fish, fried together in oil, and cocoa-nuts just gathered, by that name'.

'What a jump from Old England across the Atlantic,' he added. 'And what a contrast between old Brontë and a flock of turkeys, and your favourite dog Gull and a covey of partridges!'

The Hostes' idea of sporting ethics was very English. The clean killing of birds with a fowling-piece, or the death of a fox after a hard-ridden hunt, was a natural and noble sport, but anything that smacked of cruelty – such as bull-fighting – or killing for its own sake was despicable. One such incident in the Cape Verde Islands determined Hoste never to shoot a monkey for sport. Two of his officers had been returning from a day's shooting when they saw a female monkey running over some rocks, fired and wounded the animal.

'She fell with her young one in her arms,' he wrote to Dixon. 'On the pursuer coming up, she grasped the little one close to her breast, and with the other hand pointed to the wound which the ball had made and which had entered above the breast. Dipping her finger in the blood, and then holding it up, she seemed to reproach him with being the cause of her death, and consequently that of the young one, to which she frequently pointed. I never felt so much as when I heard the story, and it serves to show how strongly the parental feelings are implanted by Nature, even in the brute creation.'

The *Eurydice* was now ordered back to Portsmouth for repairs and fitting for further foreign service but arrived two days after George Hoste, now a young officer in the Engineers, had sailed from there with an expeditionary force bound for the Mediterranean. The frigate had passed the convoy the day after it had sailed but, of course, Hoste had not known his brother was embarked, nor that his father, who had seen him off at Portsmouth, was already on his way home to Norfolk. But there was the heartening thought that he had gone to the Mediter-ranean, where the two would probably meet, rather than the West Indies, a posting that often amounted to a sentence of death from yellow fever.

Hoste was able to meet his father before the latter reached Norfol'c by hurrying to London and staying with him at the Osborne Hotel in the Strand. Here he heard disturbing news of Dixon and of Kate, both of whom were unwell, although this was put down to the unseasonably cold weather for May. There was no time for a visit to Godwick – only a bluff, reassuring letter saying, 'How I do wish, my dear Dick, I could shake your honest old hand once more before I left England, and that we could have a hearty laugh together at Godwick' –

but his father accompanied him back to Portsmouth to see his ship and try to allay his fears for his brother and sister; the dreaded possibility for both was tuberculosis.

Hoste proudly showed his father over the frigate, apologizing for the untidiness caused by the refitting and promising to arrange a demonstration of beating to quarters and manning the guns 'with all the bustle and confusion of an action at sea but it must all be in *dumb show*'. But he was able to show him over a ship of the line, the *Princess Royal*, which was in dock, and then a new invention that he felt certain must have an application to naval warfare. He wrote to his brother that he had 'explained as far as I was able the *Steam Engine*, you never saw any person so astonished as he was'.

Certainly, Dixon Hoste was a cheering guest, reassuring his son about Dick's health so that he was able to write him a jolly letter asking, 'Pray are you in love?' and giving him gossipy details about his stay in London. But once his father had left for Norfolk, his depression returned and the optimism in his letters home seemed forced: 'What cruel cold weather we have had for May! I am certain poor Dick must be better than bobbish to stand it.'

His brother had had a relapse but rallied and Hoste was able to chide him, 'You have had a hard bout of it . . . If you would follow the example of your *younger* brother and take more *care of yourself*, it might be *better*.' There was time to brood about Kate as well ('I hope ere this that Kate has recovered her usual looks') while he awaited a convoy that he was to escort to the Mediterranean and there was little to do but go ashore in Portsmouth to play billiards and pass around the political cartoons by Gillray that his father had brought him.

When his sailing orders did arrive on 21st May they were 'such as my most sanguine hopes could wish or expect'. He was to command the escort of a convoy to Portugal and the Mediterranean, where he would put himself under Nelson's command once again. 'I am at this moment one of the luckiest and happiest fellows in the world,' he told his father. 'I know you will partake with me in the happy and glorious prospects now before me: a nice little frigate, and going under my gallant patron on the very ground which, a few years ago, was the theatre of so much honour to him . . . from whence I hope not to return till I have gained plenty of credit and plenty of cash . . . I need not tell you to think of little *Eurydice* sometimes.'

Leaving part of his convoy at Oporto, Hoste took the rest safely to Gibraltar where, to his delight, he found his brother George living in one of the transports of the expeditionary force that was there awaiting orders to sail. George was in his usual hearty spirits, boasting that he was 'no longer a lazy landlubber but fully ready to meet old Neptune in all his rage', although his passage out had been stormy and he 'cruelly seasick'. But he laughed this away with a vulgar story about all the crockery in the ship being smashed in the storm 'not forgetting a lady's *pot de chambre* which unfortunately upset with its contents'.

There was also an immediate prospect of action. The Spanish had some forty gun-boats across the bay at Algeciras and Hoste told the senior British naval officer at Gibraltar that 'the most effectual way of sickening the Dons' would be 'to dash at them with our ship-of-war boats and by boarding . . . carry them'. When the rear-admiral decided to take up this suggestion, he had second thoughts however: 'he wished me to amuse the gun-boats, which is no joke I assure you . . . as our guns are so short that our shot would not reach them and theirs would go over and over us' and was relieved to have to escort a convoy to Malta instead.

The Mediterranean was now said to be the place for prize-money: 'I understand there is plenty to be picked up on this old station now that the English fleet have left it; and the dreaded name of Nelson being gone makes it still more likely for those French and Spanish gentry to make a dash.' But when he chased a fine frigate and was about to give her his broadside she was seen to be 'a true American, which disappointed our brave tars of an expected prize'.

Nelson and his fleet were absent because, in January, the French fleet in Toulon, under Admiral Pierre Villeneuve, had broken through his blockade and escaped through the Straits of Gibraltar. The long chase to the West Indies, which was thought to be their destination, began and the two fleets narrowly missed a confrontation among the islands, whereupon Villeneuve headed back across the Atlantic with the aim of joining forces with the Spanish and other French fleets. Once this could be achieved, Bonaparte, who had now crowned himself the Emperor Napoleon, would have an overwhelming force to command the English Channel and ship an invading army to England.

Although Nelson had failed to catch him, Villeneuve's plan went awry; he was intercepted off Ushant by a British squadron and ran south to Cadiz from which the Spanish had not sailed. Nelson, after returning briefly to Gibraltar to dispose his ships in the Mediterranean, returned to England. There, at home at Merton Place with Emma Hamilton, he heard that Villeneuve was at Cadiz, blockaded there with thirty-four French and Spanish ships of the line by twenty-five British under his old friend and present second-in-command, Vice-Admiral Cuthbert Collingwood. 'I think I shall yet have to beat them,' he said.

In August, while Nelson was at Merton and in London, Hoste was at Malta, 'cooped up in this oven' with the expedition which his brother was accompanying. There was intense speculation about their eventual destination and Hoste himself thought that 'the noble Commander-in-Chief is in the dark himself' not realizing that he was in England and that the grand climax was fast approaching.

The orders that arrived for the *Eurydice* were those for which her captain longed. He was to join Lord Nelson in the blockade of the combined fleets of France and Spain in Cadiz. This would not only put him directly under his patron's eye and doubtless lead to a post of honour in whatever action ensued but he would almost certainly hear news from home as mail would be carried in the ships that had joined the blockade from England. Cut off in Malta, he and George had worried about Dixon and Kate, William asking his father to 'tell dear Kate I regularly take her Ring out of the Desk and give her a kiss by Proxy.'

Then pessimism was justified, but it was not by letter that the news arrived from Norfolk. Off Cadiz, his old friend from *Agamemnon* days, Billy Bolton, who had married Nelson's niece and been knighted for standing proxy for him at his installation as a Knight of the Order of the Bath and was now Captain Sir William Bolton, came on board as what Hoste described as 'the harbinger of the heaviest misfortune I have met with in this life'. Bolton brought the news that his brother Dixon had died.

Dixon had been dead since 19th July after a long struggle with tuberculosis and William, in an agony of grief, transferred all his anxiety to Kate, writing home that 'letters from England are to me almost as much dreaded as they were, before this irreparable loss, desired. Poor dear Kate, pray Heaven she may stand up under this misfortune, though I confess I tremble at every paper I see, for fear something still more unfortunate, if possible, may meet my eyes.'

The only consolation was the faith that his father preached from his pulpit, even if more from expediency than dedication. So William could comfort himself by writing to the parson that 'I suffer for my dearest brother but though he is gone from us now, we are taught to believe we shall meet him hereafter, and your own maxim has ever been, "The Almighty's will be done!"'

There was only one way to alleviate the pain and that was to concentrate on the war. 'I wish the Spanish Rascals would come out and give me something to do,' he wrote home. He had not long to wait because, before the end of September, he was ordered to join Captain Henry Blackwood's frigates of the inshore squadron off Cadiz. On his arrival to assume command, Nelson had changed the tactics, abandoning Collingwood's close blockade by heavy ships in favour of a squadron of frigates close off the harbour mouth, linked by a relay of ships with smart signals officers to the main fleet, waiting some fifty miles to the south-west, the object being to lure the combined fleets from harbour.

This was just what Hoste needed, telling his father, 'I can hardly think of anything else but your house. I feel most severely the loss we have suffered and know not what I should do if the active situation I am in here at present did not almost deprive me of the power of doing anything but looking after the combined fleets, who are closely block-aded in Cadiz. For these fourteen nights I have hardly had a wink of sleep. We are obliged to keep from two to three miles off the harbour's mouth and I am heartily glad I have so active a situation.'

On 1st October, Nelson summoned him to dine on board the *Victory*. To see the splendid old ship that he had first seen at Spithead during his first days at sea, and to meet in her great cabin the slight figure in the blue coat blazing with gold and silver decorations, was all that he had hoped for. The admiral was sympathetic about his bereavement and 'as good and friendly as ever', hinting that Hoste might be shortly given command of a larger ship. He listened patiently to one of Hoste's current complaints: he had detained a suspicious Neapolitan ship and sent her into Malta as a possible prize but, after a long detention, she was freed and her captor saddled with expenses resulting from the delay in her passage. The admiral asked him to put this complaint in writing and, a few days later, himself forwarded it to the Admiralty with a covering letter in support.

Then it was back to the inshore squadron and, a week later, the sort of exploit that Hoste had longed to perform for his patron. Cruising off the Spanish coast, a convoy was sighted from the *Eurydice*, which was in company with the bomb-vessel *Aetna*, and it was seen that to be escorted by a warship mounting two long twenty-four-pounder guns, heavier and of longer range than any weapon in the two British ships. Hoste at once called his boats away and these boarded and captured four of the small merchantmen under heavy fire. The frigate, meanwhile, was closing with their escort but, as Hoste reported to Nelson, 'I was induced to run the *Eurydice* closer in than I should otherwise have done ... and unfortunately took ground on a shoal about half a mile from the mainland.' But she was quickly towed to safety by her consort and the *Eurydice*'s boats ran alongside the enemy ship which promptly struck her colours. She proved to be a Spanish privateer named *La Solidad* from Cadiz and Hoste sent her to Gibraltar under a prize crew. Nelson was delighted and sent Hoste's report on the action, together with a fulsome letter of his own, to the Admiralty.

On the 13th, the Commander-in-Chief gave Hoste his new command. She was to be the frigate *Amphion* of thirty-six guns, one of the finest ships of her rate in the fleet and a favourite of Nelson's; he had once flown his flag in her, before he had taken her captain, his old friend

Hardy, with him as flag captain to the *Victory*. The *Amphion* had just joined the fleet from Lisbon and as her captain, Samuel Sutton, was in poor health, the admiral gave her to Hoste and moved Billy Bolton to the *Eurydice*.

Hoste considered his new ship 'one of the finest and most desirable ships . . . I could not, had I had the choice of frigates, been appointed to one more to my liking.' The crowning pleasure was, of course, that it had been the personal choice of his patron: 'I need not mention the kindness I have received from Lord Nelson; his present appointment speaks for itself.'

But his hopes of early glory in battle were to be dashed. The Commander-in-Chief told him that there was no immediate prospect of the enemy leaving harbour – just as he said this to the captains of ships of the line that were sent away to replenish with supplies and water at Gibraltar and Tetuan – and that he must now undertake an important mission. This was first to embark large sums of money from Collingwood's ship, the *Royal Sovereign*, and transfer it to another ship at Gibraltar from whence it would go to finance further operations in the Mediterranean; then to visit Algiers with letters and presents for the Dey.

On the face of it, the choice of Hoste and the *Amphion* for this task was a natural one. A cargo of bullion could only be entrusted to a ship that was fast and powerful. As for a diplomatic mission, Hoste had performed many such for Nelson in the *Mutine* and was known to be tactful and charming; also, if an envoy was to carry any weight with an Algerine ruler, he must arrive in a handsome ship.

The personal letter from Nelson to the Dey was short but of some diplomatic importance, the vital passage reading, 'I rely that nothing will ever be permitted to happen which can interrupt the most perfect harmony and good understanding which exists between your Highness and the Regency, and the British Nation. I am confident that your Highness will give orders for the most friendly reception of British Ships in all the Ports of your Dominions and that they shall be furnished, for their money, with every article they may want to purchase. I shall be very anxious for the return of the Frigate, that I may know the state of your Highness's health . . .'

This letter was intended to shore up the southern flank of a British maritime thrust into the Mediterranean. Shipping off the Barbary Coast had long been plagued by pirates and Algerine privateers but, until August, the British had largely been free of these problems since the Americans had been provoked into action and the young United States Navy had been cutting its teeth in action against piracy. But now a settlement had been reached and there was the possibility that the

Algerines would see in the withdrawal of the American ships and the absence of the bulk of the British Mediterranean Fleet west of Gibraltar an opportunity to renew their plundering.

Yet in sending one of his favourite young captains and ships away on such a mission at such a moment inevitably raises questions. Much speculation and some mystery surround Nelson's actions at this time and other motives must be considered. His letters from the *Victory* during October harp upon the shortage of frigates ('I am most exceedingly anxious for more *eyes*, and hope the Admiralty are hastening them to me. The last Fleet was lost to me for want of Frigates; God forbid this should') and now one of his most experienced frigate captains and best frigates would be lost to him for, perhaps, a month.

For, whatever he said to Hoste and other captains in his situation, he himself was certain that the climactic action was imminent, as his letters show. 'I have thirty-six Sail of the Line looking me in the face . . . it is believed they will come to sea in a few days,' he wrote on the 8th, and, on the 10th, 'The Enemy's Fleet are all but out of the harbour – perhaps, this night, with the Northerly wind, they may come forth.' On the 14th, the day before Hoste left the fleet, Nelson wrote in his private diary, 'Sent *Amphion* to Gibraltar and Algiers. Enemy at the harbour mouth.'

Even if the combined fleets did not sail as soon as he expected, he planned to go after them with his inshore squadron, sending in fire-ships and perhaps bombarding the harbour with Colonel Congreve's new rockets launched from catamarans, which would be exactly the sort of action in which Hoste would revel and excel.

Nelson must have recognized this and understood the disappointment and frustration that his orders would bring upon the young man. A commander who led by example and encouragement, his denial of Hoste's right to fight beside him may have been prompted by impulses of which he himself was not conscious.

Old memories and new ambitions may have been stirred, perhaps, by the chance arrival of a ship. Just before the *Amphion* sailed, the fleet was joined by the old *Agamemnon*, commanded by his Norfolk friend Berry. With her may have returned thoughts of the eager boys he had taken to sea in her twelve years before and particularly of John Weatherhead, who had shown such promise but had died off Tenerife and whose place had been taken by William Hoste. He had been the first of the young men he had fostered but whose early deaths had resulted directly from his own orders. If Hoste were to be present at the coming battle he would be likely to throw his frigate into the hottest action and fight as close to the *Victory* as he was able. So he, too, might become another sacrifice to personal loyalty and professional zeal.

Or, it might have been that, on meeting William again, he had remembered Emma Hamilton's words – 'I say he will be a second Nelson' – and had recognized that he might well prove to be his professional heir. Whether or not there were premonitions of death in action, Nelson must have recognized that an admiral, standing on the exposed quarterdeck of his flagship in 'the pell-mell battle' he planned to provoke, faced a high risk of death or wounds. If this was to be the end of his career then, perhaps, a young man able to carry on his ideas and tradition should be preserved, this once, from danger.

Oblivious to all such possibilities and speculation, Hoste was taking his new command to Gibraltar, where he transferred the bullion to the *Aurora*. There was no need for the *Amphion* to embark stores at this time but her captain went ashore on the 17th, for a shopping expedition to buy himself a smart new uniform that would be worthy of his position, including a pair of the newly-fashionable blue pantaloons and the tight cloth trousers that were beginning to replace the traditional breeches and stockings.

He sailed next day and, on the day after, witnessed the punishment of a seaman named Robert Smith with twenty-four lashes for drunkenness. On Monday, the 21st, as Nelson's fleet and the combined fleets of France and Spain were heaving slowly towards each other over the blue Atlantic swell for what was to be the Battle of Trafalgar, the *Amphion* was running along the Barbary Coast before 'light airs' and her captain was carrying out the routine reading of the disciplinary Articles of War to his ship's company.

On the 25th, the frigate exchanged salutes of twenty-one guns with the waterfront fortress at Algiers and the British consul came on board to receive Nelson's letters. The *Amphion* embarked ten live bullocks and two mules for passage back to Gibraltar, for which she sailed on the 28th. On 9th November, she was back off the Rock and Hoste heard the devastating news.

Victory had been complete. The twenty-seven British ships of the line had fought thirty-three French and Spanish all afternoon and two-thirds of the enemy ships had been destroyed or captured. But, early in the action, Nelson, pacing the quarterdeck of his flagship with Hardy, both splashed with blood and grimy with gunsmoke, had been shot by a French sniper, firing from a mizen-top at almost point-blank range. The ball tore through his gold epaulette into his shoulder, cut an artery and penetrated his spine. He died two hours and forty-five minutes after he had been hit.

At once, Hoste wrote to his father, 'I have just time to say that I am as well as a man can be, who has lost the best friend he ever possessed. I know not how to begin. I believe I said in my last, I was ordered to Algiers by that ever-to-be-lamented man, with presents to the Dey. I left the fleet on the 15th, and on the 21st the battle was fought. Not to have been in it, is enough to make one mad; but to have lost such a friend besides, is really sufficient to almost overwhelm me.'

Next day, the *Amphion* met what had been Nelson's fleet in the Straits, but now the vice-admiral's flag was Collingwood's and the flagship was the *Royal Sovereign*. Nelson's body was already on its way home in a cask of spirits on board the *Victory* to an eruption of national grief and a funeral in St Paul's Cathedral. The new Commander-in-Chief at once received Hoste with sympathy: 'He perfectly understands how and in what manner I have gained my present rank and the footing I was on with that poor, good, great man, Lord Nelson. He is remarkably friendly indeed . . . The admiral is a very different man from Lord Nelson, but as brave an old boy as ever stood.'

His dead patron had helped him recover from the loss of his brother but there was nobody who could ease this new calamity. 'I cannot get over the loss of our late noble Commander-in-Chief . . . Never shall we find his equal and never will the Navy of Great Britain furnish a man with half his abilities. I never saw such firmness, such decision, in any man in my life before,' he told his mother. Even while indulging in this unaffected display of grief, Hoste did not forget that the roots of his success had stretched beyond Nelson into Norfolk, and he wrote to his father, 'How is Mr Coke? Remember me to him; what will he say to the victory? O that I had been there!'

V

PRIZES OF LOVE AND WAR

Without the stimulus of Nelson – even of Nelson far beyond the horizon – life at sea was, for Hoste and many others, reduced to its component parts: the execution of operational orders; working the ship and her company; making the best of all weathers; and hoping for prize-money. The intensity of excitement and the exaltation of high purpose had gone – at least for a time – with the man after whom inns in Norfolk were already being re-named simply 'The Hero'.

His successor as Commander-in-Chief in the Mediterranean, Vice-Admiral Lord Collingwood, who had been raised to the peerage after Trafalgar, could hardly have been in more striking contrast. Although they had been close friends throughout their naval careers, theirs had been a friendship of opposites. Nelson had been recognized by all as being human, humorous and, by the standards of the time, humane. Collingwood, eight years his senior, was now aged fifty-five, but, because of his solemnity, seemed older and lacked the dynamism that gave such attraction to St Vincent, who was about to assume command in the Channel at the age of seventy. But while the former was known by some of his officers as 'an old bear' there was warmth within the rigidity, which became apparent in his affectionate letters home to his wife and two daughters and his fondness for his closest companion, the old dog Bounce, whom he would sometimes sing to sleep. Now, instead of tactical plans discussed and orders given across the Commander-in-Chief's dinner table, directives would be copied by clerks on board the flagship and sent to captains to read and consider in the solitude of their own cabins. 'Old Collingwood likes *quiet people*,' noted Hoste.

But Collingwood was a commander of strong loyalties both to his own friends and protégés and to those of Nelson, so that Hoste immediately reported him as being 'very friendly, but a very different man from poor Lord Nelson'. Less than a month after Trafalgar, the admiral was making his attitude clear to the captain of the *Amphion*: 'He has promised me the best cruise he can give me, and desires me to point out where I should like best to go: he says I must take a French frigate before the winter is over.' To this Hoste added pointedly in the letter to his father that, 'I am still in hopes I shall make some *cash*'.

But first, while Collingwood took his fleet to Cartagena in an attempt to bring the nine Spanish ships of the line lying there to battle, there was another diplomatic mission. Hoste had to return to Algiers to visit the British consul and, as a gesture of goodwill, take the Dey's ambassador to Constantinople. Happily for him, relations between the consul and the Dey had soured, further plans had been cancelled and Hoste was free to rejoin the fleet, which had resumed its cruising off Cadiz.

On hearing of Nelson's death, Hoste had written a letter of condolence to Emma Hamilton, explaining to his father, 'I did, however, as the only compliment I could pay to so great a friend as Lord Nelson.' He himself found comfort in Collingwood's patronage and the satisfaction that came from knowing that, although separated widely by rank and thirty years in age, the two of them had been foremost in the affections of the great man. But, by a perverse chance, there was also in the Mediterranean at that time another admiral who might almost have been a Gillray caricature of Nelson: Rear-Admiral Sir Sidney Smith.

Both had been unconventional naval officers, bursting with zeal and ambition, vanity and verve, and initiative inspired by imagination. Both were small, vivid men: Smith was described by one of his sailors as 'a weaselly man – no hull, sir – none; but all head, like a tadpole. But such a head! It put you in mind of a flash of lightning rolled up into a ball.' A French *émigré* officer spoke of him as 'a brave generous-hearted man with a fine countenance and eyes that sparkle with intelligence'.

Like Nelson, Smith could, when he thought the circumstances appropriate, disobey orders but, unlike him, such daring usually brought reprimand and recrimination on his head. Both men's vanity was easily flattered; Smith flaunted a Swedish knighthood, awarded for some freelance naval activities in the Baltic, as Nelson delighted in his Sicilian dukedom; both men were proud of the glittering plume of artificial diamonds, with a centre that revolved by clockwork, that the Sultan of Turkey had given them to wear in their hats. But, whereas Nelson's fame was firmly founded on victory, most of Smith's amounted almost to notoriety compounded of mystery and dash. This was the man who had tried to burn the French fleet in Toulon as the port fell – but his degree of success or failure was still a matter of debate. This was the man who, together with his young brother, the ambassador to Constantinople, had tried to take charge of British efforts in the

Levant over the heads of his superiors, Nelson and Keith. It was Smith who, when captured leading a daring raid on Le Havre, had not been treated as a prisoner of war but sent to Paris for possible trial and execution as a spy and saboteur and locked up in the Temple prison, where the French royal family had been imprisoned, but from which he had made a daring escape.

However, Smith had redeemed himself from these and other escapades and improprieties by his brilliant defence of Acre, which had stopped the advance of the French army from exile in Egypt northward through the Levant. The successful defence of this port justly won universal acclaim and Napoleon, to the end of his life, spoke of Smith as one who had thwarted his grand design of conquest. Hoste shared this admiration partly because he knew that Nelson's initial dislike and distrust of Smith had latterly changed to liking and trust and because his old ship, the *Theseus*, had been closely involved in the defence of Acre. It was while supporting Smith that the accidental explosion had killed so many on board, including Captain Miller, and Hoste's friend, Major Thomas Oldfield, who commanded her detachment of marines, had died a hero's death ashore. Leading a daring sortie, he had been mortally wounded and his body fought over; while his marines tried to drag him away by his neckcloth, French grenadiers gaffed him with a halberd and carried him to their lines to die and be accorded military honours when buried amongst his enemies.

Hoste thus had reason for excited anticipation when, in March of 1806, while commanding the inshore squadron of frigates off Cadiz, he was told that he would probably be detached to join the expeditionary force that was about to leave Gibraltar for the inner Mediterranean. Admiral Smith was to be its naval commander and the small army, which his brother George would accompany, commanded by Lieutenant-General Sir James Craig. Now there would certainly be action, a chance of prize-money and, perhaps, even the ghost of a Nelson touch.

The expedition was one of many strategical shifts necessitated by the political and military landslides of the past six months. While Trafalgar had broken the enemy's main fleets and ensured the safety of the British Isles for the foreseeable future, the same month had seen the defeat of the Austrians under von Mack at Ulm, and December, the crushing of the combined Russian and Austrian armies at Austerlitz. By the end of the year, Austria had accepted the French terms for peace and this included the cession all of their territory in Italy and along the Dalmation coast, so giving Napoleon control of both shores of the Adriatic and an overland route for his invincible armies to the centre of the Mediterranean.

The new year began with a disaster for the British when William Pitt, the driving force of opposition to Napoleon, died. He was succeeded by a coalition 'Ministry of All the Talents' with his friend Lord Grenville replacing him as Prime Minister and the great Whig and intimate of Coke's, Charles James Fox, as Foreign Secretary. One of the latter's first acts on joining the administration was to offer Coke a peerage but this was refused on principle and on the grounds that he could 'serve his country better as a commoner than a peer'. Instead, a viscountcy was conferred upon his son-in-law, Thomas Anson.

On 9th January, a fortnight before Pitt died, Nelson was buried in St Paul's Cathedral with extravagant ceremonial and a national sense of pride and grief. Both Coke and Fox were present and it was noticed that the latter was far from well, although there was no suggestion that, eight months later, he, too, would die.

Ironically, Nelson's funeral coincided with renewed danger to his old charges, King Ferdinand and Queen Maria Carolina of the Two Sicilies. The collapse of Austria had again opened the way to Naples for Napoleon and he was quick to act, again driving the Bourbons to refuge in Palermo and proclaiming his brother Joseph Bonaparte King of Naples. General Craig's little army was at once rushed to Sicily, arriving just in time to stop the French from swarming across the Straits of Messina.

Delighted as he was at the prospects of action in a cause that had meant so much to Nelson, Hoste was beset by anxiety for his sister Kate. She was clearly ill, probably with tuberculosis, but her brother could not bring himself to accept that she was doomed to follow Dick, although he wrote to his father that he 'began to be seriously alarmed indeed for poor Kate . . . I am afraid there is much to fear'. When letters arrived from Norfolk, he wrote to the girl herself, 'it was with a trembling hand and a beating heart I dared look at the seal' to see whether it was the black sealing-wax of mourning. But, he continued, 'my dear father had forewarned me by the writing of "good news" on the outside'.

With a miniature of Kate and a lock of her hair beside him, Hoste wrote long and affectionate letters, urging her to 'keep up your spirits, dear girl' and imagining his and the family's joy when they were again re-united at Godwick. 'I flatter myself I shall not be more happy to see your dear old Phiz than you will that black visage of mine (which a good lady of our acquaintance was pleased to compare with a Captain of Banditti)' he wrote heartily. 'I believe you would hardly know me now – I am become quite a sea monster and the main-top bowline has got so fast hold of me, I am afraid I shall never be able to shake it off.' But, hoping for peace, he joked that he wished he could 'once more be a land crab and settle myself quietly like a good, sober, discreet personage'. Amongst the bluff jocularity, gallantry as well as concern kept breaking through: 'I hope you have received the otto of roses I sent you by the *Conqueror*, Captain Pellew. He promised to see them in a fair way for Norfolk . . .'

Increasingly, it became a strain to keep up this optimism. In April, on the same day that he wrote to his father, 'I am not a little alarmed about our dearest Kate . . . You do not write in spirits, my dear father, and I much fear you are not happy. There is a vein of sadness runs through your letters, which makes me quite miserable'. To her he wrote as cheerfully as he could, 'I am in the *fidgets* about you . . . and I often wish I could give you a good hearty kiss, dear girl, for I have vanity enough to imagine that my black face making its appearance at Godwick would be a good omen of your perfect recovery.'

Hoste had heard of Pitt's death and the Grenville administration and the rise of Whig influence and asked his sister for news of its effect upon their fortunes: 'I hope they have not forgotten my father – he certainly deserves every thing they can give him for his firmness as a brother Whig.' This enquiry was clearly directed towards Coke and his circle and already he was concerned that all might not be well in the relations between 'dear old Godwick' and 'the Holkhamites'. He noted the arrival of 'a very kind letter' from Coke's daughter, Lady Andover, but was piqued by the neglectfulness of Kate's friend, his daughter Anne: 'I am both sorry and angry that Mrs Anson has not had friendship enough to make an enquiry after you during your long sickness.' Anne Anson was now a viscountess and her husband was in the House of Lords, but she did write to Kate and, in his next letter, William was referring to her as 'dear Lady A.' The patronage of Coke was as important to the Godwick family as Nelson's had been to Hoste's career and he was constantly trying to take the temperature of the relationship. Realizing that this might depend as much upon friendships between the younger generation as upon his father's mercurial charm, he asked Kate, 'Have you been to Holkham or had any more parties on the lake? I suppose not.'

To his father he was more direct in expressing his hopes. 'Let me congratulate you on all our friends being in power,' he wrote. 'I hope also they will not forget their old friends and that you will, for your services and attachment to the Whigs, be placed in a situation where you may be of service to them and your country also . . .' He was quite clear about the reward that should have been earned: 'The Prebendary I hope is forthcoming at last – at least the staunch supporter you have always been . . . merits a Bishopric, I am sure.'

Although packets of letters from Godwick might reach him after a delay of several months, Hoste heard news of national politics, of Norfolk affairs and even his own family from a variety of sources. His brother, 'Scapegrace George', had been covering the evacuation of the Bourbons from Naples and had returned to Sicily with scraps of news from home. Two Norfolk boys, one a relation, the other a friend of his aunt's, were with him in the *Amphion* and both had shown courage in a minor action in the ship's boats although the former was 'a young pickle . . . like all youngsters, careless and loves his clothes'. They passed on news from home as did young Lord James Townshend of Raynham Hall, who was a midshipman in the Mediterranean.

Early in the year, he dined and 'had a long talk about Norfolk' with Captain Benjamin Hallowell of the *Trojan*, who had been one of Nelson's 'Band of Brothers' and was clearly destined for high command. Hoste kept a good table and loved entertaining his more senior guests with political gossip from home and showing them the Gillray cartoons which were sent out by his father 'Tell my father to send me some *caricatures* . . . I durst say they have not forgot to exercise their talents on the new Administaration,' he wrote home early in the year.

As a host, he seems to have inherited some of his father's extravagance although, in his letters home, he often stressed his frugality. This spring, he told Kate, 'This horrid hole Gibraltar will not furnish one morsel of fresh Grub but at a most exorbitant price, far above the cost of my purse, and I have the pleasing prospect of a long cruize on salt beef and pork – literally nothing else but tea and sugar – and a little matter of Old Barlow's port.' Yet his accounts for this visit to Gibraltar include not only 'fowls, ducks, turkeys, sheep' but such luxuries as Souchong tea, Moka coffee, pickles, curry powder, Cayenne pepper, catsup and butter. Wine brought on board – some in bottle, some bottled on board from the cask – included champagne, burgundy, claret, Marsala, Madeira, port and a keg of Arrack. Other luxuries purchased here included Windsor soap, lavender water and *eau de Cologne*.

The *Amphion* reached Sicily at the end of May and Hoste found a situation that reflected in darker colours the crisis year of 1799. The Bourbons were back in Palermo but, this time, the French had swarmed past Naples and occupied the whole of the mountainous Calabrian peninsula that pointed at Sicily like a bayonet, its tip only two miles across the straits. The only obstacles in their way were the ships of Sir Sidney Smith's detached squadron and eight thousand British soldiers – including George Hoste – at Messina, where, wrote William, 'excepting a shock of an earthquake now and then, nothing can disturb them'.

Sir Sidney himself was away, taking the war to the enemy. First, he put reinforcements, ammunition and stores ashore at Gaeta, thirty miles to the north of Naples, where a Bourbon garrison was successfully holding the French at bay. Then, boldly sailing past Naples itself, he forced the French garrison of Capri to surrender and occupied the island. Perhaps the true importance of this capture was that whenever the newly-proclaimed King Joseph of Naples admired the view from the tall windows of the Palazzo Reale he could not escape the ominous dragonback of Capri rising out of the bay to remind him that his most implacable enemy could only be defeated at sea.

Smith now sailed south, raiding the coast and destroying enemy coastal batteries under which his shipping could shelter. Ashore, the fighting was between the French, under General Jean-Louis Reynier, and Calabrian partisans. Like all guerrilla wars between regular and irregular forces this had become a horrifying affair of ambush and reprisal, of villages razed and no quarter given. Yet this was the sort of warfare in which Smith excelled. His unconventional attitudes, which included the absence of an automatic contempt for most foreigners such as many British officers, including Hoste, displayed, made him the ideal commander to inspire and support the ragged, savage guerrilla bands that were his new allies. Indeed, he doubtless preferred such to the stiffly-drilled, rigid-minded and often ineffective allies he had had in the Austrians and the Russians.

The more conventional officers of the British Army, with whom Smith was about to work in the saving of Sicily, were aghast at what they regarded as his conceit and impudence. But a more balanced view was held by the Chief of Staff at Messina, Colonel Bunbury, who described him as 'an enthusiast, always panting for distinction, restlessly active, but desultory in his views, extravagantly vain, daring, quick-sighted, and fertile in those resources which befit a partisan leader'.

For Hoste, this dash was an echo of adventures ashore with Nelson at Bastia and Calvi and even at Tenerife. Then, in June, he had his first taste of action in the new campaign, sending his boats in to storm and blow up a coastal castle at Cirello on the west coast of Calabria. More spectacular moves were now afoot for, although Calabria was occupied by fifty-two thousand enemy troops, the British Army was about to emulate the Navy in taking the offensive.

General Craig had, because of ill-health, handed over command of the expeditionary force to Major-General Sir John Stuart, who, while realizing that he had not the strength to attempt the re-conquest of Calabria, agreed to Smith's suggestion that he take advantage of their naval superiority to attack the mainland, even if this amounted to no more than a raid. So, at the end of June, nearly five thousand troops were embarked in transports and, on the night of the 30th, were landed fifty miles north of Messina in Euphemia Bay under the close cover of frigates, including the *Amphion*, from which Hoste watched his brother go ashore for his first experience of war.

Ashore, General Reynier could only muster immediately a few hundred men more than Stuart, but they were in a strong defensive position on a hillside near the village of Maida. Stuart and Smith, realizing that reinforcements would reach the enemy in a matter of days, had determined on quick action and the two armies met on 4th July. The worth of Smith's encouragement of the partisans was now proved, for they so harassed Reynier's troops from the cover of woods that he was stung into leaving his defences and making a head-on attack, ordering two thousand, four hundred infantry to charge the advancing British.

Now, for the first time, the French met the cool and deadly tactics with which the British were to meet their supposedly irresistible onslaughts again and again in the years to come. With drums beating the *pas de charge*, the massed columns surged forward behind a swarm of skirmishers. But the British infantry prided itself on its musketry and this, if the soldiers' nerve held, could be best deployed in thin, extended lines, through which the enemy phalanxes could easily burst, yet only if they could first survive the concentrated fire.

At Maida, they did not. The British volleys crackled along the lines, cutting down the assaulting French in hundreds. For the British, it was almost impossible to miss such targets; for the French, no amount of *élan* could withstand the succession of volleys, each of which slaughtered the van of their advance. When Reynier tried to relieve his infantry by ordering his cavalry to make a flanking attack they were ambushed by a British infantry regiment that had only just come ashore and whose presence was unsuspected. Now it was the turn of the British to advance with the bayonet and the French fled, leaving some seven hundred dead, a thousand wounded and nine hundred prisoners on the field of battle. The British loss was a mere forty-five killed and less than three hundred wounded.

The news of Maida, the first decisive defeat of the French by the British on the mainland of Europe, thrilled the British nation both by its actual achievement and with the thought that what had been achieved once could be achieved again and on a grander scale. The celebrations were such as had previously been held for naval victories and an elegant new suburb of London was named in its honour: Maida Vale. Joy swept the country and, in Norfolk, was enhanced when a letter from William Hoste, written five days after the battle, arrived with an account of

George's 'steady and gallant conduct on the field of battle', adding, 'He is a fine, darling boy and will, my dear father, be a credit to your house.'

But the victory could not be fully exploited for lack of reserves and the means to sustain a campaign against an enemy that would soon recover and be reinforced. So Stuart's little army was re-embarked and re-deployed so that it could make the maximum use of Smith's command of the sea. One detachment was to be escorted northwards to make a feint attack in the Bay of Naples in the hope of tying down enemy troops that might be on their way to Calabria. Another, which George Hoste accompanied, was landed by Smith on the mainland shore of the Straits of Messina, where it captured Reggio and Scilla. A third, under a Lieutenant-Colonel McLeod, was embarked in the *Amphion*, which, after giving covering fire to the troops landing to attack Reggio, moved up the east coast of Calabria to which Reynier had withdrawn.

The enemy, it was believed, had had some nine thousand troops in southern Calabria. Of these, nearly three thousand had been lost at Maida and others from British coastal raids and attacks by guerrillas. The survivors, including any who had escaped from Reggio and Scilla, were now ordered to retire on two bases: Catanzaro, where Reynier had his headquarters, and Cotrone [now Crotone], the main supply depot. For the reduction of these, Hoste had his frigate, the brig *Crafty*, two Sicilian galleys, three armed boats from another British frigate and some transports; McLeod had his own battalion, the 78th Regiment of Foot, and a large but unknown number of Calabrian partisans as allies.

When the squadron arrived off Catanzaro on 14th July, Hoste had found all the coast from Reggio in the hands of the Calabrians and only the Bourbon flag was to be seen ashore through his telescope. Anchoring near the town, which was said to be held by some four thousand French soldiers, he met the partisan leaders, who pleaded for arms. Writing to Smith, Hoste stressed their fears that 'if we quit the country and leave them a prey to the French and Jacobins *without* arms, how are they to defend themselves? My answer to their noisy clamour is, patience and trust to your Allies and Sovereign, who will not desert you. But how long my words *alone* will have effect is quite uncertain.'

But he was able to hearten them with some effective gunnery when the French made a sortie from Catanzaro in an attempt to recapture stocks of grain and oil in warehouses on the waterfront of the harbour. They were driven back, after three hours, by the fire of the warships, leaving eighteen dead and eleven prisoners.

The British plan was to make a feint attack upon Cotrone in the hope of attracting reinforcements from Catanzaro, which would then itself be attacked by the partisans. Meanwhile, the squadron would attempt to intercept these reinforcements as they marched along the coast road and, finally, invest Cotrone itself. On the morning of 26th July, the squadron stood inshore south of Cotrone and Hoste and McLeod saw through telescopes from the deck of the *Amphion* that the coast road was, as they had hoped, crowded with French columns marching north.

Ordering the transports to make for a point farther north, as if they were about to land troops ahead of the enemy, Hoste took his ships close inshore to bombard the road. As soon as the British plan was apparent to the French commander, he ordered the leading column to wheel into the mountains that rose steeply inland. But, while his leading detachments were out of the *Amphion*'s range, the centre and rear of the columns underwent 'a brisk cannonade', broke ranks and scrambled up the mountainside in disorder.

The little squadron now moved on to Cotrone, arriving before the reinforcements from Catanzaro, and anchored before the town. When the reinforcements did arrive – with some sixty men, wounded by the *Amphion*'s fire, in carts – Hoste allowed them to take up defensive positions just within range of his guns without interference. Presumably the French commander had had little experience of the range and power of British naval gunnery for he deployed his troops in such exposed positions that, when his dispositions were seen to be complete, Hoste brought his broadside to bear, opened fire and again drove them into the mountains.

Cotrone seemed untenable to the French and, leaving a thousand men to hold the town as long as possible, the main French force continued their retreat with the probable aim of joining the garrison of Taranto, the seaport at the head of the Gulf of Taranto.

To avoid the fire of the warships, Reynier led the remains of his army into the mountains towards Cassano, burning every village they passed so that Hoste, unable to use his guns in their defence, had to note angrily, 'from the *Amphion* we plainly observed the flames and the destructive ravages of the French Army'. Then, hearing that the retreat had been joined by some of the garrison of Cotrone, who had disobeyed orders and deserted the town during the night, Hoste and McLeod decided to issue a formal summons to surrender without delay.

Accordingly, on the 30th, the ultimatum, couched in formal phrasing, was signed and sent under flag of truce to the French commander. It read, 'The Officers commanding the Naval and Land Forces of His Britannic Majesty hereby summon you to surrender the Town and

Citadel of Cotrone to the British Force now before it.

'The Officers who deliver this Summons to you are directed to lay before you such Articles of Capitulation as we are disposed to grant, and to wait One Hour for your Answer.

'Being perfectly aware of your present Circumstances, you may believe that this Summons is dictated under mature Deliberation, and with a View to saving that Effusion of Blood which must be the Consequence of a Resistance on your Part.'

Cotrone surrendered, its garrison was embarked for Sicily to await exchange for British prisoners of war and nearly fifty enemy guns were spiked or hoisted aboard the British ships. The survivors of the French army, sniped at and ambushed by partisans, continued their retreat; now, it was thought, reduced to about three thousand men in the main force. It was a decisive victory for the British; not, of course, to be compared with Maida, but important enough to warrant a lengthy report, including letters from Hoste and McLeod, to fill a Supplement to the *London Gazette Extraordinary* and a full memorandum to the Foreign Secretary. This reached the desk of Charles James Fox on the day before illness overwhelmed him and a week before his death. Perhaps among the last words read by the great Whig was the report of the young naval officer whose distant exploits were the direct consequence of Whig ambitions years before in remote Norfolk.

On 4th August, the *Amphion* anchored off Palermo, her captain ready to receive the congratulations of the King and Queen as Nelson had so often in his time. But, first, the mail came on board and there was a letter from Godwick Hall dated 4th June, the day on which Hoste had written from Palermo asking anxiously for news of his sister Kate and confessing 'I tremble every moment I look into a paper'. Now, at last, his fears were justified. His father's letter told him that Kate had died of tuberculosis.

All thought of gathering laurels at the Bourbon court were instantly forgotten and Hoste sat down to reply. 'Excuse this scrawl, I can neither write, nor do anything else,' he told his father. 'I am quite lost for the present, but trust time will enable me to overcome the remembrance of my poor sister in some measure at least . . . I think of every well-remembered object that once belonged to that dear girl; everything that was hers becomes doubly dear. I have not dared to look at the miniature since I received your sad letter, and the locket of her dear hair remains and momentarily reminds me of her.'

He was too overwhelmed to describe his victory at Cotrone, dismissing it with, 'I have lately been employed on active service with the army, and trust I have done well, to the satisfaction of all.' Ambitions and hopes of glory and prize-money were also forgotten: 'I do not know where I am going next; it is quite uncertain, and I am quite indifferent about it.'

The brother and sister to whom he had been closest were now both dead but, as the pain of the second bereavement dulled, Hoste was struck by a comforting thought. His young brother Edward, who had been born the year after he had first sailed with Nelson, was now aged twelve, as he himself had then been. This was the age to begin a naval career and, as a post captain, he was in a position to take the boy on board his ship as a 'first-class volunteer'. The thought of it was heart-warming and he wrote to his father about it: 'Let him come when he will, I have a snug berth for him.'

For the Hoste family in Norfolk, grief was eased by the distraction of politics and the prospect of a General Election at the end of the year. But, on this occasion, another triumph for Coke was by no means a certainty. Mourning his friend Fox, both as 'the greatest man in Europe, who might have saved this country from impending ruin and the shedding of torrents of human blood' and as his own 'principal inducement to an active parliamentary career', his 'feelings and inclinations turned to a private life, which had always been so much more congenial'. For Coke, a private life was a relative term because it embraced his estates, his tenantry and his absorbing interest in agriculture. Already he was famous far beyond Norfolk and England for the improvements in livestock – cattle, sheep and pigs – that he had brought about by selective breeding and he had transformed west Norfolk from a rye-growing to a wheat-producing region to the benefit of all. For him, a private life would mean concentration on his own agricultural kingdom.

Then again, Coke's own position was ambiguous. As a Whig, priding himself on a balanced view of the aspirations of all nations rather than what he regarded as the narrow patriotism of the Tories, he had been against war with France if it could possibly be avoided. But he was swimming against the tide of his countrymen's opinion and, despite his stature in the nation's affairs, that reached godlike proportions in Norfolk, many regarded this attitude as an eccentricity in an age of eccentrics. Even before Trafalgar, when the sons of so many neighbours were away at the war, it was with the greatest reluctance that Coke gave any active support to the local militia and allowed himself to be gazetted, first, as a captain of the Holkham Gentlemen and Yeomanry Cavalry and, later, lieutenant-colonel commanding the Western Regiment of Yeomanry Cavalry.

There was also dissension within the Whig party, which had hitherto presented a united front. An immediate cause of this was unexpected rivalry from Coke's nearest land-owning neighbours, the Townshends

of Raynham, for Lady Townshend was intent on her son James standing for Yarmouth, where Coke's son-in-law, Thomas Anson, was
already a candidate. It was a petty affair but aroused rancour because,
in her fierce ambition for her son, Lady Townshend wrote to, and of,
Coke in bitter terms. That some of this bitterness reached Holkham
seems to have been the doing of Dixon Hoste, who, knowing both
parties, saw himself as mediator. Towards the end of October and
shortly before the election, he visited Lady Townshend to discuss
plans for assuring the candidacy for her son and soon afterwards
she wrote him a private letter giving details of her efforts to influence
Lord Grenville himself to this end. Clearly, she trusted Dixon Hoste
implicitly, writing, 'I trust, my good friend, you will not have suffered
by your most kind desire to keep us all right; and be assured that I
shall ever remember it with gratitude and sincerity.'

There were kindly enquiries of his wife's health ('I have sent two
books, if she has not read them, they may amuse') and an affectionate
conclusion: 'Our kindest love and good wishes from us to you all,
and I am, dear Hoste, Yours heartily and sincerely, A. Townshend.'

This was in striking contrast to her sharp references to Coke and,
indeed, to the manner in which she had ended a letter to him a few
days earlier, 'You will therefore believe me to be yours, As you deserve,
Ann Townshend.'

However, Dixon Hoste's first loyalty lay at Holkham and to Holkham Lady Townshend's letter was forwarded, probably causing more
mockery than concern but at least showing, again, that the Whigs
were divided and that Fox was no longer able to inspire them and that
Coke himself was a figure of controversy.

This acrimony was reflected in the campaign itself. The Tories made
every effort to prise wider the cracks in the Whig foundations and put
up the money to reserve almost twice as many public houses for the
entertainment of their supporters than those open for their rivals.
For the six days of the campaign, Norwich was in uproar and, in the
political horseplay of electioneering, Coke was accused of responsibility
for unseemly behaviour with which he had had, in fact, nothing to do
and of which he had been in ignorance. Thus, although he came top
of the poll, with his fellow-Whig William Windham, the Secretary of
State for War under Grenville, second, and Colonel Wodehouse, the
Tory, third, there were objections to the conduct of the campaign
and a Committee of the House of Commons decided that neither Coke
nor Windham had been properly elected. Therefore the two Whigs
sought seats elsewhere; Coke being elected for Derby in place of his
brother Edward, who stood for Norfolk, and Windham standing for
New Romney. Tiresome and humiliating as this was for Coke, the

affair caused more merriment than concern and was, in any case, put to rights at the general election in the following June when both Whigs were again returned for Norfolk.

News from home slowly filtered to the Mediterranean and in the autumn William Hoste was delighted to hear that his father was frequenting Holkham again, for that remained the ultimate source of his own patronage. Sending his compliments to Coke, he now felt able to tell his father something of his Calabrian adventures. 'I long for a day's shooting at partridges,' he wrote. 'The French army, some weeks ago, gave us an opportunity of trying our skill with the great guns, of which, I assure you, we did not fail to take advantage.' Like Nelson, Hoste would joke about shooting at game-birds or 'floating marks', perhaps in the hope that his quips would be repeated to amuse the company at Holkham.

The possibility of peace was, to him, both a promise and a threat. A promise in that it would mean a return to Norfolk to see his parents 'and *les petits*', although 'it will cost me a bitter pang, the sight of the old house'. The threat was the deprivation of glory and prize-money: 'I should like to have one or two French frigates first and then peace as soon as you please' he wrote, adding, 'I am in great glee at the prospect of a good cruise, for, to tell you the truth, a prize is now so scarce an article that I begin to want *pewter* most terribly.' After the Norfolk election, the need of 'pewter' – naval slang for prize-money – was even more acute, for the campaign had been expensive and particularly so for a parson trying to hold his own with his prosperous fellow-guests at Holkham. Both father and son knew that 'pewter' would come their way not only through Lord Collingwood in the Mediterranean but through the influence of Mr Coke in London. So any means of attracting attention was seen to further this aim, William noting with delight, 'I see some of my friends have been pleased to place the captain of the *Amphion* among a list of *distinguished Norfolk naval men*!'

Proud as he might be of naval success he had to admit that 'that wretch Buonaparte carries all before him on land'. In October, Prussia declared war upon France, but five days later was crushed at Jena. Napoleon entered Berlin before the end of the month and Warsaw before the end of the year. Even the modest British success ashore in Calabria was expunged when a strong French army with heavy artillery, commanded by Marshal Masséna, re-captured all their lost ground in a campaign of exceptional brutality and were soon back on the eastern shore of the Straits of Messina. Even the fortress of Gaeta, to the north of Naples, which had held out for so long, surrendered once its spirited commander, the Prince of Hesse, was wounded. Whenever Hoste wrote home about the imminent possibility of peace, Napoleon seemed to engineer some major diplomatic coup, or crush opposing armies in a day's fighting. So, understandably, he wrote, 'Thank God there is a little piece of water between Dover and Calais, or I am afraid we should see him in London before we are aware of it.'

A Napoleonic decree which, while less melodramatic in itself, was to have a profound effect upon the war at sea was his 'Continental System', announced in Berlin towards the end of the year, by which all Continental ports were closed to British ships and Britain itself was declared to be under blockade. The French were not, of course, able to blockade British ports but the converse was possible and a retaliatory blockade of the Continent by the Royal Navy was the consequence. The result was that while the commerce of Europe withered, the British were not only able to trade freely and profitably throughout the world but, while stopping up Continental seaports, were able to smuggle British goods into the Napoleonic empire on a massive scale. The defeat of the Continental System could not be painted on canvas like Trafalgar but it was a naval victory of the same, or greater, stature.

But hopes of such success seemed to lie, at the beginning of 1808, in the distant future. The most daring naval operation by the British was an attempt to force the Dardanelles to support the Russians, by a fleet under Admiral Sir John Duckworth, which was accompanied by Sir Sidney Smith. Although the ships successfully fought their way past Turkish batteries firing marble cannonballs – some twenty-six inches in diameter and weighing more than eight hundred and sixty pounds – Duckworth followed the wrong course against strong currents and never reached Constantinople; he refused Smith's offer to go ashore and negotiate with the Sultan and, after lying at anchor for ten days, miles from the city, retreated to the Mediterranean. Although Hoste, who was having storm-damage repaired at Malta, was able to describe this as 'one of the most daring attempts in our naval annals' he could not claim it as a success and, instead, joked that 'Jack says it is strange work playing at marbles with the Turks'.

The damage to the *Amphion* was such – she was 'quite knocked up' – that she was ordered home, her captain hoping that through Coke's influence he might be given command of one of the more powerful frigates that were then building. She arrived at Portsmouth early in August and went into dock for a major refit, but by now Hoste expected to remain in command and return with her to the Mediterranean. Collingwood had asked him to return and wrote to Lord Mulgrave, the First Lord of the Admiralty, stressing the need for more frigates in his fleet, adding, 'I should be glad that Captain Hoste of the *Amphion* should come, for he is active, vigilant and knows the coast, and more depends upon the man than the ship.'

Repairs to the ship would take at least two months and there would be plenty of time for her captain to take leave but, on this occasion, Hoste did not hurry to Norfolk. Indeed, the first news of his return reached Godwick in the newspapers and his father wrote anxiously to Portsmouth asking his son's intentions. Hoste's reply, dated 11th August, apologized for not having written and guardedly gave the reason: he had fallen in love.

It was customary for ships returning from overseas stations to carry a few passengers and, on his return from the Mediterranean, Hoste had given passage to a Mrs Brooke, whose husband, Lieutenant-Colonel Arthur Brooke, was stationed at Malta. Commanding the 44th Regiment of Foot – the East Essex Regiment – he had come out to the Mediterranean with the same expeditionary force as George Hoste in 1805 and had been awaiting active employment ever since.

During the voyage an attachment developed and Hoste described to his father the 'interesting and accomplished woman', adding 'I *was* much and *am now* greatly interested in everything that concerns her.' So when Mrs Brooke invited him to accompany her to Bracknell in Berkshire, where she was staying with a general's widow, he eagerly agreed. There, letters reached her from Malta insisting on her immediate return and he escorted her to Falmouth to see her aboard a merchant ship bound for the Mediterranean. When she had sailed, he returned to Portsmouth where his father's anxious letter awaited him.

Having written to explain 'why you have not seen my black visage down at Godwick', he immediately applied for more leave and set out for Norfolk. His return was emotional, sadness at the loss of Dick and Kate competing with joy at the prospect of taking his little brother Ned to sea with him. At the beginning of October, he returned to Portsmouth to supervise the refitting of the *Amphion*, which was taking longer than expected, first making up for his initial thoughtlessness by telling his father, 'I was never happier for six weeks in my life'.

By the end of the year, the refit was complete and successful, Hoste declaring that his ship was 'now as good as new and stronger than when launched'. The *Amphion* sailed from Spithead in January, escorting a convoy of sixty sail bound for the Mediterranean. This time her captain had no regrets at leaving England after the long stay in Portsmouth dockyard – 'Six months' spell in that delectable spot is quite enough' – and there was the thought of Mrs Brooke waiting in Malta.

On this voyage there would be the constant joy of his little brother's company and, as the frigate ran down the Solent towards the open sea, Hoste wrote delightedly to his father, 'Our dear little sailor is very well and in fine feather . . . It is the most beautiful day I ever saw; and the Isle of Wight on one side, and the coast about Lymington and Southampton on the other form altogether the most beautiful prospect I ever beheld. Dear little Edward was in raptures.' Next morning, he noted, 'Ned slept in his proper hammock for the first time last night. I was obliged to lift him in after several unsuccessful attempts on his part to accomplish it.'

The convoy called at Falmouth then, when just clear of the Channel, was struck by a violent gale – 'I verily believe some old witch has got possession of the wind and is determined to blow westerly till there is not a breath in the bag', said Hoste – and the ships were driven back to shelter in Plymouth Sound, their captains thankful to have weathered two days of storm. Ned Hoste's bearing pleased his brother, who told their mother, 'Our little sailor . . . was not at all sea sick during the whole gale which was very sharp and a most tremendous sea running. He laid on my sofa singing . . . quite as unconcerned as if he had been in the drawing-room at Godwick. All our passengers were terribly sick.'

Ned himself added a postscript for his younger brother Charles, boasting, 'We had famous fun the other day when it blew so hard. I am sure you would have laughed to see us toppling about the ship. William has got the prettiest little goat you ever saw.' Goats, amongst other livestock, were often carried on board, their milk particularly necessary for children, like Ned.

Hoste now saw no hope of peace, particularly since the United States, angered by British demands that former British sailors serving in American warships should be handed over as deserters, had imposed an embargo on exports to both Britain and France. 'I think another American war inevitable . . .' he wrote. 'Nothing but war, war, war; and war I verily believe it will be till I am an old grey-haired gent, in spite of another *Norfolk Hero* having commenced his Naval Career.'

The *Amphion* joined the fleet off Lisbon, then entered the Mediterranean bound for Malta. One day out from Valetta, Ned Hoste was for the first time to see his brother perform one of those acts of daring that had already given him the reputation of a Norfolk Hero himself. A sudden gale and thunderstorm struck the ship as darkness fell and Hoste, on deck supervising the hurried taking-in of sail, saw lightning strike the main-mast and set fire to the top-gallant sail. Without pausing to give orders, he swung himself into the shrouds and scrambled aloft to the blazing canvas, where 'with the jacket he had stripped off for the purpose, and which was already drenched with rain, he succeeded in quickly extinguishing the flames'. Next day, the frigate entered the Grand Harbour, her captain doubtless wondering whether Mrs Brooke was among the crowds watching her glide between the bastions.

A week later, Hoste was ordered to Sicilian waters. There, hopes of a reunion with George Hoste, who was stationed at Augusta, were dashed when he was ordered to watch the French fleet which had managed to land a strong expeditionary force on Corfu. But the enemy, evading the British, escaped to Toulon, where he sighted them towards the end of April 'all snug'.

For a single frigate to be sent in search of an enemy fleet that was believed to be in, or near, its principal base was a mark of supreme confidence in her captain. If that fleet were met at sea, the frigate, properly handled, should be able to escape destruction and shadow her quarry. But there was always the possibility that she might be caught at a disadvantage by a squadron of frigates, each of her own speed and weight of broadside, perhaps off a lee shore. It would be Hoste's responsibility to avoid such dangers while seeking out the ultimate ambition of every bold frigate captain: a duel with an enemy frigate of equal power and resolution, until she was destroyed or surrendered. Then that captain would be the talk of England, his exploit described in the *London Gazette*, illustrated by painters and engravers, praised on ballad-sheets and his name for ever coupled with that of his ship. All England would know of 'Hoste of the *Amphion*'.

This long-awaited encounter seemed possible for Hoste on 12th May, 1808. Sailing past Toulon and the thicket of masts in its harbour on a south-westerly course in search of an enemy frigate that had been sighted off Majorca, the *Amphion* approached the Spanish frontier, the border town of Rosas and the anchorage of the Golfo de Rosas. There, at anchor beneath the guns of Fort Bouton, lay a fine French warship. She was the *Baleine*, a frigate-built, armed storeship of about eight hundred tons, manned by some hundred and fifty men and mounting thirty guns. Hoste at once cleared for action, beat to quarters and stood into the bay.

'Not a moment was lost,' he later recounted. 'We had every man ready for boarding her, and my intention was to have run *Amphion* direct alongside and boarded from thence . . . In all the actions I have ever been in, I never saw more cheerfulness and confidence than was expressed by my gallant crew. When I tell you we were exposed to the fire of three heavy batteries besides the French ship, you will conceive we had enough on our hands. Notwithstanding their fire, in three minutes I should have been on board of him; but the poltroon, seeing out intention, gave way to his fears, and rather than await an attack where he had every advantage, cut his cables and ran her on shore under the batteries of Fort Bouton and another of eight twenty-four pounders.'

To have closed with her now would have meant certain destruction by shore batteries firing at point-blank range, so Hoste anchored as close as was prudent and began three hours of bombardment at long range. Before long the enemy's fire slackened and then ceased and Hoste decided that an attempt to board her, or at least set her on fire, from his ship's boats could be risked. Bennett, his middle-aged first lieutenant, took command of the boats but, while they survived the cannon-fire, they ran into volleys of musket-balls and had to pull out of range.

After four hours, during which the *Amphion* had taken several heavy shot in her hull and had her masts and rigging much cut about, Hoste had to be satisfied. The enemy ship now lay beached and heavily damaged, her guns silenced, and it seemed unlikely that she could return to sea for months to come. It was a bitter disappointment, particularly after the first exhilarating run into the bay, when a hard-fought duel seemed certain and Hoste could savour the thought that 'if there is such a thing as true happiness in this life, I think for five minutes I have felt it'.

He was particularly pleased by the behaviour in action of his young brother. 'My little Ned behaved like a hero,' he said. 'He tells me he could beat a dozen French frigates now.'

To his father he wrote, 'Oh! had I been able to bring him out, what a chance it would have been for your boys.' There was more disappointment when no mention of the action appeared in the *London Gazette*, but Lord Collingwood's praise made up for this. A letter from the admiral telling him that the occasion had afforded him the opportunity 'to exhibit that skill and spirit of Enterprise which has ever distinguished your Services' was followed by an interview on board the flagship. 'I am confident, sir,' said Collingwood, 'that everything that an officer or seaman could do, was done; and a most gallant effort you have made indeed!'

'You may suppose, my dear mother,' Hoste wrote home, 'this language to a man, who has nothing but his sword to depend on, was highly flattering. I stood at least *three feet higher* on the occasion.' Again he praised Ned but stressed that the boy was being shown no favouritism: 'I keep him pretty tight at it, I assure you, and some say, his being my brother is the hardest duty of any youngster in the ship. I try to make him an example to all the other boys . . . He is first at everything: I need say no more. When you write to him, give him a hint how necessary it is he should be acquainted with history in general. He is so fond of the practical business, that I am obliged to exert fraternal authority to get the theory.'

Ned and the other small boys were not allowed to take part in operations that might prove 'desperate' but this protection was, at best, marginal. Hoste liked to tell the story of one occasion when the boats were about to leave the ship, manned and armed for a cutting-out expedition, and he saw Ned climbing down into one of them. At once he ordered the boy back on board as being 'too young for that sort of work' and he reluctantly returned to the quarterdeck, then went below. After the boats had pulled well away from the frigate, the lieutenant in command had felt something move under his legs, then saw that it was little Ned Hoste who had slid out of a gun-port undetected and hidden himself beneath the coxswain's bench. It was then too late to take him back to his brother.

After a visit to Malta for repairs to the frigate's battle-damage, Hoste was ordered on a secret diplomatic mission. Early in the year, France had invaded Spain and, in May, King Charles IV and his crown prince had been forced to renounce the throne and Napoleon transferred his brother Joseph from being King of Naples to King of Spain. Another royal figurehead was needed to rally Spanish resistance and this was to be the Archduke Charles, who now embarked in the *Amphion*.

That the mission was unsuccessful was no fault of Hoste's but it served to keep alive the disappointment of the indecisive action and this was made worse by news from home that there had been no mention of it in the newspapers. Five months afterwards, he was still harping on 'the dastardly conduct of the enemy' that had cheated him of fame, writing, 'Never mind, dear mother, though the *Gazette* have not it in, it shall go hard but some other day that self-same *Gazette* will do me justice.'

This frustration was made worse by the departure of Mrs Brooke from Malta to join her husband's regiment in Sicily. He was now quite frank about his hopeless infatuation when writing home, even sending her letters to his mother for her comments. 'Tell me from her letters what you think of her,' he asked. 'I wish you knew her, she is very amiable and if she was not married I should say the most captivating manners I ever knew. I almost wish I had never known her for if *Sailors* in these busy times had *time* for anything else than their duty, I don't know what the consequences might have been. But she is *disposed* and that stops everything.'

Now his hopes were pinned to Collingwood, who had promised him another cruise ('I do not know where I am going, but it will be something good') and this proved to be 'the best cruise in his command': the Adriatic. There, virtually all trade was carried on by sea and, to those naval officers seeking prize-money 'pewter', it seemed rich and virgin water. Late in June, he passed the Straits of Otranto to join Captain Campbell of the *Unité* and so successful was he in harassing both enemy trade and their shore stations that, on his return to Malta, Collingwood ordered him to resume the profitable cruising. Rightly he assumed that his was, in part, a reward for his unsuccessful efforts off Rosas: 'the only good that I know of from that day's work is my appointment to the Adriatic Station which was the best gift in the power of the Commander-in-Chief.'

His luck coincided, however, with the Admiralty's decision to reduce a captain's share of prize-money from one of just below half the total to exactly a quarter. Hoste was outraged at these 'ridiculous innovations', complaining that 'a parcel of old grograms, who are very quietly seated over their Christmas fire, do not allow for many a sleepless night of watching and anxiety that we have. They forget that in our service, when others take it by turns to watch, the captain must always be on the alert, and that if the chances are in his favour in the prize way, it is more than over-balanced by constant anxiety and care.'

Yet even a quarter-share could be considerable and, in October, he wrote home that he had sent one prize into Malta and the merchant who was her part-owner, 'poor fellow ... spoke feelingly on the subject', telling him that she and her cargo were worth £20,000. So, even if William Hoste's ambitions had been thwarted, his father's were being fulfilled and he could read, with a lightening heart, his son's letter from the Adriatic: 'I have at last got on good ground for *pewterising*; and I trust, if the war lasts, and I remain on this station a couple of years, to be able to give my good father a lift over the stones.'

VI

LORD OF THE ADRIATIC

The Adriatic was Collingwood's gift, just as the *Amphion* had been Nelson's, and from the outset it was as exciting an experience as any ambitious young captain could have desired. The Mediterranean was a dramatic theatre of war – the western basin with its direct confrontation with French power and the eastern, mysterious both in its redolence of past splendours and in present political intrigue and military gambling – but, seen in practical, professional terms by a naval officer, the gain and the glory it offered was probably to be shared with other ships of the fleet.

The Adriatic, on the other hand, was, literally and figuratively, a backwater. British ships that were ordered there from the base at Malta would pass through the Straits of Otranto – the channel, forty-five miles wide, between the south-eastern peninsula of Italy and the island of Corfu – and find themselves in a deep, often stormy trough some hundred miles wide and running five hundred miles north-west to the old mercantile heart of Europe, Venice.

The *coup de grâce* had been given to the dying Venetian Republic by France eleven years before but Ragusa [now Dubrovnik], its former commercial rival, survived between the mountains of Dalmatia and the sea. Now, the whole eastern coast of Italy from the Venetian lagoon, along the flat shores and the mountainous outcrops, and including the fortified seaports and dockyards of Venice itself and Ancona, were occupied by the French. The eastern coast of the Adriatic was in turmoil. Most of it had long been dominated by Venice but now Trieste itself, Fiume and stretches of coast around them were part of the Austrian Empire, at this time in uneasy alliance with France.

Most of old Venetian territory had just been re-named the Illyrian Provinces by Napoleon. Early in 1808, the Republic of Ragusa, having preserved a precarious independence by playing the French, Austrians, Turks and Russians against one another, finally fell to full French domination and Marshal Auguste Marmont, who had been working

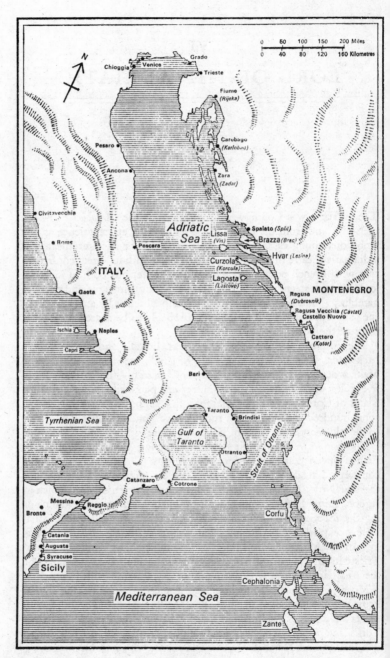

THE ADRIATIC

to this end for three years, was created Duke of Ragusa. This was a rich prize for, in the preceding years of war, Ragusan merchants had made vast profits by taking advantage of their ships' privileges as neutrals in seas where most other merchantmen could be taken as prizes by one side or the other.

So French rule extended, in name at least, southward to Montenegro, where among mountains dominated by warrior tribes rather than the *Code Napoléon*, it joined the chaotic and crumbling Turkish Empire. Far to the south again, the French occupied both shores of the Straits of Otranto, having a strong garrison recently established in Corfu.

Even after the death of Venice, the Adriatic remained an intensely mercantile sea and trade along its mountainous eastern shores was carried on almost exclusively by ships, since roads were few and precarious. It was this trade that became the prey of those British warships fortunate enough to be ordered there from the familiar rigours of the Mediterranean. There may have been no prizes on the scale of the great convoys and rich East Indiamen that tried to run the blockade into the Atlantic ports of France, or treasure-ships bound for Spain, but potential prizes abounded and would probably be to the gain of a single ship and her crew.

While some of this trade was carried by three-masted polacres or two-masted brigs, the principal carrier was the *trabaccolo*, a sturdy little sea-going ship of between fifty and seventy tons with two lugsails and a jib. These plied singly or in flotillas, sometimes under escort, carrying every sort of cargo between the Adriatic ports, having the advantage that, being small, they could not only take refuge in the little fortified harbours that abounded but could quickly and easily hide in bays and behind rocks when the sails of a predatory British frigate came up over the horizon.

Faced with capture, such small ships rarely put up a fight but, for the British, there was the excitement of speculation as to the possible cargo aboard when, all sails set, the frigate swooped upon a prize. Thus, on this cruise during the last quarter of the year, the *Amphion* took thirty-eight merchant vessels and burned six, which were not worth the trouble of taking as prizes.

Sometimes there were prisoners to be embarked and usually put ashore as soon as possible, but occasionally one warranted special attention. One such was a beautiful young Parisienne, who was apparently on her way to Italy where her husband was serving in the French Army. Hoste, who prided himself on chivalrous behaviour towards ladies in distress, was mortified that for days she cowered in a cabin, too terrified to venture on deck. It was a little social triumph when he was at last able to persuade her that she was in no danger and that her country's enemies were actually helping her on her way to her husband.

Gain was plentiful in these waters but not glory. The French had wrecked the great Arsenale of Venice in 1797 and, although it was again building warships, there was, as yet, little prospect of serious opposition. However, Hoste steered for Ancona, the enemy's main naval base, in the hope of enticing whatever might lie there to come out and give battle. As the *Amphion* ran in towards the city on its hills above the harbour, Hoste's telescope picked out masts and yards against the background of ramparts and citadels, warehouses and the domes and *campanili* of two dozen churches. They proved to belong to a frigate and a brig which together might be tempted to accept his challenge.

But, he wrote to his father, 'I . . . saw my friends lying in Ancona, to whom I sent a friendly invitation, in the name of *Amphion* and crew, requesting they would come out and try their strength, for the honour of their flag; but I might have spared myself the trouble, for all my efforts to rouse one spark of national honour failed and there they remain.'

There was one fight during this cruise. It was a skirmish between the frigate's yawl and two potential prizes, which turned out to be well armed and full of fight, putting their assailants to flight with the loss of two seamen killed and four wounded, including the officer in command, Lieutenant Jones. It was almost a routine encounter between small craft, albeit an unsuccessful one, but the night's activities became the talk not only of the *Amphion* but of the Navy because of an extraordinary coincidence.

Every ship had its own legends – tragic or comic – that were handed on in conversation over dinner in wardroom, gunroom or on the gun-decks but were particularly fresh when the event could be remembered by one who had been in the ship longer than most and could be asked to spin the yarn from memory. Lieutenant Jones was one of these. He had been in the ship when Hardy and Sutton had been captain and could talk of many officers who had sat at the wardroom table and had become part of these legends by some act of heroism, or folly, or by dying in some unusual manner.

One minor figure in the mythology was a young Irishman, Donat Henchy O'Brien, who had served in the *Amphion* as a midshipman in 1802, after the Peace of Amiens, when the ship had been hunting smugglers in British waters. After passing his lieutenant's examination in London he had returned to the ship for a few months, then was appointed to the new frigate *Hussar*. Soon after joining her, war had broken out again and the ship was ordered to Spanish waters from whence in February, 1804, she was sent with dispatches for the Channel Fleet. On passage she was wrecked off the coast of Britanny, her crew taking to the boats and making for the harbour of Brest where they were made prisoners of war.

O'Brien had first been imprisoned at Verdun but, three years later, after an attempt to escape, which took him to the Channel coast and within sight of the sails of British warships, he was sent to Bitche, a mountain fortress in the Vosges, where recalcitrant British prisoners were likely to find themselves; breaking the journey with another attempted escape which ended with capture on the shore of Lake Constance. The last that any of his former shipmates had heard of him was that he was imprisoned in the most secure and gloomy subterranean dungeon in Bitche.

Now, on 8th November, 1808, his old ship, the *Amphion*, lay off Trieste, her captain anxiously awaiting the return of his boat and O'Brien's old friend Lieutenant Jones. Then, at noon, the masthead look-out shouted that the yawl was in sight, but her progress was slow and she seemed to be badly damaged. Hoste ordered the barge, which had also returned from a sweep along the coast, to take her in tow and, an hour later, she was brought alongside, splintered by shot and with wounded men lying on her blood-stained bottom-boards. The frigate was ready to receive casualties and the wounded were hoisted in by a chair lowered by block and tackle from the mizzen yard-arm.

Hoste had at once seen that Jones had been badly hit but when another wounded man, wearing civilian clothes, was helped out of the chair he assumed him to be the master of the enemy ship that had treated his boat's crew so roughly. Controlling his anger, he ordered the stranger to be taken below when two other lieutenants, Bennett and Phillott, who had been in the ship as long as Jones, recognized the wounded man as the former Lieutenant O'Brien, their old shipmate. The mood instantly changed and O'Brien was gently helped below to the surgeon, Mr Moffat, who found that a musket-ball, striking his right arm, had laid bare the artery and that amputation might be unavoidable. Hoste's clerk gave up his cabin and, for more than a fortnight, O'Brien was confined to the cot and during this time, as his wound healed and, being free from infection, amputation became unnecessary, he told his remarkable story.

In September, O'Brien, with three companions, had escaped from Bitche by lowering themselves by rope some two hundred feet from the walls of the fortress. They crossed Germany and reached the Austrian frontier near Salzburg, where the present alliance with France was unpopular and their pretence to be American was readily accepted. One of the escapers had fallen ill and had to be left behind, but O'Brien and the others reached Trieste, which, together with Fiume, was still under Austrian control, the only Adriatic ports not occupied by the French.

The British vice-consul was still in residence and, with his help, they chartered a small boat to take them out to the British frigate which was known to be blockading the port, cruising some distance from shore. After a night at sea they sighted a warship's boat, hailed her and to O'Brien's amazement were told that she belonged to the *Amphion* and was looking for enemy shipping. Explaining that two of them were escaped naval officers, they were taken on board the yawl and O'Brien, as he later put it, 'instantly recognized Lieutenant Jones, an old friend and shipmate of 1802. I immediately made myself known to him and this excellent fellow exultingly expressed his gladness that he should have been the officer that had had the good fortune of picking us up.'

Jones explained that the *Amphion* had only relieved the *Unité* off Trieste the night before and talked about the prizes they had taken, while O'Brien told him about their escape. It was a fine morning and, soon after sunrise, when the officers were deep in their talk, two strange vessels were sighted against the mountains of Istria to the east of Trieste. Jones immediately set course for them and, as they drew near, it was seen that one appeared to be a large rowing-boat crowded with men which seemed to be pulling for shore and away from a schooner flying Venetian colours. Jones concluded that the greater part of the latter's crew were making their escape, realizing that capture was inevitable. The little British yawl made directly for the schooner, Jones determined 'to board and make a hand to hand affair of it'.

O'Brien was asked to fight with the small detachment of marines on board. 'Who can conceive my pride and elation when I thus found myself participating in the glories of my profession, and reflected how short a time had elapsed since I had been either a prisoner in a dungeon, or a sort of Nebuchadnezzar wandering in the fields and forests,' he was to recall. 'A ship's cutlass, a black musket, were good substitutes for my chains and padlock.'

The yawl fired several shots at the schooner which, to the surprise of the British, fired back with a cannon, probably a six-pounder, and her decks could now be seen crowded with more than twenty men. O'Brien fired his musket at their officer (they were now close enough to see that he wore the insignia of the *Légion d'honneur*) and felled him. At that moment a volley from muskets, blunderbusses and big musketoons struck the yawl: two sailors fell dead, another mortally wounded and four others hit, including O'Brien.

Seeing the effect of the schooner's fire, the second enemy boat, also manned by more than twenty men, put about and made for the yawl. Jones, despite his wound, remained in command and, seeing the hopelessness of fighting two enemy vessels, each more powerful than his own, sheered off, the retreat being covered by one marine sniping from the stern while O'Brien bit off the caps of cartridges and passed them to him with his left hand. This was effective enough to allow their escape and sad return to the *Amphion*.

Hoste immediately took to O'Brien, admiring his courage and enjoying his robust humour, so that, after the Irishman had taken passage to Malta, returned to England and come out again to the Mediterranean, fifteen months later, he appointed him as his third and junior lieutenant.

The *Amphion* herself returned to Malta for a brief refit before Christmas but, in the first week of 1809, was ordered to return to cruise and blockade in the Adriatic. But now the war there was about to change, for the Austrian Empire seemed intent on throwing off French domination and challenging Napoleon again with its vast armies. This would bring them into direct conflict with French power on both shores of the Adriatic and there would be heavy work for the Royal Navy.

All seemed to depend on Austria. The news from Spain was bad. Madrid had fallen and the British expeditionary force had had to be evacuated from Corunna after a harrowing retreat, at the end of which its commander, Sir John Moore, whom Hoste had known during the brief Calabrian campaign, had been killed. Despite the spasmodic resistance of the Spanish peasantry, it seemed impossible that they could have any effect against French armies without massive support from outside and this would be impossible to provide.

Austria declared war, as expected, in February soon after Hoste had returned to the Adriatic station. He tried to show optimism but he had had too much experience of both the Austrians and the French in the field to expect much of the former and even a disastrous name, von Mack, from the end of the last century, when Nelson had saved the Neapolitan monarchy, was being bandied about again. Hearing that the Austrian armies were about to march and that Trieste and Fiume would again be open to the British, he wrote to his father, 'Pray heaven the Austrian arms may be successful this time! but I have my doubts. Treachery, treachery, has formerly ruined them, and still we see the chief cause of their ruin, General Mack, now recovering his courage through Vienna . . . We shall have some amusement this spring, no doubt.'

Just before war was declared by Austria, the *Unité* sailed for Malta, leaving Hoste the senior officer in the Adriatic, where he was later joined by the brig *Redwing* and soon the British ships were in action. An enemy brig of six guns and a *trabaccolo* had been sighted at anchor in a creek in the Dalmatian island of Meleda [now Mljet], covered by guns and some four hundred troops ashore. Hoste at once sent the boats of both ships in to attack under command of his first lieutenant, Charles Phillott, who had relieved Bennett. As they approached the shore, the enemy fired their cannon once, then fled, allowing the British to collect their prizes, and destroy the shore batteries and storehouses of oil and wine at their leisure.

Hoste was becoming familiar with these islands that ran in a long archipelago from Fiume [now Rijeka] to Cattaro [now Kotor], providing sheltered leads for shipping plying up and down the Dalmatian coast and innumerable places for quick concealment when his sails were sighted. As the *Amphion* approached these islands, their presence would often first be sensed by the wind-borne scent of pines and wild herbs. Then their silhouettes would appear, often in monochromatic planes, one behind the other, like theatrical scenery, and he was coming to recognize their peaks and ridges and remember their names. At night, when the darkly wooded outlines of mountains were only faintly visible, blocking out the stars, the shoreline could be seen as a pale band of limestone where the sea had washed the rocks bare, a band that would be deeper on coast exposed to the full force of Adriatic storms, where the waves broke higher and the vegetation had retreated.

The distant glimmer of lights along a waterfront, or high on a mountainside among the stars, could, taken in juxtaposition, give a skilled pilot an idea of his position. All along this coast and on the islands were little seaports that were small echoes of Venice, their slim *campanili* standing above a huddle of houses roofed with apricot tiles and the proud insignia of the Lion of St Mark rampant in stone above citadel gates. On the mainland, the most important of these, south of Fiume, were Zara [now Zadar], Spalato [Split], where the medieval city had been built in and around the ruins of the Emperor Diocletian's palace, Ragusa and Cattaro. The islands, too, were often places of importance, renowned in their own right: Brazza [Brac] for its stone quarries, Lesina [Hvar] for its Venetian theatre and Curzola [Korcula] as the birthplace of Marco Polo.

The attention of Hoste – and, indeed, of Lord Collingwood, his captains in the Mediterranean Fleet and subsequently the Board of Admiralty – was now drawn to the most remote of these islands, Lissa. The importance of Lissa [Vis] had been recognized since seafaring began by traders, pirates, navies and fishermen. There were Neolithic remains on the island and the mark of several civilizations: Roman and Byzantine, and that of Venice, which held it from the beginning of the fifteenth century. To British naval officers, Lissa was to the Adriatic what Malta was to the Mediterranean, a strategic base offering shelter from the sudden storms that whirled out of the coastal mountains and a secure anchorage in a sea which shelved sharply to more than four hundred fathoms.

Lying some thirty miles to the south-west of Spalato, Lissa was the most distant island from the Dalmatian coast and, when visibility cleared before rainfall, the coasts of both shores of the Adriatic could sometimes be seen from its highest peak, two thousand feet above the sea. Covering nearly two hundred and forty square miles, the mountainous island possessed two deep-water harbours: one on the northern coast, the other on the east.

The former, Porto San Giorgio, was a near-perfect harbour, running from a narrow entrance, able to take the biggest ships, for one and a half miles across a wide and sheltered bay to the town of Lissa itself. There was a safe anchorage within, quays in front of the Venetian merchants' houses in the town of Lissa and its suburb of Cut and, on the western shore, gently-shelving bays which would be ideal for careening the bottoms of heeled ships. While both harbours were sheltered from the strong *fugo* winds that blew from the south-east in spring and autumn, the ferocious *bora*, which howled out of the mountains to the north-east, blew straight into the mouth of San Giorgio, although ships might be able to leave by warping into a little bay near the entrance, or be towed out by their boats. In that season, the anchorage in Comisa Bay on the far side of the island was secure. This was sheltered by mountains and had the few facilities of a fishing village and the island's only fresh-water springs, that bubbled, slightly brackish, from the rocks near the shore. Yet Comisa [Komiza] was open to the north-westerly *maestral*, which blew in summer, and, as this was the season of most intense maritime activity, Porto San Giorgio remained the harbour of greater value.

So Lissa became the lair from which British frigates could most easily pounce upon enemy trade and hardly a day passed when Hoste did not take a prize, or burn a merchant vessel that was not worth the inconvenience of manning with a prize crew. From here, too, raids on the enemy's coast could be mounted and he became bolder in accepting the risks of shore batteries and of putting his landing-parties ashore to face infantry.

Ancona itself was too strong to tempt a raid although Hoste often reconnoitred it, finding in April that the enemy squadron in the harbour had been increased to three frigates and five brigs, all ready for sea. But there were other smaller, fortified harbours that he felt confident of seizing, or at least, of cutting out shipping from under their guns.

This confidence increased with the arrival of reinforcements. This had become necessary since it was suspected that the enemy squadron in Ancona might be used to evacuate Marshal Marmont from Dalmatia should the Austrians appear likely to drive his army into the sea. It arrived in the form of two frigates, the *Spartan* and the *Mercury*, the captain of the former, Jahleel Brenton, now becoming senior officer in the Adriatic. Hoste immediately took a liking to the new commodore, despite his own loss of status, describing him as 'one of those few characters I have met with whom I should wish to make a friend of . . . I need not say more of him than that he reminds me a thousand times a day of my much-lamented brother.' In a ship still excited by O'Brien's escape from captivity, Brenton, also a former prisoner of war, was at once lionized as having been the undaunted senior naval officer amongst the British captives.

The little squadron assembled at Trieste and four days later were in action, attacking the port of Pesaro to the north of Ancona. Seeing the masts of shipping in the harbour, Brenton took his three ships in to within half a mile, anchored and manned the boats, forming them in two divisions, one with field-guns, or carronades, mounted in their bows, the other with incendiary rockets.

The commodore then summoned the town to surrender, but its Governor hesitated, hoisting a flag of truce while hastily mustering his garrison. So the flag of truce flying from the *Spartan* was struck and fire opened, dispersing the assembling enemy troops and sailors who could be seen desperately trying to unload the cargoes from merchant ships. The British boats then pulled into the harbour, landed the marines, then positioned themselves to enfilade the streets running inland from the quays. That done, the landing-parties blew up the fort and brought thirteen laden *trabaccoli* out of the harbour.

In the months that followed, the *Amphion*, alone or in company, was constantly appearing off enemy ports – Ancona, Zara, Rimini, Venice itself and many smaller places – sometimes seizing a prize within range of their shore batteries, sometimes sending boats inshore to launch a few impudent rockets, sometimes to put a landing-party ashore to blow up a fort or spike guns.

Then, in early summer, the scale of the Adriatic war suddenly assumed ominous proportions. The Austrians suffered a series of reverses, culminating in the shattering defeat at Wagram in July, that were to deliver the whole of the Adriatic seaboard to France. Three ships of the line, the *Northumberland*, *Excellent* and *Montagu*, under Commodore Hargood, arrived to join Brenton and Hoste, but they could do nothing to prevent the fall of both Trieste and Fiume.

The loss of the former was particularly galling because the Pesaro prizes were lying there and less than half could be saved by the daring of a midshipman, who narrowly escaped capture. The amount of prize-money thus lost to the three frigates was estimated at £10,000.

More serious was the presence of four Russian ships of the line in the harbour, since Russia was in temporary alliance with France. The British had planned to cut them out but contrary winds so delayed their approach that by the time they could work into the bay, the ships had been warped into positions from which their broadsides commanded the harbour mouth. This was also covered by heavy batteries, while the waterfront swarmed with several thousand French infantry.

Between the beginning of this second cruise that Collingwood had given him and the arrival of Brenton, Hoste had taken twenty-nine prizes. Reports of this had reached Malta, from whence he feared exaggerated rumours would get to London and, eventually, Godwick. His share had been satisfactory but not extraordinary since he had taken the precaution of adopting the custom of sharing his prize-money with another captain, who would do likewise, so increasing the chance of some gain but reducing that of anything remarkable.

Letters from his father had pleaded new poverty and the need of financial help so, in June, he wrote a tactful letter. 'Now, my best of fathers,' he began, 'hear me on a subject which concerns us both very intimately, and to me is a very delicate one. I will candidly lay before you my situation in respect to money matters, and you shall act and decide yourself afterwards. You have heard most probably that at least I have realised a fortune and that I have gained lots of pewter. Everyone tells me the same; I am very sorry to say i :xists only in idea.

'Since my sailing from England in 1808, I have received prize-money to the amount of £6,000, half of which goes to Captain Briggs, who has shared with me all the war . . . I give you my honour this is all I received. I expect another £1,000, perhaps more or less.' Hoste's own share had been forwarded to his agent in London, Isaac Clementson of Clement's Inn, to purchase stocks and shares. Now, he told his father, some of this would be sold and £500 'in hard money' be made available to him.

He wrote also to his father about the course of the war in Europe but not, as before, about home politics beyond saying, 'my chief reason for wishing the outs in is the chance of its being attended with no small advantage to yourself'. Instead of speculating on Whig fortunes, he wrote, presumably to his father's disappointment, 'It is not often, I assure you, I think of politics, particularly of party. Lord Nelson used to say, Sailors had no business with party; that who was in, or who was out, ought to be the same thing to them.'

But now that he enjoyed the patronage of Nelson's successor, Collingwood, he had less need to curry favour with Coke and the landowners for any immediate purpose other than the prospect of some partridge-shooting when he returned to Norfolk.

He had good news of young Ned, who had taken an active part in a second attack on Pesaro. On this occasion, the landing-parties were commanded by Brenton and Hoste in person, the latter being accompanied by his small brother, who 'shared in the danger and honour of the day'. Once ashore, the British had 'some smart work for an hour or two' and almost ran out of ammunition, the *Amphion*'s party suffering several casualties.

The most dangerous action in which the boy took part was the storming of Cortellazzo at the mouth of the river Piave, where the French had stationed a flotilla of Venetian gun-boats to protect the trade between Venice and Trieste.

Towards the end of August, Hoste planned a raid on this base with the intention of blowing up the fort, spiking the guns and cutting out the gun-boats and *trabaccoli* lying under its protection. Accordingly, having remained out of sight of land all day, he crowded sail after dark, anchored off the river mouth at one in the morning and, by three, had his marines and seamen, under the command of Lieutenant Phillott, on shore about a mile from the fort. When this had been carried, success was to be signalled by blue flares, upon which the *Amphion*'s armed boats would at once pull for the harbour to board the shipping which would then be caught between the fire of the British and that of the captured battery of twenty-four-pounders on shore.

Hoste noted the sequence of events in a pocket journal. '27th Off Cortelazzo a.m. 12.30. Anchored. Sent the boats mann'd and armed in Shore under the command of Lt Phillott: 3.25 Saw a firing of Gt. Guns and Musquetry in the direction of Cortalazzo, at 3.35 a Blue Light in the same direction; at 3.55 another; and ditto with 3 lights. At day light obs. our Men in possession of Fort Cortolazza and 6 of the Enemy's Gun boats and several Market Vessels. Got them out of the River. 5.40 p.m. Sailed with the Gun boats.'

The laconic jottings give no suggestion of the excitement of the night assault with bayonet and cutlass; the capturing of the heavy guns behind their ditch and stockade; the firing on the gun-boats as the frigate's boats materialized from the darkness; the spiking of the great guns and the explosions that destroyed fort, battery and barracks. The British had lost not a man.

Of his own part in the affair, Hoste was extremely modest, telling his mother, 'You know, on these occasions, the *Captain*, after planning the business and disposing of his force, has *nothing to do* but wait the event . . . Little Ned was in my own gig and as happy as a *prince* in being so actively employed. He is a fine brave boy.'

Soon after this, the *Spartan* was ordered back to the Mediterranean and Brenton offered to take Ned with him. Hoste hesitated, then agreed, because 'a man like Brenton is as likely, and much more so, than our friend Lord Nelson was when I first went with him, to turn out as great a character. He will have all such advantages in being with Brenton in learning French, Italian, drawing, etc., etc., that I should not have been doing him justice to have kept him.'

Before the end of the year, Hoste was professionally, as well as personally, alone when the ships of the line were withdrawn and he found himself 'once more lord and master of the Adriatic.' Now he could again expect the lion's share of any prize-money, noting that between June, 1808, and Christmas, 1809, his ship had taken or destroyed two hundred and eighteen enemy vessels. 'It looks well on paper,' he complained, 'but has not put much cash in our pockets, owing to the difficulty attending their being sent to port.'

The nearest port where prizes could be assessed was now Malta, and the difficulty in getting them there was partly the shortage of British seamen to make up so many prize crews and partly the weather. Over Christmas, the weather was appalling but the *Amphion* continued cruising and capturing. On Christmas Eve, Hoste wrote to his mother, 'I wish I was one of your snug Christmas fireside party, instead of being half frozen to death by one of these cold north-east winds, that literally blow through my lantern sides, and I have never felt it so cold in England.'

But, three days later, he wrote to his father in a buoyant mood: 'I hope you have had as pleasant a Christmas as we have had; though so severely cold that water froze in the cask, and a hard gale of wind, we were taking prizes, and as happy as princes. Can there be a greater proof of the pusillanimity of our enemies in this part of the world, than to allow one frigate and one sloop to annoy the trade in the manner we do? I will give you their force. At Ancona, three frigates, two brigs and two schooners: at Venice, one frigate, three brigs, two schooners and gun-boats innumerable; at Trieste, four Russian line-of-battle ships, two frigates, and six French gun-boats and one galley.

'What think you of their enterprise after that? The truth is, they are afraid of the weather, and are very badly manned: we are all well manned and do not care a fig about the weather.'

This was true at the beginning of 1810 but would not be so by the end of the year. British naval activity had had a disastrous effect on the economies of the countries bordering on to the Adriatic and, while it had had no effect upon the French occupation of its shores there were signs that, in time, it might. While all the ports were ostensibly shut to British trade, this was carried on by those the French described as 'smugglers', traders operating under British licence and protection.

They defied the Continental System by landing their goods in Europe wherever there were no naval or coastguard forces to stop them and the activities of Hoste and his brother-captains had seen to it that these were few.

The continual raiding of the coastline and the destruction of forts, shore batteries and signal stations had also given heart to the indigenous patriots, the potential partisans on both western and eastern shores and given the Ragusans hopes of an eventual return to independence and the Austrians a faint optimism in the face of their disastrous confrontation of the French.

All this amounted to more than a political and economic irritation. Realizing that the British Navy would continue to thwart his ambitions in the Levant and beyond, Napoleon was considering a grand strategy by which his Army of Dalmatia, greatly strengthened, would march south-east into the Turkish Empire, with or without its consent, through the Balkans, across the Bosphorus, into Asia Minor and erupt into Asia itself. But without control of the Adriatic, and with the abiding danger of having a British expeditionary force put ashore in Dalmatia to cut his communications, such possibilities would have to remain grandiose dreams.

So the Emperor decided that the British must be expelled from the Adriatic. The ships for this purpose were now available both from the French fleets and from the Arsenale at Venice, which was now back in production under French direction. To man them, plenty of seamen were available from blockaded or destroyed merchantmen and these could be stiffened by trained French ratings and attempts were being made to revive the Venetian naval profession under French control. Well aware of the value of personal leadership, Napoleon picked the future commodore of his Adriatic squadron with particular care. The man he chose was as much a son of the Revolution as Hoste had been a child of the twin pillars of English society, the Church of England and the Royal Navy. His name was Bernard Dubourdieu.

Seven years older than Hoste, Dubourdieu had a reputation for professionalism and daring that the former would have envied, especially so because he had fought and taken a frigate – a British frigate at that – in single combat. Now, at the age of thirty-seven, he was physically hard, fierce-tempered, his face – small, tight mouth; strong, straight nose and large, alert eyes – framed by thick side-whiskers that grew down from hair worn short-cropped, as was Hoste's.

The son of a master-cooper, he had gone to sea in a merchant ship at the age of sixteen. Conscripted into the Navy in 1792, he had quickly been recognized as a potential officer and rated, much as Hoste had been, *aspirant*. A year later, he had seen active service in the Mediterranean on board the frigate *La Topaze* but she had been one of the prizes taken by Hood at Toulon and Dubourdieu was among the prisoners sent to Gibraltar. After eighteen months in a prison hulk, he planned an escape and succeeded. Under cover of darkness, he swam to and boarded a small sailing-boat in the harbour and, with her, collected twenty other Frenchmen from the hulk before pushing off in search of a sea-going ship to seize. This proved to be the transport *Le Temple*, of ten guns, but, surprised by Dubourdieu and his men, who were armed only with a single hatchet, the captain surrendered. He was forced to make the necessary recognition signals to the guardships as his captors sailed his ship between the British warships at anchor in the roads and steered for the Atlantic. Dubourdieu made his escape and arrived safely at Lorient with his prize.

Two years later, he was captured again when his ship, the corvette *La Gaieté*, bound for Cayenne, was taken by the British frigate *Arethusa* and, this time, spent seventeen months imprisoned in England. Released in 1799, he was sent to Egypt in a frigate and again lived up to his dashing reputation, taking soundings in the approaches to Alexandria under fire from a British squadron and running the blockade to carry dispatches to France. Sent to the West Indies, he again distinguished himself both in repelling an attempt to board his ship by the boats of a British ship of the line and in rescuing the crews of ships that had been swept on to a reef by a tidal wave. In 1806, he was promoted to *capitaine de frégate*, made a member of the *Légion d'honneur* and appointed Commandant at Martinique.

Returning to France a year later, he was given command of a frigate and took thirteen British prizes and some three hundred prisoners on a cruise in the Mediterranean. Soon after, he was confirmed as *capitaine de vaisseau*, the equivalent rank to post captain. It was in 1809 that he fought his frigate duel, his own ship, *La Pauline*, losing no men killed after fighting the *Proserpine*, which lost ten killed, for more than an hour and forcing her to strike.

This action won Dubourdieu the Cross of the *Légion d'honneur* and again brought him to the notice of the Emperor, who was looking for an aggressive officer to take command of the squadron he was forming in the Adriatic. The news that he had been chosen for this appointment was given to Dubourdieu by Decrès, the Minister of Marine, who, after some flattery about his 'noble and powerful ambition to seek out the most extraordinary occasions for bringing the enemy to battle', told him that it was the Emperor's wish that he put himself under the command of Prince Eugène Napoleon, the Viceroy of Italy. He therefore travelled from Toulon to Milan to be given formal orders to take command of the squadron, consisting of five frigates – three French and two Venetian – and three Venetian brigs, that was to assemble at Ancona. But first he was to visit Venice to discuss and plan the new naval construction programme with the French director of the Arsenale, Tupinier, because future contingencies would include the building of ships of the line in order to keep the British south of the Straits of Otranto.

The appointment of a commander for one Adriatic squadron coincided with that for the other. At the beginning of 1810, Hoste had been joined by Captain James Gordon in the frigate *Active*, of thirty-six guns, and, after seeing a little brisk action in one another's company, the *Amphion* left for Malta, arriving after an absence on active duty of thirteen months. The crew had been sickly and Hoste himself in poor health but this was forgotten when he was summoned by Lord Collingwood to be given his orders. The admiral, now in his sixtieth year, was clearly a sick man – he was, in fact, to die of cancer on his way home to England in the following month – but he had one more act of patronage for his old friend's favourite. There were plenty of frigate captains senior to Hoste in the Mediterranean but Collingwood told him that he had been so pleased with his activity in the Adriatic that not only was he to return there in the *Amphion* but he was to command a squadron of three frigates and a sloop. Bursting with pride and gratitude, he told his father, 'I stand at least *two feet* higher'.

Before returning to his station in March, Hoste saw his brother George, who had travelled from Messina to meet him. He seemed much matured; he still had 'a good deal of the *colt*' but was 'a little more steady which makes him the pleasantest companion' and his elder brother noted that the two of them had grown out of their youthful habit of quarrelling over trifles.

Also at Malta he met Donat O'Brien, whom he had rescued from Trieste and who was now a lieutenant. Phillott, the first lieutenant of the *Amphion*, had been promoted commander, and been succeeded by Jones and the third lieutenant, William Slaughter, had taken his place so that O'Brien delightedly accepted the offer to become third lieutenant of his old ship.

Back in the Adriatic, O'Brien noticed the changes in the character of the war after an absence of more than a year. 'The enemy's naval force was now rapidly increasing in the ports both of Venice and Ancona,' he wrote later, 'and it was evident that the French Emperor was about to make an effort, either to inflict some serious injury on our commerce, or to interrupt our naval superiority in the Adriatic.' Soon he became accustomed to the aggressive routine of the ship: 'We used to heave-to, or stand close inshore off their ports, and under easy sail, and sometimes we would detain, board and destroy their coasting vessels and do everything in our power to exasperate them and induce them to come out.'

In April, the *Amphion* was back at Lissa with nine prizes. Port St George, as the British now spoke of it with proprietorial familiarity, had become of even greater strategical and commercial importance since Hoste had begun to use the harbour. Instead of trying to get prizes back to Malta they could be brought here to await the availability of prize crews, or the departure for Malta of a frigate which could take several in tow.

Here, too, foreign traders could operate under British licence, which would be granted if the bulk of their cargo was made up of British goods. It was also a base for privateers; some, perhaps, little better than pirates but all adding to the perils of those hoping to trade for the benefit of France and subjugated Europe. Thus the population of Lissa, which had been about twelve hundred before the arrival of the British frigates, began to grow as Adriatic seamen arrived in search of employment. Although the French encouraged the commissioning of privateers themselves to prey upon the licensed traders, these had no protection against patrolling British warships. The consequence was what Hoste described as 'an almost total stagnation of trade in the upper part of the Adriatic.'

The pattern of prize-hunting and the recruiting of skilled seamen to enter British service was described by Hoste's contemporary Charles Pemberton, who served in the frigate *Alceste* in these waters. 'This proved too narrow a sea for Pietro Camiso's ambition to sail in; and he advanced himself to the dignity of *capitano* of a *trabaccolo* of Pola, *La Madre di tutti gli Angeli*, which fetched and carried between that port, Venice and Fiume. It was an unlucky day for Pietro, when, seduced by the yellow smile and oratorical jingle of additional *zecchino*, he bargained to navigate 'The Mother of All the Angels' to the mouth of the Tagliamento, there to take in a cargo of bricks for Chiozza [Chioggia]; for within one hour of his tripping his anchor, he, and his deeply laden *trabaccolo*, were prize to certain boats of his Majesty's ship *Alceste*, which picked up 'The Mother of All the Angels' as she was yawing about in the fog. So Pietro and his *trabaccolo* did not go to Chiozza that time, but, altering course, following in the frigate's wake, made fast to a hawser, with five other victimized small craft, like bosses on the tail of a boy's kite, and in this order entered Porto San Giorgio at Lissa, where 'The Mother of All the Angels' was safely delivered of her bricks.

'But, even now, Pietro Camiso could turn his wits to account; for being familiar with every nook in the Dalmatian Islands, and experienced in the depth of water in every inlet and bay along the coast from

Spalato to Trieste, he soon forgot his grief for the loss of his *trabaccolo*, in the profits which accrued on his services as pilot, in our along-shore expeditions and boat-marauding excursions; and many a countryman and countryman's neighbour of Pietro's dropped into the open jaws of the foe, which lay, as per direction given by Pietro, to catch them.'

Hoste's first cruise as commodore of the squadron was highly successful and, a month after taking up the command, he wrote home from Lissa to say that 'my darling *Amphion*' had taken or destroyed forty-six vessels 'which will bring us a little pewter'. 'If I stay two more years in the Adriatic,' he added, 'I may scrape enough together to set the Hoste family at the dear old house as happy and as comfortable as I hope they ever have been.'

Then, as prizes became rapidly more scarce, he and his captains became increasingly bold in their attempts to cut out ships from fortified harbours. One such was taken by the *Amphion* in broad daylight from under the guns of Fiume. The year before Hoste had spent a few days ashore there, staying with a Flemish family, while recovering from a bout of fever, and had flirted with a pretty daughter. She had spoken no English so, he had told his mother, 'I am obliged to chatter French; but that and a beautiful woman I by no means find annoying'. Now Fiume was occupied by the French but, as his frigate ran in to seize her prize, he was close enough to the town 'to distinguish with our glasses the family that were so kind to me. We hoisted our colours as we passed the house which was asking how they were in our language, and a wave of the ladies' white handkerchiefs answered, "Very well".'

The squadron now consisted of the *Amphion*, the *Active* and the *Cerberus*, of thirty-two guns, and the sloop *Acorn* of eighteen. This was already inferior in fire-power to the ships being made ready for Dubourdieu at Ancona and Venice.

On one such reconnaissance of both Ancona and Venice, Hoste led his three frigates on to the eastward in search of a convoy which, he had heard, was carrying naval stores to the Arsenale. He found the enemy lying in a river just above the small town of Grado, protected, it was reported, only by the shoals that sheltered the shore, two ruined forts and, it was said, twenty-five French soldiers. He at once planned a night attack by his boats.

The boats of all three frigates were to assemble at midnight, but only those of the *Amphion* and *Cerberus* were ready and, rather than await the *Active*'s boats, Hoste ordered the attack to begin. The landing was made, and the marines and seamen marched towards the town covered by carronades mounted in the boats, which pulled slowly along the shore under the command of O'Brien. Then, at daybreak, it was discovered that the estimate of enemy strength had been dangerously wrong. A strong force of French infantry supported by armed peasants debouched from Grado and, when the British took cover from their fire in some hillocks, assumed this to be a retreat to the boats and charged with the bayonet. There was fierce hand-to-hand fighting which ended suddenly when French resolution collapsed, some running away and more than forty surrendering. The landing-parties, which had now been joined by those from the *Active*, took possession of the town, fought off a counter-attack – taking more than twenty prisoners – and turned their attention to the prizes.

Some of these were too heavily laden to be taken out over the sand-bar. But five laden prizes were sailed to Lissa and about fifteen small craft were brought out, loaded with the cargoes of eleven larger ships which had had to be burnt at their moorings. The British had lost four marines killed and the French ten, eight of whom had died from bayonet wounds.

By the end of July, Hoste knew that some sort of demonstration could be expected from the Ancona squadron. Now they were ready for sea and two frigates and a corvette at Venice had moved to Chioggia, from which they could run down the Italian coast to a rendezvous. So his squadron was constantly on the move, each ship taking a spell for replenishment and rest at Lissa. There was little recreation beyond swimming, fishing and walking in the terraced vine-yards above the little town. Then it was noticed that the promontory, forming one side of a little bay which had already been named English Harbour, and on which stood the *campanile* and church of a sixteenth-century Franciscan monastery, offered enough flat land for a game of cricket. Ned Hoste, who had re-joined his brother ('My dear boy Ned . . . grows tall; but, like myself is one of Pharaoh's lean kine'.) became captain of the *Amphion*'s Eleven.

'We have established a cricket-club at this wretched place,' wrote Hoste, 'and when we do get anchored for a few hours, it passes away an hour very well. Teddy is the head of the party.'

Games of cricket and the brisk routine of patrols were interrupted at the end of September, when it was learned that the enemy's squadron had assembled and been joined by its latest reinforcements off Chioggia and had sailed under the command of Commodore Dubourdieu. The squadron consisted of two French frigates of forty guns, *La Favorite*, Dubourdieu's ship, commanded by Captain Antoine La-Marre-la-Meillerie, and *Uranie* (Captain Pierre Margollé-Lanier), the forty-gun Venetian frigate *Corona* (Captain Pasqualigo), the thirty-two-gun Venetian frigates *Bellona* (Captain Baralovich) and *Carolina* (Captain Palicuccia) and the French sixteen-gun brigs *Jéna* and *Mercure*. On 6th October, Hoste, having detached the *Cerberus* to Malta, himself accompanied only by the *Active*, sighted this squadron off Ancona.

As he stood south-west towards the port, he could see some ships partly under sail, others getting under way. At first, he could not identify them or their exact number and, knowing only that he would be outnumbered, held his course. At noon, Dubourdieu made sail to meet Hoste, one division of three ships on the starboard tack, the rest close-hauled on the port tack so as to take advantage of any shift of the south-easterly breeze. By one, the opposing forces were close enough for accurate identification and it was obvious to Hoste that to continue on his course would be suicidal. Reluctantly he tacked his two frigates and stood away to the north-east.

Dubourdieu continued his pursuit for an hour then, perhaps because the wind was rising and he was as yet unsure of the ship-handling qualities of his captains in bad weather, put about and made for Ancona. Expecting the enemy to enter harbour and remain there until the coming gale blew itself out, Hoste made for Lissa in search of reinforcements. Arriving there three days later he found the *Cerberus* on the point of departure for Malta. Taking her and the *Acorn* under his command, he again steered for Ancona, to accept battle this time, but the gale was followed by three days of calm so that he did not sight the high skyline of the city until the 20th. Then, as telescopes were focused on the harbour from the four British ships, it was seen to be empty but for a guardship, a brig and a few gun-boats.

Where had Dubourdieu gone? Corfu seemed the most likely destination, for it was from there that any attempt on Sicily would be mounted. So, crowding sail, Hoste steered south-east. He planned to call briefly at Lissa, on the chance of more news of the enemy, before making for Corfu, hoping to arrive there before Dubourdieu to offer him battle before he could enter the harbour.

Then, next day, Hoste stopped and questioned a Sicilian privateer, which, he was told, had just been chased by the enemy squadron that was most certainly making for Corfu. Abandoning his plan to stop at Lissa, Hoste pressed on down what he believed to be Dubourdieu's wake.

At dawn next day, instead of sighting the enemy's sails against the sunrise, a fishing-boat was seen and hailed. She had left Lissa only the day before and had no news of Dubourdieu. So Hoste sailed on towards Corfu all that day and the next and on the following morning he was in sight of Brindisi. But the wind was now blowing strongly from the south-east and it seemed unlikely that the enemy would have beat against it towards Corfu and more likely that they would have run across the Adriatic to the Gulf of Cattaro where an enemy convoy bound for Corfu was thought to be assembling. There, further disappointment awaited; the anchorage in the outer basin of the great sea-loch was empty.

The frustration of the chase was reminiscent of Nelson's blind pursuit – guided only by intuition – of the French fleet in 1798, the excitement heightened by the hope that this, too, might end with a climax as decisive as the Battle of the Nile. It was always possible that Dubourdieu had left the Adriatic to join an attempt upon Sicily. But now the wind was blowing even harder from the south-east into the mouth of the Adriatic and Hoste believed that the enemy must still be to leeward, somewhere on the fifty thousand square miles of sea to his north-west. Thus, the most likely place to pick up news would, as usual, be Lissa. There was another possibility that was almost too humiliating to consider and that was that Dubourdieu's destination had not been Corfu, or Cattaro, or Sicily, but the island of Lissa itself.

The familiar hunched hills rose out of the sea, the squadron ran towards the mouth of Port St George. Before they could enter, the mast-head look-outs could see that that humiliating fear had been justified. They could see the burned-out wrecks of ships. So without waiting for details of what was so obvious to the eye, Hoste immediately crowded all sail to the north-west for Ancona.

As he was later told, Dubourdieu and his squadron had arrived at Port St George at the very time the Sicilian privateer had been telling Hoste that the enemy was sailing towards Corfu. An attack upon Lissa had been uppermost in the commodore's mind; the Minister of Marine had urged him to destroy the base that was proving so ruinous to their trade, adding, 'You are in a most favoured position – make the most of it and be promoted to rear-admiral.' Yet he dare not risk a stand-up fight with a British squadron less than half the strength of his own. This was realism, not cowardice. Dubourdieu knew that Hoste commanded frigates that were the equal of any; his crews were as well-trained and experienced in gunnery as they were in seamanship. His own ships' companies, on the other hand, were a mixture of French and Venetian professionals and Italian and Slav conscripts who had spent little time at sea and seen little or no action. To lead them into battle with the British at the very beginning of his own training programme was out of the question, although he expected the prospects would be quite different after a winter spent working up their gun-drill and seamanship.

So it was that Dubourdieu planned a raid on Port St George while the British frigates were away. He embarked a battalion of French infantry, sailed from Ancona and cruised southward down the coast of Italy. Then, on the night of 21st October – the fifth anniversary of Trafalgar – he heard from fishermen that the British squadron had left Lissa on a cruise to the southward. It was the time to strike. Next morning, the Franco-Venetian squadron was off the north coast of Lissa and Dubourdieu in *La Favorite* led the *Bellona* and *Corona* – all three ships wearing British colours – into the harbour, leaving the *Uranie* and three smaller ships outside to watch for the return of Hoste. A little after noon he anchored and sent seven to eight hundred troops ashore to occupy the port.

On this morning, there were no regular British warships in the harbour, but a midshipman of the *Amphion* had been left in charge of some prizes, two ships which were awaiting transfer to Malta, and half a dozen privateers. Recognizing the frigates as they entered the harbour for what they were, the midshipman gave the alarm and the crews of the privateers and almost all the people of the town took to the hills, scrambling up the narrow paths through the vineyards and scrub to watch events in the harbour below. Only the mayor and council of Lissa remained in the town for, as Napoleon claimed it to be part of the French dominions under British occupation, they felt they had little to fear.

Dubourdieu lay in the harbour for six or seven hours, and he and Hoste reported his actions during that time very differently. In his report to Prince Murat, Napoleon's son-in-law, who had been proclaimed King Joachim Napoleon of the Two Sicilies – or, perhaps in a propaganda version of this that was made public – Dubourdieu claimed a dazzling success. He took some thirty vessels, he reported, including ten privateers, as prizes, burnt another sixty-four, of which forty-three were laden, and restored a number of prizes taken by the British to their original French, Illyrian and Italian owners. There had been no resistance and, he claimed, the hundred men of the British garrison had surrendered.

Hoste, on the other hand, later reported that Dubourdieu had burnt two British and three Sicilian privateers and had taken away with him the two British prizes and a privateer schooner. There had, he said, been no casualties to the British or their allies.

What is certain is that, late in the afternoon, a fishing-boat put into the harbour with the news that they had been hailed by the British squadron that very morning. Dubourdieu at once ordered his troops to re-embark and his ships to weigh, these manoeuvres being so precipitate that the anxiety of the watchers in the hills turned to laughter and, the midshipman later reported, had the British squadron then appeared off the harbour mouth the islanders would have taken up arms against the French.

But for Dubourdieu it had been an unquestioned victory and was hailed as such throughout France and dominated Europe. His letter, or, perhaps, an exaggerated version of it, was published in *Le Moniteur* together with the claim that the British squadron, which was said to consist of three frigates, two corvettes and two brigs, had avoided combat, so disappointing his own officers and men, who were eager for battle.

If disappointment had been felt, it was shared on board the *Amphion*, where O'Brien noted afterwards, 'It was a bitter drug of disappointment; and none felt it more severely than our gallant captain. I dined with him that day, and saw the big drop trickle down his manly cheek. Never was there a more gloomy, melancholy dinner-party, or dinner-table, than this.'

The following day was hazy with a light wind and a heavy swell over which the British frigates softly swooped towards Ancona. That night O'Brien was on watch and, the haze having cleared, was sweeping the horizon with his night-glass when he sighted some dark shapes ahead. This was confirmed by a midshipman and O'Brien hurried to wake Hoste.

'I shall never forget the ecstasy with which he sprang from his cot exclaiming emphatically, "We have them at last, thank God! Thank you, O'Brien . . . Let the officers be called and all get quietly to their quarters; back your mizzen top-sail that Gordon (of the *Active*, the next astern) may get near enough to communicate without noise and I shall be on deck in a moment".'

No drum beat to quarters or boatswain's call squealed as the *Amphion* cleared for action and went to action stations with no sound but whispered commands, the patter of bare feet and the creak of block and tackle. The mizzen top-sail had been backed and as the *Active* came up with her quarter, the news was passed in a quiet voice to Captain Gordon, who then slowed his own ship to tell Whitby of the *Cerberus*. At first light, the frigates' gun-crews stood silently closed-up, their guns loaded and run-out. Slowly the shape of the sails ahead materialized. They belonged to fishing-boats.

When the squadron reached Ancona, it was seen that, as expected, the enemy were lying alongside the mole, safely under the guns of the citadel; indeed, they had been entering the harbour before their pursuers had been out of sight of Lissa. It was hard to bear, especially when it was realized that the account in *Le Moniteur* would reach London long before Hoste's own report would arrive at the Admiralty via the flagship of the Mediterranean Fleet. The French version, which would soon be the talk of the clubs and would doubtless be reported in the county newspapers, boasted baldly that 'the English squadron, though superior to the French in force and numbers, most sedulously avoided measuring strength with it'.

Disaster followed humiliation for Hoste. Back again off Ancona, after a visit to Lissa, the *Amphion* and the small frigate *Volage*, which had just relieved the *Cerberus*, collided. The British had spent the day lying off the port in line of battle, but just out of range of the shore batteries, in the hope of provoking Dubourdieu to come out. At dusk they stood out to sea as the wind increased and a gale seemed imminent.

'At about nine in the evening, I had given my night orders and turned in,' Hoste told his father, 'when, about half an hour afterwards, I was awoke by the officer of the watch with the *pleasing* intelligence that a large ship was on board of us. I instantly jumped on deck and found the *Volage*, one of the squadron, had by a sudden change of wind and violent squall got on board us and was damaging us considerably. It was really the most serious moment I ever experienced and for some moments I thought both ships must go to the bottom.'

The bows of the *Volage* had crashed into the *Amphion* amidships, then scraped down her side, smashing superstructures and rigging, until her anchor hooked over the quarterdeck bulwark, so that the two ships ground and heaved together until the thick anchor-rope could be hacked through and they lurched apart. Both were so badly damaged that Hoste could only leave Gordon to watch Ancona in the *Active* and himself take the *Volage* in tow and set out into the storm, bound for Malta dockyard and repairs.

The *Amphion* was away on passage and in dock for more than two months and her captain feared that, at last, the ship was no longer fit for such hard service. 'As the last gift of Lord Nelson, I should prefer remaining in her to anything else,' he explained. 'But now she is quite gone by; I still *esteem*, though no longer a *lover*, and I hope my ever lamented patron would, if he were still afloat, say I had done justice to his gift.'

But Dubourdieu's successful raid on Lissa, and his own failure to intercept him or bring him to battle, was only one of the shadows to fall on Hoste's prospects. Collingwood had been succeeded by Admiral Sir Charles Cotton, whom he did not know and who had had no Nelsonian connections: 'Sir C. Cotton is very civil but he is not, like my Lord Collingwood, *in my way*.'

During Hoste's absence in Malta, he had, of course, been replaced as senior officer in the Adriatic and it seemed that he had had his chance of glory and missed it. He tried to forget his disappointment by joining the social jollities of Malta: 'we are all gaiety at this place and nothing but masquerades and balls – no less than five next week. One would suppose that the Tarantula had made cruel devastation amongst the fair ladies of Malta, for dancing is the order of the day, and night, too.'

He also tried to comfort himself with thoughts of home, which he would see again if, as he expected, he was ordered to take his battered frigate back to England. 'I begin to think that I could be happy enough in dear old Norfolk without going further in search of honour or riches,' he wrote to his mother. 'I hope to have a lick at the partridges next season.'

VII

VICTORY AT LISSA

To his surprise Hoste was not ordered to Portsmouth but back to the Adriatic. His unique experience of that sea had been recognized but he could expect none of the favours that Collingwood had shown him. He could not hope to resume his status as senior officer while a seventy-four-gun ship of the line was north of the Straits of Otranto and naturally expected to take orders from Captain George Eyre of the *Magnificent* while he was there. But he was put out when Admiral Cotton decided that his decision to appoint O'Brien as his first lieutenant – 'as is his birthright', Hoste said – was incorrect and, without consultation, ordered that he should be replaced by Lieutenant David Dunn, who was eight months his senior. It says much for the morale of the *Amphion* that O'Brien's disappointment and Hoste's petty humiliation did not become a source of rancour.

They sailed late in February, 1811, and, after coming up with the *Magnificent*, which Hoste boarded to meet Eyre, the *Amphion* anchored in Port St George on 7th March. Little had happened since he had last been there but, now that winter was over, some further attempt on Lissa could be expected from Dubourdieu and Hoste had been drafting plans for the fortification of the island, particularly shore batteries to command the harbour mouth.

Now the routine of cruising and blockade had to be resumed and, next day, the *Amphion* sailed for a short excursion south to the islands of Pelegose and Tremiti and the mainland of Italy before returning to the waters off Lissa, where she joined forces with the *Active*, *Cerberus* and the little *Volage*. Eyre in the *Magnificent* was far distant, so Hoste took command of the frigate squadron for another run across to Ancona to taunt Dubourdieu.

The four ships were to spend the night off Lissa under easy sail, then set out together at first light. As they rode out the hours of darkness, the ships beat slowly into a stiff north-westerly breeze with the *Active* some way ahead to windward. The *Amphion* had just tacked about a mile off the north shore of the island and set the main-sail when, at three o'clock, the watch on deck heard the distant reports of two guns fired in quick succession and saw a blue flare to windward. This was the signal for an enemy and Hoste at once answered it with a blue light. Almost immediately the signal, that they assumed had been made by the *Active*, was repeated and answered.

The *Cerberus* and *Volage* were in company with the *Amphion* but it was not until five o'clock that they sighted the *Active* to the north-west. It was not only the British frigate that emerged from the grey morning light. Beyond her lay the largest squadron of warships any had seen in the Adriatic. As each set of masts and yards became distinguishable from the next, Hoste was able to identify them as being five frigates, a corvette, a brig, two schooners, a small gaff-sailed xebec armed coaster and a gun-boat. Dubourdieu had accepted the challenge at last.

The British ships at once cleared for action, and Hoste ordered the squadron to make all sail and, tacking together, steer towards the enemy. As the three more easterly ships came up with the *Active*, their captains became aware of two certainties. One was that Dubourdieu's squadron was at least twice as strong as their own. The other was that, this time, it showed every sign that it would stand and fight. 'The disparity, to all appearance, was overwhelming,' noted O'Brien, 'but, strange to say, there was not a soul in the *Amphion*, from the chief down, who did not anticipate a complete victory.'

On board *La Favorite*, Bernard Dubourdieu had known that he had been sighted since the *Active* had fired her signal guns but he did not know that other ships were in her company until first light. Then he saw, six miles to the south-east, three more frigates flying British colours from their mast-heads between him and Port St George, which was his goal. In order to reach this he would have to fight them and this he was now ready to do.

The battle that was about to begin was the direct result of an order from the Emperor Napoleon. At the beginning of February, he had ordered that Lissa again be attacked and that, this time, it should be seized and held. Whether the expedition sailed from Ancona, or assembled at the small port of Lesina some twelve miles north-east of Port St George, was a matter for Murat and Commodore Dubourdieu to decide. It was only essential that Lissa be captured. The Emperor brushed aside the former's protest that, even if the island were captured, the British would simply move their base to another island with a sheltered anchorage, such as Curzola or Meleda; while these might be less well placed strategically, they would enable the frigates, privateers and traders to keep the seas. To this Napoleon replied that both the islands Murat had named were protected by his forces at Ragusa and that the attack he wanted must go ahead.

Napoleon had originally ordered that the expeditionary force should number one thousand, five hundred soldiers but, in the event, only about a third of that number assembled at Ancona under the command of a favoured Italian officer, Colonel Alexandre Gifflenga who had been aide-de-camp to Murat. These, together with six heavy cannon, two field-guns and two mortars, with which to defend the captured Port St George against British counter-attack, were embarked in the squadron which sailed from Ancona on the evening of the 11th of March, while Hoste was away cruising far to the south of Lissa.

The force that Dubourdieu now had under his command seemed more than adequate for his mission. The main fighting strength lay in six frigates, three French, three Venetian. His own ship, *La Favorite*, the *Flore* (Captain Peridier) and the newly-joined *Danae* were all ships of more than a thousand tons, mounting forty-four guns and manned by some three hundred and fifty men. Of the Venetian ships, the *Corona* (Captain Pasqualigo), was another big ship of forty-four guns, newly built at the Arsenale of Venice, while the *Bellona* (Captain Duodo) and the *Carolina* (Captain Baralovich) were standard frigates of thirty-two guns and complements of two hundred and twenty-four.

In addition to these were the brig *Mercure* of sixteen guns, two schooners, the xebec and the gun-boat; this small, secondary squadron mounting a total of thirty-six guns.

Against two hundred and seventy-six guns and nearly two thousand men of Dubourdieu's frigate force, Hoste had only his four frigates, together mounting only one hundred and twenty-four guns and manned by less than nine hundred men. The *Active* (Captain James Gordon), his most powerful ship, carried only thirty-eight guns and was smaller than any of the enemy frigates. His own *Amphion* and the *Cerberus* (Captain Henry Whitby) were thirty-two-gun ships and the *Volage* (Captain Phipps Hornby) mounted only twenty-two guns.

The one British advantage was their skill and experience in seamanship and gunnery, which Dubourdieu's squadron, despite intensive training over the past months, could not hope to match. So confident of this professionalism was Hoste that he intended that his squadron should fight in one tight formation, each ship ready to respond instantly to his signals in the initial stages before the battle broke up into gunnery duels and boarding, one ship against another, when signals would not be seen through the smoke.

At six o'clock, the British were beating towards the enemy in line ahead, the *Amphion* leading, followed by the *Active*, *Volage* and *Cerberus*, all sails set. The enemy, having the advantage of the wind, were bearing down to meet them and it soon became clear that Dubourdieu was dividing his force, intending to meet the British in more than one division.

When the opposing squadrons were about two miles apart, still just out of gunshot range, Hoste experienced such exhilaration that it had to be shared. He had never overcome his despair at having missed fighting at Trafalgar but, now that he was out-numbered as Nelson had been, a sudden rush of memories came to him – the *Agamemnon*, the *Captain* and the *Theseus*; St Vincent, Tenerife, the Nile – and on impulse he called his signal midshipman. Nelson's last words to his fleet had been a signal that was now known to all England so he would emulate his friend in this as he hoped to do in battle. He gave an order and signal flags raced up the *Amphion*'s halyards spelling out his message, 'Remember Nelson'.

No telescopes were needed to read the signal in the three ships following close astern and as the two words were repeated and shouted down to the gun-decks, the magazines and the surgeons waiting below on the orlop decks, the sailors manning guns on the weather-decks sprang into the rigging and cheered. 'Never again so long as I live shall I see so interesting or so glorious a moment,' remarked Hornby of the *Volage*.

But it was not only Hoste who remembered Nelson. Dubourdieu had made a study of his unconventional tactics, particularly those at Trafalgar. He, too, wanted to produce 'a pell-mell battle' – as had Nelson – in order to make use of his principal advantage: manpower. Even with his massive preponderance in weight of metal, he dare not risk an action that could be decided by the accuracy and speed of gunfire, in which British experience would probably prove decisive.

But in men he outnumbered the British by more than two to one and he felt so confident of the aggressive zeal that he had been trying to transmit to them, that a decision, hand to hand, by boarding seemed the way to overwhelm the British, who could then be met as equals, man to man. So, to create his *mêlée*, Dubourdieu adopted the tactics of Nelson at Trafalgar, forming his squadron into two divisions; the windward led by himself in *La Favorite*, followed by the *Flore, Bellona, Mercure*, the xebec and a schooner; the leeward division consisting of the *Danae, Corona, Carolina*, the schooner and the gun-boat.

Dubourdieu's two immediate subordinates, Captain Meillerie and the commander of the expeditionary force, Colonel Gifflenga, were less confident than he. The latter, fearful of exposing his infantry to naval gunfire before they could even begin their business of taking, occupying and holding Port St George, had the night before asked if he could land his men before the risk of action at sea came with morning. His request was refused. Then, as they watched the squadron haul apart into the two divisions, Meillerie turned to Gifflenga and said, 'Colonel, would not it be better were we to wait an hour longer and form our line?'

But the commodore had no such doubts. Sensing their apprehension, he turned to them and said, 'This is the happiest day of our lives. We have the advantage of two frigates over the enemy and are as well manned as he is.'

In remembering Nelson, Dubourdieu also remembered Captain Jean-Jacques Lucas of the *Redoutable*, who had so trained his ship's company in close combat, grappling, boarding, sniping and throwing grenades, that when the *Victory* had run alongside her, one of his snipers had succeeded in turning the British triumph sour by killing their Nelson. He would now adopt the tactics of both men: Nelson's to produce the occasion to implement Lucas's. He, Dubourdieu, leading his windward division, as Nelson had done, would, sword in hand, lead his men into action as Lucas had and teach Lord Nelson's pupil, Captain Hoste, a lesson of his own.

Seeing the enemy ships form into two divisions to bear down upon him, each in line ahead, Hoste remembered the dangers of a loose and ragged line against such tactics; the breaking of the Spanish line at St Vincent and 'the Nelson Touch' at Trafalgar. He therefore made the signal for his ships to close up tight, the bowsprit of each almost touching the stern of the next ahead. His ships now advanced slowly, under only topsails and topgallants, ensigns and Union Jacks flying from mast-heads and stays as well as the regular red ensigns at the mizzen peaks. Then Hoste ordered his own commodore's pendant to be hoisted to the main-mast, shouting as the flag flew upward, 'There goes the pride of my heart!'

The squadrons were now little more than a mile apart, rippling over the water towards each other at right angles; Dubourdieu seeing Hoste's four ships against the hunchback mountains of Lissa, Hoste seeing Dubourdieu's squadron coming at him across a wide arena of sea, its horizon jagged with the hills of islands – Brazza, Lesina and Curzola – and, in the distance, the great grey shapes of the mountains of Dalmatia.

At nine o'clock, the opponents came within range of each other's long-guns. There was absolute silence in the British ships but for the wind in the shrouds and the splash and hiss of bow-wave and wake. Then Hoste shouted to O'Brien, 'Try a single shot from one of the main-deck guns at Dubourdieu's ship!' The eighteen-pounder fired, its smoke blowing back over the deck, and a plume of water spouted below *La Favorite*'s bowsprit. The next order to fire would be for a broadside, double-shotted, and there was no doubt that it would strike home.

Dubourdieu was steering his division towards the stern of the *Amphion* to break the line between her and the *Active*. But the two ships were so close to one another that they almost seemed to be linked and when the first broadsides thudded along the British line in flashes of flame and billowing smoke, he abandoned the manoeuvre as impractical. Instead, he altered course a few points to starboard to lead his division ahead of Hoste's ship, then to put their helms over and run down the far side of the British line so concentrating the fire of both his divisions on it – just as Nelson had destroyed the French fleet in Aboukir Bay.

The broadsides of both the *Amphion* and the *Active* now concentrated on *La Favorite*, inflicting such damage that Dubourdieu doubted whether any of his ships could complete the evolution before their masts, rigging and sails were so cut about that they would drift helplessly and be blown on to the rocks of Lissa, on which waves were breaking only a few hundred yards beyond Hoste's line. He therefore changed his plan a second time and decided to stake everything on immediate boarding and a decision by hand-to-hand combat.

Now, at the last moment, the commodore felt a spasm of doubt. Turning to Colonel Gifflenga, he said, 'This is a glorious day – but I have been somewhat too rash. However, courage!'

It was the supreme moment of ambition and patriotic ardour for Dubourdieu. His choice meant death or glory within a few minutes and, shouting to his coxswain to steer for the *Amphion*'s quarterdeck, he waved his sword and called for boarders and gun-crews to follow him. The British watched in amazement as the French ship bore down on them through the smoke, her forecastle and bowsprit swarming with boarders, cutlasses, pikes and pistols ready, while at their head stood their commodore, unmistakable in the blue, white and gold of his uniform, sword in hand.

There was a brass howitzer mounted on the quarterdeck of the *Amphion*, five and a half inches in calibre and loaded with seven hundred and fifty musket-balls. When *La Favorite* was little more than ten yards distant and her boarders about to spring, this was fired. As the smoke blew back, the enemy's forecastle was seen to be wrecked and scattered with broken bodies. Almost all the eager boarders had been cut down by the single blast of shot and among the dead and dying lay the brave Dubourdieu, the captain of the ship and most of his officers.

The French officer surviving aft by the helm ordered the coxswain to sheer away from the British ship and try again to work round her bows. Nothing could have suited Hoste better and, knowing what would happen to *La Favorite*, he ordered his ships to put about simultaneously, so steering away from the shore while the shot-shattered enemy drifted past to be blown on to the rocks.

Deft as Hoste's manoeuvre was, his ship narrowly avoided joining *La Favorite* for her jib-stay and halyards had been shot away and the sail itself, upon which the evolution largely depended, flapped uselessly. Seeing this, the seaman, who was captain of the foretop, caught the halyards, swarmed and swung up among the rigging like a monkey and in a feat that seemed to the first lieutenant 'almost superhuman'. He rove the halyards to the mast-head block, and slid down a stay to bend them to the bowsprit end, so that the sail again filled and swung the ship out of danger.

The frigate had escaped the rocks by a few dozen yards and was now on an opposite course, the last of the line instead of the first. But the second ship of Dubourdieu's line, the *Flore*, still attempted to succeed where he had failed, Captain Peridier steering for the *Amphion*'s stern to rake her with a broadside before running up her far side. As she approached, a French seaman scrambled out to her fore yard-arm swinging a blazing fire-grapnel to throw into and set fire to the British ship's rigging. At once the marines of the *Amphion* fired their muskets on him, several shots striking the grapnel itself but without effect. With one final swing the sailor threw the grapnel but in his excitement he had misjudged the range and it fell hissing into the sea between the ships, while he himself ran along the yard and jumped off the far yard-arm into the sea.

A moment later, the *Flore* passed within pistol-shot of the stern windows of Hoste's elegant cabin, each gun in her broadside firing as it came to bear. O'Brien, commanding the main-deck guns, had anticipated this and, since his broadsides now had no target, shouted the order for his men to lie down between the guns 'while', as he said, 'the *Flore*'s shot rattled along the decks without doing injury to the men thus protected'.

Then, as the *Flore* bore up on the *Amphion*'s lee-quarter, the *Bellona*'s Captain Duodo put his helm over and ran up the British ship's windward side so catching her between the two, as Nelson had caught so many at the Nile. Again Hoste demonstrated his superb seamanship; making more sail, he suddenly surged ahead and out of the trap, put his helm hard over, cut across the bows of the *Flore* and opened his broadside on her lee side so that she completely shielded him from the fire of the *Bellona*. A few minutes later, the *Flore*, her decks a ruin of splintered woodwork and corpses, struck her colours.

Key to plans opposite:
British: Amphion, A; Active, B; Volage, C; Cerberus, D.
Franco-Venetian: Favorite, 1; Flore, 2; Bellona, 3; Danae,, 4; Corona, 5; Carolina, 6; Mercure, 7; small warships, 8, 9, 10, 11.

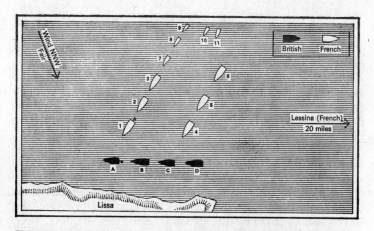

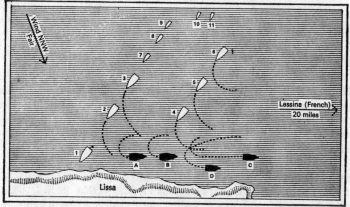

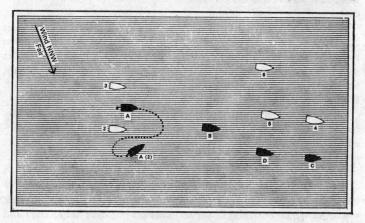

THE BATTLE OF LISSA

As she did so, the *Bellona* sailed under her consort's stern to engage the *Amphion* but was herself raked with gunfire from bow to stern. After taking a succession of broadsides she, too, surrendered but Hoste's boats were so shattered by gunfire that he found difficulty in getting prize-crews across to either ship. Seeing this, Peridier ordered the *Flore*'s colours to be hoisted again and he made sail and escaped into the smoke.

The *Amphion* herself had suffered much, shot about in masts and yards, sails and rigging and in the hull, her decks running with blood. Hoste himself had been blown off his feet when a chest of musket-cartridges on the quarterdeck exploded, his face scorched and the skin burned off his hands, while the face of Dunn, his first lieutenant, was completely flayed by the explosion. Later a shot or splinter struck the telescope from Hoste's hand, then a musket-shot hit his right arm. He refused to go below to have it dressed and when the surgeon appeared on deck to examine his wound he immediately sent him below with orders that he should not be bothered about his injuries until after the action.

When young Ned was hit beside him and sent below to the surgeon, Hoste did not even send to enquire after his wound but just ordered another youth to take his place. Some minutes later, Ned re-appeared on deck with a bandaged hand and resumed his action station. Reports were coming in of heavy casualties in all parts of the ship, but there was no time to attempt a count.

Meanwhile, the enemy's lee division had been concentrating on the other three British ships. As Hoste had been putting his squadron about, a shot had jammed the *Cerberus*'s rudder so that the little *Volage* wore first and found herself leading the British line. Seeing this, the captain of the *Danae*, avoiding the heavy broadside of the *Active*, which was now lying third, led his three big frigates at the *Volage* expecting a quick and easy conquest. But, while the French ships mounted long eighteen-pounders, the *Volage* carried carronades which, although short-range weapons, fired thirty-two-pound shot and these now smashed into the *Danae* as she came up for the kill, forcing her to haul off.

As the *Danae* opened fire from longer range, Captain Phipps Hornby of the *Volage* ordered his gunners to increase the charge in the carronades in the hope of reaching the enemy and this they did until the guns leapt so violently in recoil that they broke their breechings and upset. This left the little ship with only one six-pounder cannon to defend herself against the frigates' broadsides. She would certainly have been destroyed had not the *Active* come up at this moment to her rescue, at which both the *Danae* and *Carolina* put their helms over and made all sail for the open sea and steered after the *Flore* for Lesina.

Meanwhile, the *Cerberus*, which had been engaging both the *Corona* and the *Carolina*, had suffered heavily from the rapid and accurate fire of the former but when the *Active*, the most powerful of the British ships and still undamaged, came up, even the brave Captain Pasqualigo joined in the flight of the other two Venetian frigates with Captain Gordon in pursuit.

It was now about noon and the battle had drifted from the coast of Lissa out into clear water and it was there, mid-way between Port St George and the harbour of Lesina that the last duel was fought. The *Corona* was sailing slowly, much cut about in sails and rigging, while the *Active* swooped after her under a full press of canvas. Pasqualigo knew that he could not escape but he was determined to uphold the honour of Venice – he boasted a Doge among his ancestors – and waited for Gordon, turning to present his whole broadside to his pursuer.

The duel between the two frigates lasted for two hours and was hard-fought. At first, the *Active*, unable to bring many guns to bear herself, had to allow the Venetian broadsides to rake her from the bow. Gordon could not close with his enemy for more than an hour and, when he did, she fought on, slowly making towards the batteries of Lesina, until Pasqualigo realized that his ship was so wrecked that she could never reach safety and surrendered.

At half past two in the afternoon, the Battle of Lissa ended and, as the gunsmoke drifted away, the outcome could be assessed. Obvious to all in the British ships was that this had been, in its way, as decisive a victory as Trafalgar, for all but two of the enemy's main squadron were captured or destroyed.

When Dubourdieu's ship, *La Favorite*, had run on to the rocks, some two hundred of her crew had escaped to the shore after setting fire to her; she burned throughout the rest of the battle, the explosion of her magazine in mid-afternoon signalling the end of the action.

When the *Bellona* had surrendered, Hoste wanted to make sure that she did not also try to escape and sent one of his aides-de-camp, Midshipman Cornwallis Paley, to ask Lieutenant O'Brien to try and launch a boat and take possession of her. All the boats seemed shattered but finding a light one less damaged than the rest, O'Brien with Midshipman Kempthorn and four seamen carried her bodily to the ship's side and got her into the water. Immediately she began to sink but, if four men baled with their hats and the fifth paddled, she made some way and O'Brien even thought of trying to chase the fugitive *Flore*. He shouted to Hoste on the quarterdeck for permission to do this but was told to make directly for the *Bellona*.

O'Brien scrambled up the ship's side to be met by her first lieutenant with the news that Captain Duodo was lying, mortally wounded, in his cabin. O'Brien's first thoughts were for the seaworthiness of the prize and of the danger of fire. Questioning the gunner about this risk he was told that Duodo had ordered him to conceal some barrels of gunpowder forward in the cable tier and that, if the ship were compelled to surrender, these should be detonated to sink the ship. But the captain had been wounded before he could give the order to fire the train.

Now O'Brien went aft into Duodo's cabin and found him lying on his back with a ghastly wound in his stomach. Grasping the lieutenant's hand, he wept and thanked him for his kindness to a vanquished enemy. Promising any help within his power, although there was none, O'Brien next inspected the main gun-deck and later recalled the scene: 'It would be difficult to describe the horrors which now presented themselves. The carnage was dreadful – the dead and dying lying about in every direction; the cries of the latter were most lamentable and piercing. The surgeon, a herculean man, with an apron and his shirt-sleeves tucked up, attended by his assistant and others, bore a conspicuous part in the tragedy, being busily employed in examining wounds, ascertaining the bodies from which the vital spark had actually fled, and superintending their interment, or rather launching out of the ports!

'Strange to say, every man stationed at one of the guns had been killed, and it was supposed by the same shots (our guns being double-shotted) which passed through both sides of the ship into the sea. At another gun, the skull of one poor creature was actually lodged in the beam above where he stood, the shot having taken an oblique direction; in short, the scene was heart-rending and sickening.'

The prisoners were now assembled on deck and among them O'Brien found two Portuguese and one of these being the quarter-master, he was sent to take the helm of the ship as being the most trustworthy. But there was no more fight in the *Bellona*, and the little prize crew ordered her ship's company to make her ready for the passage to Port St George. 'In a short time we found ourselves in a somewhat better condition,' O'Brien said afterwards. 'The dead nearly all thrown overboard, with some who were not quite lifeless, but of whom not the slightest hope of recovery could be entertained, as the surgeon and his assistant repeatedly assured me. The sprung and shattered spars from aloft were sent down; the sails, which stood in need thereof, unbent and replaced; and the decks shovelled and cleared from the heaps of gore and ordure with which they had been encumbered.'

The *Bellona* had had about seventy officers and men killed and about the same number badly wounded and, although her masts and yards were still standing at the end of the action, her hull seemed 'a mere shell', such havoc had been wrought by the *Amphion*'s raking fire. The *Corona*, which had fought so long and hard, had suffered about two hundred casualties and had been 'cut to pieces', both aloft and in the hull, and her main-mast badly damaged by a fire which had finally been put out by the British prize crew.

When *La Favorite* ran on to the rocks and took fire, some two hundred of her crew scrambled ashore, leaving about one hundred and fifty unaccounted for. The survivors marched on the town of Lissa where they were met by two midshipmen from the *Active*, who had been left behind in charge of prizes, leading a scratched-together gang of privateer crews and to them the French surrendered.

The losses to the *Flore*, *Danae* and *Carolina*, which had escaped, were never even guessed at by the British, although the *Flore* was known to have suffered severely. All the small ships of the Franco-Venetian squadron managed to escape, one of them after an attempt of remarkable daring. While the battle was at its height off the mouth of Port St George, the captain of the Venetian schooner, which mounted only one gun, realized that the merchant shipping in the harbour would be unguarded while Hoste's squadron was otherwise engaged. So, shrugging off the possibility of shore batteries, he ran into the harbour to be amazed and delighted to see that the ship closest to him, a Sicilian privateer of fourteen guns riding at anchor, at once hauled down her colours at his approach. The surrender of the brig by her captain, Clemento Fama ('"Fama" indeed!', joked the British afterwards) was seen by the *Active*'s two midshipmen, who at once took a boat, pulled out to the privateer, ordered her captain out of the way and fought off the marauding schooner, so saving the shipping and prizes in the harbour.

The British loss, although far lighter than their enemy's, was heavy for a squadron manned by only eight hundred and seventy-nine officers and men: fifty killed and one hundred and thirty-two wounded. The *Amphion* had suffered most heavily with fifteen killed, including two midshipmen and the boatswain. One of the midshipmen, John Spearman, was a particular favourite of Hoste's and was killed at his side. The boy was commanding one of the quarterdeck guns and had turned to ask his captain for another target and Hoste 'having given a moment's attention to point the gun, turned his head to his young *élève*, and he was no more'.

On the evening of the battle it was clear that a gale was in the offing – as it had been after Trafalgar – and the squadron made its way into Port St George with its two prizes. First there were the wounded to be disembarked and Hoste directed that the surgeon of the *Bellona* should take charge of all enemy casualties and that comfortable quarters should be found for the mortally-wounded Captain Duodo; he was taken to the house of a priest where, soon after, he died.

While his crews were busy repairing the worst of the battle-damage and making the ships ready for the passage to Malta, Hoste set himself the task of trying to persuade Captain Peridier of the *Flore*, now safe in Lesina, to acknowledge that he had surrendered and to give up his ship. He sent a letter under a flag of truce to Peridier, 'as a man of honour', insisting, 'You know, Sir, I might have sunk you, had I not considered you as having surrendered, and so might two of my squadron also. By the laws of war, the *Flore* belongs to me, and the purport of my present truce is to demand her restitution in the same state as when she struck.'

A reply came from the frigate's acting captain, Peridier having been wounded in the battle. 'I cannot surrender His Majesty's frigate to you . . . because she did not strike her colours as you are pleased to state,' he wrote. 'His Majesty's frigate had her flag cut by shot. Her state not allowing her to continue any longer the engagement, her captain thought proper to withdraw from it. If you should not consider my answer satisfactory, I request you will address yourself to my Government.'

There was nothing more that Hoste could do beyond return the letter because it had been 'neither signed nor dated (I presume through mistake)' and to tell whoever found himself in command of the *Flore* that 'by the laws of war, his frigate belongs to my Sovereign, and his sword to me'.

This was a small blemish in the blaze of glory that Hoste now prepared to enjoy. On 25th March, the squadron sailed out of Port St George with its prizes – O'Brien commanding the *Bellona* – and received their first congratulations from Captain Eyre who had arrived to blockade the fugitives in Lesina with the *Magnificent*. Making for Malta, they ran into heavy weather on passage, the *Bellona* almost rolling her yard-arms under and the prisoners, who out-numbered the prize-crew by three to one, helping to bale the leaking ship.

The victorious entry into the Grand Harbour of Valetta took place on Sunday, the 31st. Hoste's rank did not warrant an official welcome, with the garrison paraded on the fortifications, but the entire garrison did turn out, together with, it seemed, the whole population to crowd the ramparts and flat roofs and cheer; as O'Brien described it, 'a continued hurrah and *vivas* were kept up from the time we entered the harbour until the ships were anchored and sails furled'.

A round of congratulatory parties, fêtes and balls now began and, at all of these, the British captains were accompanied by their honoured

Venetian prisoner, Captain Pasqualigo; 'for which he appeared truly grateful', said O'Brien. Official letters of praise from Admiral Cotton were read to the mustered ships' companies, but for Hoste the richest reward was in letters comparing his achievement with Nelson's.

At Palermo, Rear-Admiral Charles Boyles, also a Norfolkman, whose father had been the Customs officer at Wells-next-the-Sea near Holkham, had been responsible for passing on the news of Lissa to the Commander-in-Chief and to the Admiralty and now wrote: 'Your distinguished bravery will for ever immortalise your name and make our county of dumplings and dripping rejoice to think they have, still preserved for its protection, a brilliant spark from the shrine of our immortal countryman, Lord Nelson.' He added, knowing well the influence radiating from Holkham Hall, 'I have written to Mr Coke to give him an opportunity of telling your father and mother of your noble deeds.'

Lord Radstock, whose son, the Honourable William Waldegrave, was a 'first-class volunteer' in the *Amphion* and had been wounded in the battle, wrote, 'When I look at you as the truly worthy *élève* of my incomparable and ever to be lamented friend the late Lord Nelson – and I contemplate the giant steps with which you have pursued him in the path of Glory – as an Englishman, my heart gladdens at the bright prospect and my admiration and respect for your character in proportion.'

Just before reaching Malta, when he was allowed to use his injured right arm and take up a pen, Hoste wrote to his father: 'We are all recovering from our *hard* KNOCKS. You will read my letter in the *Gazette*. It will do my brave squadron justice *this time*, at least . . .

'It is gratifying to me to observe the regard they all have for my dear old *Amphion*. She was the last gift of my poor Lord Nelson. I hope I have not disgraced his memory in the care of her, though she is cruelly knocked about.'

The day after arriving in Malta, he wrote to his mother: 'If I was to tell you of our reception at this place yesterday, you would laugh at me and call me a vain, foolish man . . . Yesterday was the proudest day of my life . . . I could not help thinking, when amidst all the honours . . . of that dear old house in Norfolk and that if you and my dear father could have witnessed the scene, it would have gladdened your affectionate hearts.'

His ecstatic response to the praise ('You might have knocked me down with a feather, and I certainly did not exactly know whether I wore my own hair or a wig') raised the sights of his ambition and he confided to his mother: 'They tell me here, I shall have SIR added to the Hoste. Now, my dear mother, believe me, on the word of a sailor, that I have not the vanity to expect the BART., and that the KT. I would not accept *on any account*. I would rather be a poor gentleman than a poor knight.'

With the possibility of a baronetcy in mind even a letter from his father confessing to desperate financial difficulties did not unduly depress him. Now that he could expect great rewards, he instructed his agent in London to sell all the shares he had bought with his prize-money 'at any loss' and make any amount of the proceeds available to his father, to whom he wrote a comforting letter, saying that all possible help would be forthcoming. But he also gently warned against extravagance.

On 2nd June, the *Amphion* and the *Volage* sailed for England with their two prizes; Dunn, now recovered, going to the *Bellona* to take over from O'Brien, who again became first lieutenant of Hoste's ship, and a lieutenant from the *Cerberus* taking command of the *Corona*.

Much excitement was aroused by the arrival on board the *Volage*, as a passenger for England, of the celebrated Lord Byron after his long sojourn in Greece and the Aegean. Byron at first delighted in the company of naval officers and was excited by Hoste's account of the Battle of Lissa and particularly by his praise of Pasqualigo, the Venetian, since he already had his narrative poem, *The Doge of Venice*, in mind.

While on board, he wrote his *Farewell to Malta*, in which he gave his opinion of that island,

> *Adieu, ye joys of La Valette!*
> *Adieu, sirocco, sun and sweat!*

and of Army officers,

> *Adieu, ye females fraught with graces!*
> *Adieu, red coats, and redder faces!*
> *Adieu, the supercilious air*
> *Of all that strut "en militaire"!*

and of naval officers,

> *Farewell to these, but not adieu,*
> *Triumphant sons of truest blue!*
> *While either Adriatic shore,*
> *And fallen chiefs, and fleets no more,*
> *And nightly smiles and daily dinners,*
> *Proclaim you war and woman's winners.*

His host, Captain Phipps Hornby, he found, 'one of the best marine productions in my recollection . . . a gentlemanly and pleasant man and a Salamander in his profession, fight anything'. But, as the days passed in 'the gentle dullness of a summer voyage', this novelty palled and he wrote to his friend John Hobhouse, 'as I have got all the particulars of his late action out of him, I don't know what to ask him any more than *you*'. His fellow-passenger, an Army doctor, was actively boring and Byron confessed, 'I yawn and swear to myself and take refuge in the quarter-gallery', this being the officers' lavatory.

But he amused himself talking with the sailors and listening to their songs and ballads, writing to Hobhouse, 'Take a mouthful of saltwater poetry by a Tar on the late Lissa Victory:

> *If I had an edication*
> *I'd sing your praise more large,*
> *But I'm only a common foremast Jack*
> *On board of the Volage! ! ! !'*

At last, the *Amphion* was home. On 11th July she anchored off the Needles but, instead of running up the Solent to Portsmouth, was ordered round to the Thames. She anchored off Gravesend then sailed up-river to Greenwich, where she lay under the eyes of the naval pensioners, many of them veterans of Nelson's victories, at the Royal Naval Hospital. Then, a few miles up-stream, there was London and, embedded in the heart of it, the focal point of every naval officer's ambitions, the Board Room of the Admiralty, where the news from Lissa had already been announced.

When the frigate arrived and the welcomes began, one of the first visitors was Dixon Hoste himself, brimming with pride and gratitude, to congratulate his sons and be introduced to the other officers. For the occasion he had written a ballad of the sort with which he liked to flatter Mr Coke, calling it *Lines Written on the Return of the* Amphion *to England*:

> *Swift glides yon vessel o'er the sportive main,*
> *Proud of her freight, exulting in her Fame;*
> *And well she might – for noble Hoste she bore,*
> *Whose deeds outrival those in days of yore;*
> *Amphion is her name – From Lissa's strand*
> *She longs to gain once more her native land . . .*

VIII
THE BOLD BACCHANTE

The hero's return was something of an anti-climax. He was received cordially by Charles Yorke, the First Lord of the Admiralty, in Whitehall but there was no talk of a knighthood, let alone a baronetcy. The four captains would be awarded the gold Naval War Medal, enscribed 'Lissa', with the blue and white ribbon to wear on their coats, and that was all. Hoste was, however, told that he could recommend officers for promotion and himself take the pick of the new frigates under construction for his next command and name the station where he would like to serve.

Even the triumphal return to Norfolk was a disappointment. He was, of course, treated as a celebrity, the heads of the county families coming to offer their congratulations at Godwick Hall, but the jollities seemed hollow once he had grasped the full significance of his father's penury. He had written from Malta in the days of exultation after the battle and told him to draw freely on his prize-money and had instructed his prize-agent to pay whatever might be necessary. He had expected that his father might ask for some hundreds of pounds but now he found to his horror that he had taken and spent all the 'pewter' he had saved since his first award of prize-money. This amounted to several thousand pounds, which he had planned to spend on the purchase of a small country house in Norfolk and to provide a modest income from investments.

Although there was to be neither officially-recognized glory nor a fortune for him, Hoste did find satisfaction in concentrating again on his profession. As his next ship, he chose the *Bacchante*, a frigate of thirty-eight guns, then building at Deptford on the Thames. Dunn, who had been promoted to commander, was to take charge of her until she was ready for sea, then O'Brien was to be her first lieutenant.

About twenty other 'old *Amphions*' were to join her and nearly all the midshipmen, including Ned Hoste, Waldegrave and Paley. There were also new first-class volunteers to be chosen and now the choice was wide. Since Trafalgar, a career in the Royal Navy had become fashionable, something for the younger sons of the aristocracy to take up, and no longer a profession for those of naval families and impoverished parsons. Hoste was flattered when Coke's son-in-law, Lord Anson, the great-nephew of the famous admiral, asked him to take his son Charles and he readily agreed.

Another volunteer from a naval family was Edward Pocock, the grandson of Admiral Sir George Pocock, whom Hoste had hoped to emulate. The son of a naval chaplain, whose wife had had useful naval connections, George Pocock had survived many years of hard service in the West Indies and Indian Ocean and his dogged professionalism had paid handsomely. As commander of the squadron that had supported Clive on the Coromandel coast of India and, later, in command of the fleet that took Havana at the end of the Seven Years War, Pocock had amassed a vast fortune in prize-money and retired to a mansion on the river at Twickenham. It was poignant to have young Pocock in his charge, when Hoste's own modest ambitions had been dashed by his father's profligacy.

In November, the *Bacchante* was launched before what O'Brien described as 'a joyous and brilliant assembly'. In March, fully rigged and provisioned, she sailed round to Portsmouth to make the final preparations for service in the Mediterranean, which her captain had chosen as his station. Hoste was particularly pleased that he had, as his chaplain, the Reverend William Yonge, an old friend who had known Nelson and was a lively companion. 'He is fit for an admiral,' Hoste wrote of him. 'He has intelligence and fire enough for a Nelson, though I do not mean to say but that he makes an excellent divine.' This admiration was mutual, Yonge writing of Hoste, 'I never met with anyone who possessed such real love for active service, except Lord Nelson; there is a great resemblance between them, which I dare say will increase every day.' He also looked forward to his captain's companionship: 'His manners are particularly pleasing and cheerful. He has read a great deal; his taste leans to poetry; our best poets are familiar to him and he repeats with facility their most striking passages.'

Hoste was delighted with his ship's company and this was remarked upon by both Yonge and O'Brien. 'This morning, the whole ship's company were drawn up on the quarterdeck,' wrote the chaplain, 'The day was beautiful, the crew, the finest set of young men I ever saw collected together on so small a spot. What pride a man must take in commanding such a party! Hoste is in raptures with them.'

The eagerness with which some of his old ship's company had sought to stay with their captain had been shown by David Buchanan, the chief boatswain's mate of the *Amphion*, who, before she sailed for England, had been offered promotion into another ship. 'No, thank you, sir,' he had replied. 'If it's all the same to you, I'd rather be chief boatswain's mate with Captain Hoste and spill my blood in the lee scuppers than be boatswain of the finest first-rate in the Service.'

O'Brien felt so confident in the morale of the sailors that he gave all the 'old *Amphions*' twenty-four hours' leave to celebrate the first anniversary of the battle of Lissa with a dinner in Portsmouth. James Bealy, the quartermaster, had written a song about the battle and this, together with another by a seaman in the *Volage*, was sung:

> *There now, my boys, brave Hoste did say,*
> *We'll conquer, or like Nelson die . . .*

Then every one of the roisterers returned to the ship before their leave expired.

But not all the ship's company could be trusted to resist the temptation to desert and Yonge noted, 'In consequence of the men having received their pay, we are to drop down to St Helens, as a greater security against deserting, which they are apt to do when they have money in their pockets and nothing to lose by going.'

Most of the ship's company were English but there were about two dozen foreigners, including eight Americans, and, as was usual on the lower deck, an Irish contingent that could be relied upon to make a good showing in 'a mill' – as they called close-range combat – and to appear regularly on charges of drunkenness.

Hoste was reluctant to order the brutal ceremonial of flogging and Yonge wrote that his captain 'cannot bear to punish men, and so great is his dislike to it, that when we meet at breakfast, I can always tell by his looks when there is to be any punishment in the course of the morning'.

But such punishment there had to be and Hoste had decided that it should be so ordered that its effect would be more marked, while not casting a continual depression over the ship. No longer would men be flogged as soon as their sentence had been passed so that, as in his early days commanding the *Mutine*, this could become an almost daily routine. Instead, whenever possible, punishment would be inflicted on several men during one morning – although this might mean that some would have to spend several days in irons – so that the cruel spectacle would become only occasional but even more of a memorable warning to others.

After swinging at her anchor in St Helen's Bay for more than a month waiting for a Spanish grandee, who was to travel as a passenger to Cadiz, while Hoste 'fretted himself into a bilious attack' at the delay, the *Bacchante* eventually sailed on 3rd June. She reached Cadiz – now a friendly port – during a bombardment by the besieging

French, disembarked her passengers, entered the Mediterranean and reached Minorca at the beginning of July. In Port Mahon, all was warlike bustle with an expeditionary force getting ready for a landing on the Spanish coast. However, the main force of the Mediterranean Fleet was off Toulon and the *Bacchante*'s departure was hastened by reports of enemy ships in the offing. Five minutes after Hoste had returned from dining with Admiral Hallowell on board his flagship in the harbour, the frigate was under sail. 'I never saw a more animated scene,' remarked Yonge. 'The men at the capstan fairly ran the anchor up at a trot; all was alacrity and eagerness; and Hoste was delighted with this appearance and spirit of his crew.'

Off Toulon, they came up with the Commander-in-Chief, Vice-Admiral Sir Edward Pellew, who had succeeded Cotton the year before. Hoste was delighted with his reception for Pellew had been the most dashing of all frigate captains and now his own name was being coupled with the admiral's in a most gratifying manner. What pleased him particularly was that, without prompting, he had commented upon the lack of any suitable reward for the victory off Lissa, especially now that the Board of Admiralty were 'making knights by the gross'.

'I was received by the chief most graciously,' Hoste told his mother. 'He said, "Is that ribbon all they intend doing for you? They ought at least to make you a baronet." I said I would rather he should wonder why I was not one, than why I was.'

Pellew confirmed that he was to return to the Adriatic as 'his birthright' and there he went, fighting and capturing a French privateer and her prize on the way.

Early in August, the familiar outline of Lissa materialized through the heat haze. But it was not the place that Hoste remembered, although he took pleasure in steering the ship close inshore to show Yonge where *La Favorite* had beached and blown up and point out her guns still lying scattered on the rocks. The chaplain was impressed as the harbour opened before them and Hoste explained that it could shelter ten ships of the line; but less so with the town, which he considered 'a most miserable hole, small, confined and dirty'. Then, as some of the leading citizens came out in boats to board the *Bacchante* and welcome Hoste, he noted with satisfaction that they 'appeared delighted at his return and said that they felt themselves quite secure again now he was come back, though there was a seventy-four in the harbour at the time'.

Now, since that battle, Lissa had been generally recognized as being of the utmost strategic importance. In the summer of 1811, Napoleon had ordered that another attempt should be made to capture it, but

Murat had pleaded that this would be impossible in the face of British naval opposition until the new ships of the line under construction at Venice were ready for sea. Expecting another attack, the British decided to implement Hoste's ideas for fortifying Port St George and, at the same time, to formalize the status of the island as a major British base by giving it a Governor, a constitution, laws of its own and the means to enforce them.

On 24th April, Lissa had been formally taken over. Three frigates, the *Eagle*, *Apollo* and *Havannah* entered Port St George and landed the first Governor, Lieutenant-Colonel George Duncan Robertson, his staff and a garrison. There was a parade along the waterfront of the town past the balconied houses built by Venetian merchants. First came two companies – each of two hundred and twenty men – of the 35th Regiment under a Major Slessor and Captain MacDonald, next two hundred and sixty Swiss mercenaries under Captain Balbier, then two hundred and eighty Corsicans commanded by Captain Gerolini and finally three hundred Italians of the Calabrian Corps proudly wearing the battle-honour 'Maida' on their caps.

After marching past the Governor, the troops paraded in the paved court in front of the sixteenth-century church of San Spilice, the Union Jack was hoisted, Colonel Robertson waved his hat and called for three cheers and the thump of saluting-guns from the frigates boomed and echoed round the limestone hills.

Later in the day, Robertson met the city fathers and discussed the constitution, which was to be based on old Venetian and Croatian law as well as British. A magistrate's court was to be set up and Captain Balbier was appointed Chief of Police. Taxes were to be levied and duty was to be paid on imports, exports and the landing of fish; there were to be mooring fees. The economic warfare which Lissa had supported would no longer seem much like smuggling and privateering but would be regularized under the rule of law.

Initially, the British would live on board their ships but Robertson began renting houses and soon Lissa and its suburbs had the appearance of a busy garrison town with fourteen taverns and six billiards rooms along half a mile of waterfront.

The Governor had been appointed by, and was answerable to, Lieutenant-General Lord William Bentinck, who had served in the Peninsula and was now in Sicily as Commander-in-Chief of British land forces in the Mediterranean. He was responsible for the garrison of Lissa and any small expeditionary force that it might furnish, but the senior operational commander in the Adriatic was now Rear-Admiral Thomas Fremantle, flying his flag in a 'seventy-four', the *Milford*. He usually had two other ships of the line and more than half-a-dozen frigates under command.

It was Fremantle who most actively supported the creation of a fortified naval base at Port St George. Army engineers drew up plans for a massive fortress, to be known as Fort George, mounting a dozen of the heaviest guns, and its building by Italians and Croatians began immediately, the foundation stone being formally laid by Robertson. Three smaller forts, like the round Martello towers on the south coast of England, were built on commanding heights above the harbour and named after Bentinck, Robertson and Wellington. Even the hills upon which they were built were named after British officers, Fort Bentinck standing upon Mount Hornby, so called in honour of the captain of the *Volage*.

When Hoste returned he was flattered to find that the small island off the harbour mouth, where he had landed some guns after Dubour-dieu's first attack, had now been properly fortified with a round tower built by the crew of the *Milford*, a battery of guns, a small barracks and a signal station and that it had been named Hoste Island.

Of the greatest professional interest was the new dockyard which was being built under Fremantle's direction. The admiral had made his headquarters in buildings taken over from the Franciscan monks on the little shingle peninsula running out into English harbour at right-angles to the quays of the town. He had bought some land for £50 including buildings that could be used for storehouses and a hospital and enough of a gently-sloping beach to take a ship of the line, heeled over for the careening of her bottom. An old ship was beached in deeper water and sheer-legs mounted on her so that frigates could lie alongside for the stepping of new masts. Such were the facilities that Fremantle could boast to Pellew that 'already have the *Achille* and *Eagle* had as complete a refit here as they could have had in Portsmouth harbour, or any place without docking, and this without the desertion of one man, or the sickness which is generally the consequence of a refit at Malta'.

Another advantage was that instead of a ship in need of a refit being three months absent at Malta and on passage there and back, the ships remained at their forward operational base, forming part of its defences. This appeared particularly important to Fremantle in view of the alarming rate of re-armament at Venice. In July, one of his frigate captains, Hollis of the *Achille*, reported two enemy ships of the line, a frigate and three brigs in the Venetian lagoon, another three of the line and a frigate in the water at the Arsenale and from three to five of the line on the stocks. Even this, he feared, might be an under-estimate because ships in the dockyard 'cannot be seen from the mast-heads of this ship for houses and public buildings' and, as only trusted artificers were allowed into the Arsenale, much of this information came from fishermen who had come from Venice to trawl in the open sea.

So Fremantle usually kept two of his three 'seventy-fours' off Venice to prevent a sudden sortie. They had to be close inshore because only one enemy ship could leave the lagoon at a time and this could be caught and destroyed at once – as the *Victorious* had destroyed the new *Rivoli* at the beginning of the year – rather than allow a squadron to break out and form line of battle.

The third British ship of the line was at Lissa – together with whatever ships were in the dockyard – leaving the frigates to cover both shores of the Adriatic and blockade Corfu. This disposition of Fremantle's force and the setting up of the dockyard at Lissa was supported by Pellew but not by the Board of Admiralty, who wrote to the Commander-in-Chief that their Lordships did 'not approve any further expense being incurred in the establishment of a Yard at Lissa, and that they desire no appointments may be made there, as they cannot think an Establishment to be at all necessary so near to Malta'. Fremantle was mortified but his initiative was vindicated soon after when plague broke out at Malta and the Lissa dockyard came fully into its own.

The regulation of Adriatic trade as a means of economic warfare also brought the admiral into conflict with others. He disagreed with the decision to levy taxes and port dues on traders using Port St George and overruled the Governor in insisting that it revert to a free port. At sea, he allowed merchant ships to sail under British licences that had been transferred from others, which led to their abuse by those carrying other cargoes destined for ports under French control and not those for which permission had been granted. This large-scale flouting of the licence system was clear to Hoste, who drew the Commander-in-Chief's attention to it by letter but was himself sharply rebuked by Fremantle for confiscating one particular cargo: 'the transfer of a licence from one mercantile house to another is not evidence of its misapplication'.

During one acrimonious exchange, Hoste's pride was outraged by the admiral's sarcasm and he later wrote to him, 'Your asking me if I came there to be complimented and that you would compliment me for an hour if I wished it was so insulting to the feelings of a gentleman that I know not how to account for the language.'

From the day he joined Fremantle's flag, Hoste's relations with him were strained. Hitherto, he had always assumed that any friend of Nelson's would be a friend of his and Fremantle had been with his patron at Tenerife, Copenhagen and Trafalgar. But the admiral, while brave and able, was choleric, intensely ambitious, somewhat coarse-grained and well aware that he had been a contemporary of Nelson's and had fought alongside him as a fellow-captain in the battle with the *Ça Ira* when Hoste had only been a midshipman.

So he had not taken kindly to a letter from the captain of the *Bacchante* announcing his arrival in the Adriatic by stressing his pleasure at serving with another 'friend of poor Lord Nelson', who would understand how close their relationship had been. This presumption – as it must have seemed – was made worse by a complaint against Captain Rowley of the *Eagle*, under whose command the more junior captain had temporarily found himself. Hoste, plainly offended that, after his former triumphs, he should have to take orders from a less experienced officer in the sea that he saw as his birthright, reported that Rowley's behaviour towards him had been ungentlemanly. He was not to know that Fremantle referred to the senior captain as 'my friend Chas Rowley'. The admiral must also have been aware that Hoste knew the Adriatic better than he did and nettled when the victor of Lissa suggested obliquely that his squadron was not so active as it might be.

That relations between the two were not always sour was due partly to the admiral's recognition of the captain's professionalism and zeal and partly to the latter's impulsive generosity. Once, when the *Bacchante* anchored in Port St George, Hoste heard that the roof of Fremantle's house had leaked during a rainstorm and that he was living in damp discomfort, so immediately invited him to stay on board his frigate.

In the summer and autumn of 1812 it was clear that Napoleon had become so heavily committed to his invasion of Russia that daring offensive action on other fronts might succeed where, a few months earlier, they would have been folly. There were also reports of serious unrest along the Dalmatian coast and, particularly, among the Montenegrins in the mountains around the Gulf of Cattaro. It therefore seemed to Hoste, remembering his success in supporting the Calabrian partisans, that the time to clear the enemy from that coast was at hand and he asked Fremantle for a mere two hundred soldiers or marines to help him do this. But Fremantle was cautious; he did not believe the reports of unrest and had just written to tell Bentinck that he could not undertake amphibious operations against the Dalmatian coast without an expeditionary force of ten thousand men. So Hoste's request was regarded as something of an impertinence and the admiral's only reply was to tell him that he was required for service elsewhere.

This was to be on the most unexciting and unprofitable station in the Adriatic: the blockade of Venice. It was particularly unwelcome to Hoste because he had never fully recovered from the 'inflamation of the lungs' and the malaria, which had occasionally troubled him since his time in the *Mutine*, and the damp air blowing off the Venetian lagoon and marshes was regarded as particularly injurious to those with such tendencies.

At Port St George it was said that the only two captains who knew how to chase and take prizes were Rowley of the *Eagle* and Hoste. The latter now showed, on his first cruise, that the patrol off Venice need not be as unprofitable as it was reputed to be and snapped up a small convoy and its escort of gun-boats. On his second cruise, in September, contrary winds gave him an excuse to avoid Venice and he ran across to the Italian coast below Ancona where, near Vasto, he sighted a convoy of eighteen merchant vessels escorted by nine gun-boats armed with long twelve-pounders.

At the sight of the *Bacchante* bearing down upon them, the merchantmen ran themselves on to the beach, their crews taking up firing positions in scrub along the shore, while the gun-boats anchored to give covering fire. As the water was too shallow to allow the frigate close inshore, the boats were called away under command of O'Brien and an assault landing was launched. The enemy had formed a strong line with the sterns of their ships to the beach so presenting small targets and with the guns mounted in their bows. The British soon came under fire but replied only with cheers until the range was about fifty yards when they fired their carronades, loaded with grape-shot and canister, re-loaded and fired again and then boarded through the smoke.

The attack was a complete success – the largest and most complete capture of a convoy in the Adriatic since the campaign had begun – and the prizes, most of which were carrying cargoes of oil and almonds, were assembled for the passage to Lissa. But by evening the north-easterly wind blew up into a Boreas gale – the *bora* – after dark, scattering the prizes. There was no hope of collecting them in such a storm, so the *Bacchante* returned to Lissa to hope for their safe arrival.

When the frigate anchored, only four of the prizes had arrived so, next morning, Hoste and Yonge climbed into the hills to watch for their 'lost sheep' and were rewarded by seeing all but two sail into the harbour. One prize crew had lived for two days on raw salt beef, another, after two days without water, had survived by dipping ship's biscuits into the sweet oil that was the cargo.

It had been a pleasant day in the hills, looking down through the trees and vines to the *campanili* and jumbled roofs of the town and the harbour and counting the sails of the prizes as they appeared tossing across the wild sea.

During their walk, the two men stopped at the church of St Cyprian, standing by the path from the town of Lissa to Fort Wellington. The priest, whom they woke from his *siesta*, showed them with pride the miraculous wax figure of the Virgin, reciting the wonders it was said to have performed.

Such an event had occurred on the day of the Battle of Lissa, he said, clearly unaware of his visitors' identity. One of the figure's accomplishments, wrote Yonge afterwards, was 'the interest it evidently took in the success of Hoste's action. The lady was sometimes pale, sometimes red, as the tide of victory appeared to ebb and flow; so at least said the padre, and with the utmost seriousness, though he did not know that he was talking to Hoste: had he been aware of it, perhaps we should have been treated with a miracle. I do not see why the image should have shown any fears about the matter; a personage endued with such powers, ought, I think, to have foreseen the issue.'

The friends returned in good humour and Hoste went aboard Fremantle's flagship to report on the safe arrival of most of the prizes. While there he heard the report of a gun close at hand and a moment later was told that it had been fired from his own ship and that the eighteen-pound shot had narrowly missed the head of the flag-captain, who had been looking out of the window of the quarter-gallery lavatory.

Hurrying back to the *Bacchante*, Hoste was greeted with horrifying news. A lighter had moored alongside the frigate so that oil jars salvaged from sinking prizes could be loaded into her and some of the young volunteers, among them Charles Anson, had climbed down into her to be taught the process of loading. After watching for a while, the boys started a little horseplay and the boy Anson was on the deck of the lighter immediately in front of the muzzle of one of the *Bacchante*'s loaded main-deck guns when it fired, killing him instantly.

Nobody had touched the gun, which was not even primed, and no cause was ever found for the accident which blew apart the grandson of Coke of Norfolk. 'Poor lad,' wrote Hoste to his father. 'He was universally beloved, good-tempered, obliging and the most innocent-hearted creature that ever lived. Had he been my own son, I could not have been more attached . . . Poor Lady Anson! how much I feel for her.'

There was nothing to be done but give the boy a funeral to befit his family's rank. Had he died at sea, his body would have been launched over the side, sewn up in a hammock with a round-shot at his feet; had he died at home, Dixon Hoste would have presided over the laying-up of his coffin in the Coke mausoleum at Tittleshall church. But now he was taken across the harbour of Lissa in a sad procession of the *Bacchante*'s boats to a small cemetery sheltered by pines and there Hoste and Yonge conducted his funeral. There were stone-masons nearby, building Fort George, and they cut a stone slab to lie on his grave and chiselled into it the words, 'Hon Charles Anson AD 1812.'

The death of young Anson was particularly poignant because it had been caused by an inexplicable accident, unconnected with any warlike operation; unlike the death of poor Midshipman Few, who had sketched the Battle of Lissa for the marine artist Thomas Whitcombe. While bringing a prize to port on a stormy night, he was knocked over the side by the gybing boom and drowned.

Hoste, like Nelson, took particular care of his young volunteers and midshipmen, holding them back from the most dangerous expeditions, then, as their seamanship and physical strength increased, gradually allowing them to court danger. Until now he and they had been lucky: two midshipmen had been killed in the Battle of Lissa, but otherwise there had been no violent deaths. The dangers had, however, sharply increased. Partly this was the weather and, through this winter season, the Adriatic was constantly whipped by sudden, violent storms; and partly because of the swarms of enemy gun-boats that now protected coastal shipping and were usually ready to stand and fight.

So, for the young officers and aspirants, there were more risks and more narrow escapes. The two midshipmen commanding the missing prizes from the Vasto convoy were both lost: one drowned, the other to die as a prisoner in Italy. Another, Midshipman Rous, son of the Earl of Stradbroke, was saved, when his prize capsized in the same storm, by another midshipman, Waldegrave.

After the death of Anson, these losses continued. Although the *Bacchante* was supposed to be carrying out the routine of blockade – off Venice until Christmas and then off Corfu – her captain sought any opportunity of boarding enemy ships at sea or cutting them out from under coastal batteries. On one of the latter occasions, on the coast of Istria, where he said he had found himself 'from contrary winds', he had cut out a single *trabaccolo* from a bay where it had sheltered, defended by four or five hundred soldiers on shore.

One of the former, that amounted to a minor naval engagement, took place early in January. On the 6th, the *Bacchante*, accompanied by the brig *Weazel*, attacked and captured five French gun-boats bound for Otranto to collect the pay for the Corfu garrison and, two days later, they took six merchant vessels. The fight with the gun-boats was fierce, because their guns were mounted on swivels enabling them to traverse the weapons while maintaining formation, and Ned Hoste showed great zest in command of a gig. Thus, as small warships, they were useful captures and Hoste ordered prize crews to take them to the island of Zante, which was in British hands. One of the gun-boats, the *Calypso*, was commanded by Midshipman Pocock, the grandson of the admiral, and the last seen of him and his prize crew was as they set course for Zante into a gathering storm. The *Calypso*, Pocock and his men disappeared without trace; the midshipman, heir to vast prize-money from the Coromandel coast and Havana, having his brief naval career recorded in the frigate's logs and journals and on a marble plaque in Twickenham church beside the placid Thames.

Another prize was commanded by Midshipman Cornwallis Paley, a popular boy who had served as a volunteer in the *Amphion*. His prize crew consisted of three seamen and a lad and three Italian prisoners were left with him to help work the ship. After leaving the *Bacchante*, an Italian stowaway surrendered himself to Paley, begging for mercy and pleading that he was the owner of the cargo and had not been able to bring himself to abandon it without an appeal for its restoration. Paley apparently found him good company, and they continued towards Zante until becalmed off Corfu, when the stowaway suggested that his captor anchor and take his sailors below for dinner. So, leaving the lad and the Italians on deck, the others went below. The moment they were out of the way, the prisoners stabbed the boy to death and began clamping down the hatches to keep the rest of the prize crew below. Hearing the commotion, Paley jumped up from the dinner-table, ran up the ladder and forced open the hatch. As his head and shoulders appeared, one of the Italians seized his hair, pulled his head back on to the hatch-coaming and cut his throat.

As the other three British sailors pushed up the ladder and out on to the deck they were each cut down with an axe; one killed, the others horribly wounded. The Italians had only intended to kill the boy and, keeping the others imprisoned below, to sail the ship to Corfu; so the wounded men were not killed but handed over to the French authorities, who eventually sent them back to the *Bacchante* where they told their grisly story. Paley, they said, had not died immediately but had also been put ashore at Corfu, where they had helped him walk to the French headquarters. A military surgeon had treated his gashed throat but the wound had turned septic and he died.

Next month, more triumphs and disasters followed. At two o'clock on the morning of the 13th, the *Bacchante* came up with eight merchant vessels escorted by two French gun-boats, heavily armed. The whole convoy was captured by a boat attack commanded by Lieutenant Silas Hood, whom Hoste had chosen as first lieutenant, succeeding O'Brien, whose promotion to commander was imminent. It was a long, running fight and Hoste's report of it to the admiral began, 'My dear Sir, For these last forty-eight hours we have been doing nothing but burning, sinking and destroying the enemy's vessels.'

One gun-boat, *La Vigilante*, had on board General Bordé, who was on his way to take command of the garrison at Verona. In hope of avoiding detention, he claimed to be 'a *simple* passenger', as Hoste put it, adding, 'I am not to be duped by his French humbug.' Indeed, it had been by intercepting at sea letters written from Corfu by the general and his staff that the British had been able to reckon the position of the convoy on the 13th.

The loss of the young men deepened Hoste's depression for, in addition to his difficult relations with Fremantle, he was beset by personal disappointments and worries. Hearing that a new list of baronets was about to be announced, Dixon Hoste wrote with his customary over-optimism and exaggeration to his son with the news that his name was on it. Hoste replied, 'I think you are too sanguine about the title you say the Government intends to confer upon me . . . I cannot deny that I should feel gratified at the honour . . . though our family wants nothing to make it more honourable or ancient, yet I shall feel a noble pride in the reflection that I have added to the arms the insignia of the baronetcy.'

Hoste's name was not on the list – although his friend Jahleel Brenton's was – and he gently reproved his father, 'The total of baronets is come out, I see, and I am not included . . . You let your good wishes for my welfare carry you a little too far.' He expressed delight at Brenton's honour but wondered whether there might not be 'some concealed story' for the absence of recognition for the victor of Lissa, which 'is allowed by all my brother officers to stand as an action of the most brilliant nature, and all tell me, the first of the kind.'

There were also persistent, though unfounded, reports that he was to be taken away from his beloved frigates and given command of a ship of the line, where he would spend most of his time under the eye of an admiral and have little chance to show dash, or initiative, or collect prize-money. The latter was as necessary as ever since his father's improvidence continued. Just before leaving England in 1812, he had agreed to lend his father another £3400 and he was still, nearly a year later, making smaller payments – one of £20, another of £100 and so on – through his agent in London.

But now the full extent of his father's profligacy became apparent and, aghast, he wrote to him: 'I have received a letter from my Agent, which gives me much concern. It grieves me to find that my Father should deceive me, that *even the Interest* of the Money I came forward with two years ago should not be paid, how then can the Principal? I assure you I feel quite hurt that there should be occasion for me to say a word on the subject.'

Yet even this reproof was added as a postscript to a letter that seemed as affectionate as ever, ending, 'God bless you and remember me to all, my dear Father'.

Another worry was the elder of his two surviving sisters, Jane, who had now reached marriageable age. She had grown into a pretty and intelligent girl and her wit had made her a welcome guest at Holkham, where she became a particular friend of Thomas Coke's youngest daughter Elizabeth. She was also being courted but her mother had told William that she was doubtful about one ardent young man's intentions. To this Hoste replied, 'You can't conceive how anxious I am about Jane . . . I hope the young man is not playing the *rogue*, I hate your *shilly-shally* gentlemen, and if there is one character more detestable than another, it is that of trifling with the affections of a girl till she is made to esteem and love *him* who had actually had no serious intentions than going farther than a *flirtation* – By heavens he had better not trifle with the happiness of my Sister or he may live to regret it . . . no Sister of mine shall be the subject of *tea-table tattle*.'

Poor health – notably recurrent bouts of malaria – plagued him and, on one occasion, deprived him of some social recognition. In April, the *Bacchante* put into Malta, where her captain was received as a celebrity. His victory off Lissa was now part of Mediterranean legend and he himself made such 'an imposing impression' that the Governor and senior officers determined to give a ball in his honour. Yet, much as he loved a sociable occasion, Hoste felt too ill on the evening of the ball to attend and sent a note to the only other captain in the harbour, William Dillon of the armed troopship *Leopard*, asking him to take his place.

Dillon was reluctant because he had been wounded in both legs and was shy about hobbling round a dancing-floor. But Hoste pressed him to go, saying that the ball was to honour the Navy as a whole. 'I instantly made my arrangements,' Dillon said later, 'but, not intending to trip it on the light fantastic toe, I put on a stout pair of military boots.' In the event, he had to open the ball with a senior officer's wife but was then allowed to sit out the rest of the evening.

Increasingly, Hoste turned away from family worries and professional slights to the company of his brother-officers. He had himself chosen all those in the *Bacchante* as potentially congenial companions and his friendship with Yonge was now such that when the boats were sent inshore on a raid the chaplain would accompany the captain to the vantage point of the main-top to watch the fighting.

The captain's table and the wardroom were enhanced after the capture of *La Vigilante* by the presence of the French general and his staff, whom Yonge found to be 'gentlemanlike, pleasant and well-informed men, particularly the general, who is tolerably impartial in politics for a Frenchman'. There were many discussions about the war and European affairs, General Bordé maintaining that Napoleon had only undertaken the subjugation of Europe and the invasion of Russia to thwart British ambitions 'without any idea of individual benefit to France, but out of pure generosity to Europe in general'.

He also forecast a threat to Europe from Russia: 'a most formidable nation . . . dangerous to the liberties of Europe . . . she possesses men, arms, courage, abilities and inclination.' The British officers were surprised at the thoughtfulness of their prisoners since they had been brought up to think of French naval officers as fops or firebrands. 'The Revolution, I fancy, has effected a considerable change and they are become much more serious and reflecting,' was Yonge's comment.

Goodwill was engendered particularly by a coincidence revealed by the general's aide-de-camp, Richardot. On discovering the name of the frigate's captain, he had presented him with the compliments of a Madame Vallié. Hoste was surprised and puzzled. Then the Frenchman asked if he remembered, back in 1808 when he commanded the *Amphion*, capturing a merchant ship carrying corn and, as a passenger, a beautiful young Parisienne on her way to join her husband who was an artillery officer in Italy.

This had been Madame Vallié and Hoste might remember that despite his courtesy to her she appeared terrified and had refused to leave her cabin to walk on the quarterdeck. This, he now revealed, was because she had been told that 'the English were cannibals and devoured their prisoners of war. Possessed with this notion she would not show herself on deck, that she might not excite the appetites of the sailors. She had even congratulated herself on being taken in a vessel laden with wheat in the hopes that such a supply of food, somewhat more natural, might defer her fate long enough to afford a chance of escape.'

Finally, however, she was convinced that the British were as gallant with ladies as they seemed and thereafter held them – and particularly their handsome captain – in 'the highest esteem'. Since her release she had constantly repeated this entertaining story and, only the night before Richardot had sailed from Corfu, her husband had told him that if he was to be captured by the British on the voyage he hoped it would be by Captain Hoste.

When the ship returned to Lissa after a patrol there were social diversions to be had in the other ships of the squadron and ashore. Lissa itself had changed dramatically since Hoste had first anchored there. Now, above the harbour mouth, stood the gleaming walls and ramparts of Fort George, completed this year. Over its gates was carved its dedication to 'George the Third. By the Grace of God King of Great Britain and Ireland, etc.' and within, off its two courtyards were officers' quarters and barracks. Below were magazines, a vast cistern for rainwater and a narrow passage, that could be used as a sallyport during a siege, running down to the water's edge. It was a fortress of which any naval base would be proud.

The town itself had become relatively sophisticated now that it was a recognized seat of government. Many of the resident British officers and officials had brought their families to live in rented houses in the town and the Governor and Admiral Fremantle both had comfortable residences. Even the indigenous population had changed, abandoning their national dress for clothes cut from the cheap English cloth that was passing through the port to be smuggled into Continental ports.

The officers of the other frigates, met ashore, tended to be good company for many of them were young men of some social standing who had used their influence to serve under a dashing frigate captain and were therefore men of spirit as well as education. Some were linguists, others had knowledge of the Classics and therefore of their Adriatic surroundings, others were artistic or musical. One of Rowley's officers in the *Eagle* was Lieutenant William Innes Pocock, the son of the fashionable marine artist Nicholas Pocock and a distant kinsman of poor Midshipman Pocock. He was himself an accomplished artist as well able to commemorate some brisk action with a lively watercolour as conduct a survey and draw charts.

All the ships' companies were in some degree musical even if this only meant the ability to play the fiddle or sing a shanty. The officers were, like their counterparts ashore, accustomed to entertaining themselves with musical evenings and it was this that led Hoste to devise – probably with Yonge's help – his secret musical code.

There were known to be French spies among the crews of merchantmen passing through Lissa, just as there were in any coastal town occupied, or visited by, the British. It was therefore important that messages should not be written in plain English and sent by messenger, just as talk of plans must not be allowed in public places. Therefore Hoste recorded in an inside page of the little notebook, which was both a pocket signal book and muster book, what he described as his 'New Secret Telegraph'.

A message written in this cypher would appear to be a simple musical score. However, as his key showed 'the apparent notes of music' were linked with the numbers of flags in the standard signal book, punctuation being marked by bars and sentences by double bars. There were variations, which could be agreed upon between signal officers, such as reading from right to left, and musical symbols could be used to represent the names of ships. Characteristically, the example that

Hoste chose to give in his pocket-book translated as, 'I shall attack after dark'.

Means of secret communication at sea, or within sight of hostile telescopes, were also devised. The most simple of these was to signal a rendezvous, this indicated by the hoisting of a French flag and a numeral that would relate to a particular place: 99 for Lissa, 57 for the channel between Lissa and Lesina, 78 for Fiume, 49 for the Gulf of Cattaro and 50 for Ragusa.

While Hoste was making so remarkable a success of what had seemed likely to be dull blockading routine, without, as he complained, a word of congratulation or thanks from Fremantle, the admiral was engaged in a major counter-offensive against the French. Early in 1813 he had used his strategic reserve of the 35th Regiment to seize the islands of Lagosta [Lastovo] and Curzola, making the latter an advanced base for further operations and imposing on it the sort of formal British rule as Lissa now had. In May, the *Bacchante* was given her first cruise – as opposed to a patrol – since Fremantle had taken command in the Adriatic and Hoste was ordered to sail in the Gulf of Fiume and among the islands.

But his luck did not hold. Almost immediately, a convoy of seventy *trabaccoli*, mostly laden with wheat, was reported near Carlebago [Karlobag] but could only be reached by a narrow, shallow channel, which had never been navigated by a ship the size of the *Bacchante*. Hoste was not deterred but, when severe head winds necessitated constant tacking, the attempt seemed hopeless and he sent his boats ahead under oars. The crews pulled for thirty hours against the wind and current but, by the time they reached the anchorage, the enemy had heard of their approach and the convoy – thought to have been worth at least £50,000 in prize-money – had sailed six hours before the exhausted British arrived.

However, Hoste took Carlebago after a brisk bombardment, then moved up the coast to anchor off Zara, which had been the destination of the corn convoy, in the vain hope of snapping up some of the fugitives. Then his luck did change. Making for Lissa, strong adverse winds offered an excuse to run across to Ancona and, off the Italian coast, a large convoy was sighted and seven of the frigate's boats were sent inshore after it. The convoy proved to have almost as many escorts as merchant ships – eleven gun-boats and fourteen merchant vessels – and a fierce hand-to-hand fight followed as the British boats ran through a barrage of grape-shot and musketry to board. Hoste and Yonge were, as usual, watching from the main-top, and the former reported, 'Teddy and Lord Radstock's son, Waldegrave, both boarded the French commodore, and carried him *l'épée à la main* –

excuse my French.' The boarders lost three killed and six wounded but Yonge recorded, 'You may cut sailors to pieces, but you cannot conquer their spirit. One of them had his right arm shattered while in the act of boarding a gun-boat; instead of retreating, he took his cutlass with his left hand and continued to press forward as long as he could stand, holding up the bleeding remnant as a signal for his comrades to avenge him.' The *Bacchante* returned to Lissa with nine prizes under her guns.

The strategic balance in the Adriatic was changing again. Napoleon's invasion of Russia and the destruction of his army on the retreat from Moscow had absorbed so much of his military effort that it had been possible to clear the French from most of their Illyrian Provinces north of Ragusa by the time Austria felt confident enough to again declare war on France in August. Now an Austrian army under General Count Laval Nugent, an Irish soldier of fortune, was to advance on Fiume and Trieste to cooperate with Fremantle in cutting the enemy's lines of communication with the Balkans and beyond.

Even before the declaration of war, Fremantle had, without Austrian help, achieved half of this aim by storming Fiume with landing-parties from his squadron, which consisted of his flagship, three frigates and a brig. The seamen and marines, led by Rowley of the *Eagle* and Hoste, first took the fort and batteries then 'boldly dashed on through the town, although annoyed by the enemy's musketry from the windows of the houses and a field-piece placed in the centre of the great street'. All the enemy guns were taken but no prisoners, since the garrison had taken to its heels.

Rowley was made Governor and Hoste Lieutenant-Governor of Fiume but the appointment, and indeed the occupation, was short, as the squadron was to move along the coast to attack other French positions. It was not until the end of August that Austrian troops marched into the town and garrisoned it.

The *Bacchante* played her customarily active part in the coastal operations and, in September, was off the coast of the Istrian peninsula awaiting the proposed Austrian attack on Trieste. After cruising off the port, just out of gun-shot, they heard heavy gunfire ashore at daybreak on the 10th of the month, but could see nothing through the haze. Then, as Hoste was sitting down to breakfast, a boat came alongside with a message from a senior Austrian officer, Baron d'Aspré, to say that the town had fallen to their attack and he would be grateful for advice on ways of assaulting the castle, which was still held by the French.

Hoste at once called for his gig and was pulled into the bay. The town was silent as the boat entered the harbour, past the twenty heavy guns mounted on the mole and under the fourteen cannon of the shore batteries. The bulk of the citadel above the town was now showing through the haze as the gig ran towards the quay and Hoste rose to step ashore. At that moment all the batteries opened fire, shot lashing the water round the boat. Hoste shouted to the coxswain to put his helm hard over and to the seamen to pull for the open sea.

Watching with horror from the *Bacchante*, the officers realized that there was nothing they could do to help. Under such fire at point-blank range the boat would be smashed at any moment and, it seemed, only a miracle could save it. 'We were obliged to remain trembling spectators of the scene,' said Yonge, 'watching every shot as it pitched and rebounded over the boat. Several fell so near, that we lost sight of them in the splash of water occasioned by the force and size of the ball.'

What had happened, it later emerged, was that d'Aspré had, in fact, taken the mole and the quayside but that the French in the citadel had counter-attacked, driven them out and again manned their guns. Seeing the boat put off from the British frigate, they had held their fire until its destruction seemed certain.

Miraculously, Hoste escaped – 'not a hair of him or his crew was touched' – and Yonge's apprehension turned to admiration as 'with that coolness which never foresakes him, he contrived to steer the boat so as to give the shot the least possible chance of hitting him, and he even stood up in the boat with the flag in his hand, as if in defiance.'

This melodramatic escapade and theatrical flourish was appropriate in that it marked the opening of a performance in this theatre of war which would present, against a background of spectacular scenery, William Hoste as its leading player.

IX

THE SUMMITS OF CATTARO

In the autumn of 1813, Napoleon's dreams of conquest in the East – a grand march through the Ottoman Empire to the Levant, Egypt and, finally, India itself – were kept alive by his possession of two great fortress-cities that commanded the way eastward. One was Cattaro, with its magnificent natural harbour leading to the way, through Montenegro, deep into the Balkans. The other, Ragusa, which had out-lived Venice as a centre of international commerce and shipping and, even under French domination, retained much of its ancient cunning and prestige.

The British now controlled the Dalmatian coast and islands to the north of Ragusa and had taken both Fiume and Trieste. Yet these two cities remained as a reminder that Napoleon might, despite the disasters in Russia and the imminent invasion of France from Spain by the British under Wellington, still surprise his enemies once again by some brilliant strategic stroke. While the French flag flew over Cattaro and Ragusa, the threat to all that Nelson and Sidney Smith had achieved remained.

For more than a year, Fremantle had appreciated this and had considered the action he could take. As early as July of the preceding year, Colonel Robertson had reported that the native population around the Gulf of Cattaro was ready to rise against the French and would do so if British support were forthcoming. But a condition of this was a promise that, in the event of failure or the withdrawal of the British, the entire insurgent population would be evacuated to escape reprisals. Fremantle dismissed this offer as impracticable and wrote to Bentinck in Palermo that he could not attempt to take Cattaro and Ragusa without the use of that expeditionary force of ten thousand men.

Otherwise, all he felt capable of attempting was the blockade of both places and, at the beginning of 1813, he felt that this might eventually prove decisive. However, in August he was confessing to Pellew that he had been over-sanguine in his expectations: 'I observe that the French, finding it impossible to get supplies by their coasting vessels, have been employing lately hundreds of natives on the publick roads, and that they now get their Corn and flour upon mules into those places; the labour and expence of this mode must be excessive; I am however afraid my expectations will not be realised.'

Then, early in October, Fremantle received a disturbing report from the captain of the ship on blockade duty off the Gulf of Cattaro. This was that the population had, without waiting for British help, revolted against the French, whose troops were reported to be besieged in their forts and garrison towns. Immediate action was essential for the most important political and strategic reasons because the gulf and its hinterland were claimed by both Austria and Russia. It seemed that, while the more civilized inhabitants of the coastal towns favoured the former, the warlike Montenegrins in the mountains supported the latter. With reports arriving of a Russian army advancing towards the Adriatic to help fight the French, it was clearly of the utmost importance that they should not occupy Cattaro and Ragusa before the Austrians.

The most urgent action would have to be at Cattaro. Little, it seemed, could be attempted but, by supporting the *Bocchese* – the traders and seafarers of Venetian descent in the coastal towns of the *Bocca di*

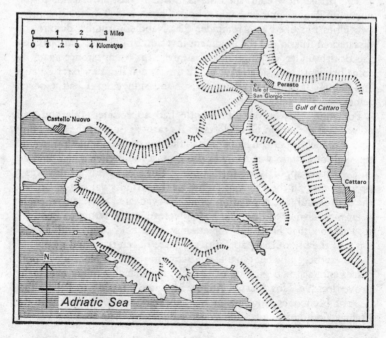

THE GULF OF CATTARO

Cattaro – against the wild Montenegrins, the situation, whatever it proved to be, might be stabilized pending the arrival of an Austrian expeditionary force.

The man for such a task was obviously Captain Hoste for, however cool their personal relations, Fremantle realized that no British officer knew the coast better and he had also had some experience of diplomacy. So the admiral reported to the British Ambassador in Vienna, Lord Aberdeen, that he was sending Hoste in the *Bacchante* 'with some money, arms and ammunition to take management of the whole concern'. He then stressed that the Austrians must act quickly because the Montenegrins were 'a lawless banditti not to be depended upon, and because the Dalmatians consider them as bad as the French . . .' Aware of the anarchy and confusion that would probably arise from 'the animosity of such a body of people without order or discipline', he was dispatching the frigate but urged that the Austrians send a senior officer and some troops to join Hoste as quickly as possible.

Since Fremantle's early days in the Adriatic, Hoste had been offering to attack any French garrison, including Cattaro and Ragusa, if he were given a striking force of two hundred soldiers or marines and now, summoned on board the flagship to receive his orders, he repeated this request. If he were to have any chance of reducing the French fortresses – the citadel of Cattaro was said to mount ninety guns, and was only one of several fortresses in the gulf; Ragusa was thought to be defended by a hundred and fifty cannon – then he must have a detachment of marines and some guns and mortars. His request was refused and he left the admiral's cabin surprised and disappointed but, as he said later, 'in no way daunted by an apparent determination on the part of another to prevent the success of an enterprise which himself was projecting.'

Fremantle's refusal was probably due primarily to his belief that nothing could be achieved against enemy positions of such strength and that the most that could be attempted was a holding action until the arrival of the Austrians. Yet, since he had persistently given the most successful and experienced of his captains the most mundane missions, there may also have been an element of animosity and even jealousy in giving him so thankless and seemingly hopeless a task.

So, after a stop at Lissa for ammunition and supplies, the *Bacchante* stood for Ragusa to take under Hoste's orders the sloop *Saracen*, of eighteen guns, which, with three gun-boats, had been blockading the coast under command of Captain John Harper. Eight years older than Hoste and the son of a naval officer who had been killed in action, Harper, whose many experiences of action had included the Battle of the Nile and who had served in the Adriatic for more than four years, had not had the advantage of influential patronage. His promotion had been slow so that he had not even attained the rank of post captain. But he was a brave and efficient officer and was undismayed when Hoste told him that he intended to take both Cattaro and Ragusa with nothing more than a frigate and a sloop and whatever help he could get from the partisans ashore.

On the morning of 13th October, the two ships entered the Gulf of Cattaro. Seen with the sun rising above the mountains of Montenegro, the mouth of the great harbour was difficult to discern and could well have been no more than another channel between two islands or a bay sheltered by headlands. Once past the mountains guarding the entrance, the ships were in what was, in effect, an inland sea, as isolated from the Adriatic as was that sea from the Mediterranean.

Within the gulf was an unexpected danger, always present whatever the risks of war. This was the weather; for although the sequence of deep basins were sheltered by mountains from some of the gales that swept the Adriatic, they engendered their own ferocious squalls, thunderstorms and the heaviest rainfall in Europe. This was at its worst from early autumn to early spring and already, in September, the *Bacchante* had been struck by lightning.

The horror of this and the consequent risk of fire was, at this time, described by a captain of the Royal Marines in the *Eagle*. Southward bound and having just passed the Gulf of Cattaro in search of a reported French frigate, the weather had suddenly changed. 'The weather became perfectly calm and the sky so much overcast that it was impossible to distinguish an object on deck. In the space of twenty minutes a most violent storm commenced from the north-west accompanied with incessant thunder and lightning to a most alarming degree. While the hands were aloft taking in sail, a piercing shriek was heard from the main-top. By a kind of sympathy, the panic became general and the most dismal howlings and cries were heard throughout the ship. It was truly awful. A fire-ball had struck the main-top, knocked off one of the iron hoops, the bolt of which was completely severed as if it had been nipped by a pair of shears, and wounded eight men. They were brought down in a state of insensibility – their shirts and stockings burnt to a cinder and their bodies mangled in a most shocking manner – literally flayed alive.'

Not only could such dangers be expected in the twenty miles of basins and narrows that led up to the town of Cattaro at their head, but squalls could strike without warning, tearing off sails, snapping masts, or twirling a moored ship round her anchor. As in the case of the *Eagle*, the sky could suddenly seem to turn midday into midnight and grey torrents of rain could, for hours, blot out mountainsides only a few hundred yards distant.

The enclosed, dangerous and claustrophobic waters into which Hoste now led his little squadron of a frigate, a sloop and three gunboats was already in warlike turmoil. Entering the vast outer basin of the gulf that ran more than ten miles from north-west to south-east, he found himself in a superb natural harbour, up to some twenty fathoms in depth, bordered by gently-sloping mountains that gave it the appearance of an arid Scottish sea-loch. Opposite the entrance stood the town of Castello Nuovo [Herzog-Novi] and its fortresses.

Like the other towns of the gulf, this had changed hands many times in its history, having been ruled by both Venetians and Turks and occupied by the Spanish and, briefly, by the Austrians and Russians, before falling into French hands in 1807. It was defended by two forts: one on the waterfront; the other a massive circular keep above the town, known to the British as Spanish Fort because of its origins.

Of more than one thousand, five hundred enemy troops known to be on the shores of the gulf, nearly six hundred were at Castello Nuovo. Of these only about thirty were French, most of the others being Croatian levies under French officers. The town itself mounted only seven guns – one a twenty-four-pounder – but Spanish Fort, above it on the hillside, was defended by fifteen.

At this point the gulf was some two miles wide and although the far shore was just within the extreme range of the shore batteries, they could not hope to prevent the British ships from passing, even in daylight and clear visibility. Thus Hoste would be able to continue into the widest part of the outer basin and to the narrows that ran north-east to the inner basin, and from there the gulf assumed its most sinister and threatening form.

These narrows, only two hundred and thirty yards wide, between steep mountains and subject to strong, unpredictable winds and strong currents, opened up an awe-inspiring view.

Directly ahead, beyond the narrows and across the inner basin, the stately little town of Perasto [Perast] stood beneath a wall of grey limestone mountains. Its *campanili* and *palazzi* proclaimed past wealth, for this had been a great commercial port and the home of famous ship-builders, sea-captains and navigators. Between the narrows and Perasto lay two small islands: on one, man-made on a rocky reef, stood a church; on the other, San Giorgio, had been built a modest Benedictine abbey and a fort, mounting sixteen guns – seven of them twenty-four-pounders – that commanded the narrows and the inner waters. Perasto and San Giorgio were each defended by a garrison of about seventy-five Croatians and Italians under French command.

If the narrows could be navigated and forced, the gulf beyond was something to chill the heart of the most experienced seafarer. 'It is impossible to figure to yourself . . . a scene more grand and awful,' Yonge recorded. 'The sides of the basins . . . are nothing but lofty mountains, whose summits, blasted by the fury of the Boreas, are generally enveloped in clouds.'

To the north-west of Perasto, the gulf ran into a dead-end, shut in by bare mountains, its water, when still, sometimes boiling with mushrooms of smoothly-swirling water from an underground river. To the south-east, it ran towards another apparent wall of mountain, then turned sharply south to where, more than five miles from Perasto, the fortress-city of Cattaro itself clung to the mountainside at the head of the gulf.

Once a city of the Greeks, Romans, Byzantines, Slavs, Serbs, Hungarians, Croatians and Bosnians, Cattaro had, for some three and a half centuries, been under the rule of Venice. Its stone *palazzi*, churches, merchants' houses and its massive walls, thirty feet high, that ran up the steeps to the fort of San Giovanni on its peak above the town, had the style and stability of their Venetian builders. It was a city of such spectacular and melodramatic presence that it could remind the arriving visitor more of the wildest imaginings of a romantic landscape painter than of a mercantile and military town, the entrepôt and guardian of the Balkan hinterland.

The fort and ramparts of Cattaro mounted sixty-five guns and were garrisoned by more than seven hundred troops, again mostly Croatians and Italians, with French officers, artillerymen and gendarmerie. The commander of all French forces in the gulf, who had his headquarters here, was a formidable veteran of Napoleon's Continental campaigns, *Général de Brigade* Etienne Gauthier. Until the rising of the Montenegrins there had been so little activity that, in 1812, he had applied for transfer to a more active theatre but his request had been rejected by the Emperor himself. Now, at the head of his garrison within the walls of Cattaro, he faced the possibility of a British attack with a confidence based as much on the formidable natural defences of the gulf as upon the fighting qualities of his soldiers.

On 13th October, Hoste sailed past Castello Nuovo, a few cannon-shot splashing into the water short of his ships, which returned the fire more as a matter of principle than for effect. Once out of range, he anchored and began to assess the state of whatever uprising had taken place. It became apparent that the Bocchese had surrounded Castello Nuovo and Spanish Fort, but, lacking artillery, were unable to attempt more. Meanwhile, at the head of the gulf the Montenegrins, led by their Metropolitan Archbishop Petar I – otherwise Pietro Petrovich – had invested Cattaro but were similarly thwarted by the defences. It was also clear that the Bocchese and the Montenegrins, while sharing a hatred of the French, would not fight as allies. The former, supporting Austrian claims to sovereignty, feared and hated the latter whom, as partisans of the Russian cause, they regarded as dangerous savages.

'The Montenegrins are a most extraordinary people,' wrote Yonge, 'and have stormed several places that were deemed almost impregnable and they have inspired much terror into the French . . . and give them no quarter, but they are such a ferocious set, that no one likes to have anything to do with them.'

Hoste's first task was, however, to support the insurgents in the reduction of Castello Nuovo to secure his free access to the open sea, then to take the forts dominating the narrows before their defences could be strengthened. So, sending Harper with the gun-boats and ship's boats, manned and armed, to attack San Giorgio, he set about frightening the garrisons of Castello Nuovo and Spanish Fort into surrender.

On the morning of the 14th, Hoste sent a boat ashore under a flag of truce with a summons to surrender to the commander of Spanish Fort, to which he replied that he must be given time, promising a decision by five in the afternoon. But, at five, he pleaded that his reply could not be given until next morning and, rather than begin the laborious process of preparing a siege, Hoste agreed reluctantly to wait.

Meanwhile, Harper had succeeded brilliantly. Bocchese partisans had already landed on San Giorgio and occupied the monastery but had been unable to storm the fort. But when its garrison saw, advancing towards them through the narrows, a flotilla of British boats, packed with marines and gun-crews standing ready by their cannon and carronades in the bows they lost heart and told their commander, a French colonel and a member of the *Légion d'honneur*, that they would kill him unless he surrendered immediately. This he did and, after some dispute as to whether the Bocchese or the British should take possession, it was Harper who herded the prisoners into his boats and left a small garrison to hold the island for King George.

While awaiting a reply from the French at Castello Nuovo and Spanish Fort, Hoste went ashore to meet the Montenegrin Archbishop who was coming to a house near the anchorage for the purpose. His reputation preceded him, Yonge noting that he was said to be 'of a very different nature to his adherents. He is a man of education; has been some time in Russia and is very much respected by everybody. His influence is almost unbounded with the Montenegrins, except in the article of plunder. He has made several overtures to our Government for assistance, which have not been listened to till now.'

When Hoste and his party, including the chaplain, landed, the Archbishop had not arrived but they were met by a party of chieftains who promised to support the British with any number of armed men they required.

'The right reverend soldier arrived about two,' reported Yonge. 'A very handsome man he is; tall; of a commanding figure; and of mild, but majestic aspect. He wears a long white beard, and is about fifty years of age: his manners graceful and easy. He wore a purple silk robe and cassock, with a red ribbon, like that of the Order of the Bath, and a star upon his breast; and when he goes to battle, he is covered with orders and stars. His patron is the Emperor of Russia. There were but few Montenegrins with him and those, I take it for granted, the best of the flock.'

Hoste's first impressions of Archbishop Petar were equally favourable. He was clearly a man of culture as well as action and, as a *Cavaliere di Russia*, enjoyed social as well as ecclesiastical standing. 'A very shrewd, clever man,' he described him to Fremantle, although his immediate followers were '500 desperate Banditti'.

There seemed every hope that he would provide any number of irregular infantry, and men for working-parties would be made available if and when a siege became necessary. As a first step, they agreed that a summons to surrender would also be sent to General Gauthier at Cattaro and terms for this were drawn up and the summons sent off by boat under a flag of truce.

As much as Hoste liked the formidable prelate, he disliked another priest who now made his appearance as the only representative of the Austrian Government in the Gulf of Cattaro. This was the *Abbate* Jacobo Brunazzi, whom the British naval chaplain described as 'a sort of commissioner . . . an intriguing, self-sufficient priest, who would rather do mischief than do nothing. His tongue never ceases, and, like most others who are continually talking, says many things that are either false or foolish, or perhaps both.'

It seemed, at first, that while the Montenegrin leader would do all he could to defeat the French, the principal aim of the Austrian commissioner was to stall Hoste's efforts until the arrival of an Austrian expeditionary force.

Next morning, the commander of Spanish Fort sent a messenger to ask Hoste for more exact terms of capitulation. He was told that the garrison might surrender with the honours of war, the officers would remain under parole until exchanged for British prisoners, the Croatians would be sent home but that the French and Italian soldiers would remain prisoners of war. The commander objected to this last condition, asking that they be returned with their arms and ammunition to a

French port. At this Hoste lost patience, replying that the fort and town had just five minutes to surrender on his terms or face the consequences. Realizing that this might mean an assault and massacre by the Montenegrins, who had now joined the Bocchese round Spanish Fort, the French commander surrendered at once.

Next morning the British took possession to the satisfaction of the French officers, who said that at least they could claim some credit for surrendering to the Royal Navy rather than to guerrillas.

It had been a brisk and successful operation but Hoste was dissatisfied. For several months he had been in poor health and under strain and he now became increasingly irritated with his allies who were proving more troublesome than his enemies. On his arrival in the gulf he had published a proclamation calling for unity: 'The advantages which England, in freeing this country from its oppressors, offers to its inhabitants is happiness and tranquillity . . . We wish only that you should unite hand and heart in the cause with us, and never put the sword to its scabbard till your country is freed from her oppressors . . . But I warn you at the same time that the English flag will be no support to those who take up arms under the cloak of expelling the French, and . . . basely turn them against their friends and brethren.'

To appease the rival factions, he ordered that the *Bacchante* should fly the colours of both Austria and Russia from her mast-heads and warned the Montenegrins that, unless they maintained discipline in Castello Nuovo, the latter would be hauled down. As few as possible were allowed into the town but only a promise of extra rations from the frigate took their minds off loot, Yonge remarking that 'a small allowance of biscuit tranquillized the Montenegrins'.

The next move against the French was fraught with problems. The *Bacchante* had not even been able to pass the narrows into the inner basin because of calms and contrary winds and, even when this proved possible, it was difficult to see what could be achieved against a fortress-city as formidable as Cattaro. However, Hoste decided that the guns on the island of San Giorgio should be taken by boat to the head of the gulf to support the irregulars besieging the city, although he recognized that its capture would be 'a business of great labour and difficulty, if at all practicable'.

But, to Hoste's amazement and anger, the dismantling of the battery commanding the narrows achieved what neither his exhortations nor fear of the French had done in uniting the Bocchese and the Montenegrins. Their apprehension – a natural one in view of the fate of the Calabrian partisans – was that having removed their defences, the British might decide to withdraw their warships, so leaving them at the mercy of a French relief force, or whoever coveted their towns. The leaders of the Bocchese therefore sent Hoste a tactfully-worded letter, saying that 'if the cannon was taken away for the purpose of reducing Cattaro, they cannot but approve of such determination; but if the contrary, the Community urge that the said artillery may be disposed of for the defence of their province, but not to be transported elsewhere.' A similar message was received from the Archbishop of Montenegro.

Hoste was outraged by what he considered insolence. To the Bocchese, he replied, 'Do not disgust us with trifling complaints, or ill-grounded suspicions . . . I return you the letter you sent me; I should be sorry to retain in my possession such a testimony of your distrust and want of confidence.' To the Archbishop he wrote, 'The guns shall be given back to the inhabitants; they were intended to be got up the mountains to act against Cattaro, but I shall not undertake that measure now.'

The Montenegrin prelate he had addressed with courtesy but he had lost all patience with the Abbot Brunazzi, whom he accused of pursuing Austrian policies against Russia and 'forgetting the necessity of unanimity against France'. For the first time he threatened him with arrest for subversion and responsibility for the 'anarchy and confusion', which, he told him, 'your intrigues, Sir, have so much assisted to produce.' To Fremantle, he added, 'If I had my way, I'd hang him.'

To the admiral he reported his exasperation with 'such a litigious, turbulent people' and that he was planning to abandon his attempts against Cattaro. A small garrison would remain in Spanish Fort and the *Saracen* would be left to blockade the inner basin and Cattaro, while he himself sailed northward to see whether he could achieve more against Ragusa.

Accordingly he told the Bocchese and the Montenegrins that he was not authorized to interfere with their internal affairs and, having returned their guns, would leave, although he would visit the gulf from time to time to keep an eye on the French. He sailed on 26th October – his temper not improved by the frigate running aground at the mouth of the gulf – and expressed his relief at being rid of Balkan politics. 'The archbishop is playing a deep game,' noted Yonge. 'His evident aim in paying court to us is to procure powder and ammunition . . . but I am mistaken if a hundredth part of it will be expended against the French. Unless some power sends a large regular force, he and his hordes will overrun Cattaro . . .'

While these allies had earned Hoste's irritation they were worth more than Yonge's contempt in describing 'our illustrious allies' as being mostly 'mere savages, with just wit enough to be above bits of glass and rusty nails and therefore the more intractable.' Seeing the arrival of the British as a threat to their own conflicting aims, each determined to make the maximum use of what support was offered, without helping the British to occupy and, perhaps, annex the region themselves. They therefore formed their own alliance of convenience, calling their joint council the Central Commission for the Civil Affairs of the Bocca di Cattaro, and presenting Hoste with a façade of unity.

The only regular force that would be available for the siege of Cattaro was Austrian and there were reports that they were advancing south from the conquered Illyrian Provinces and were about to lay siege to Ragusa itself. So, to hear the latest news, Hoste, after calling briefly at Ragusa, stood for Lissa and lay off the harbour mouth, awaiting a boat which brought out a major of the 35th Regiment with a report that the French had evacuated Spalato, which could be occupied without delay. This was a stimulating prospect, for the capture of a major city, even without a fight, would be reported in the newspapers at home.

It would also relieve some of Hoste's frustrations, for he had, at Ragusa, finally lost confidence in his bold plans to capture both the great fortress-cities. He had just confessed this to Fremantle, writing, 'I don't flatter myself with hopes of taking Cattaro except by blockade ... Shot are of no use. It is on the pinnacle of a high mountain. General Gauthier has retired there with 600 men and 2 months' provisions.'

Then he had continued. 'The short time I was off Ragusa was sufficient to convince me of the strength of the Ragusan forts ...' Austrian plans to besiege and capture first this city, then the other, would, he added, 'make you laugh could you see the place, which in the opinion of Captain Harper and myself is impregnable.'

In his depression he had even asked if he could be relieved and ordered to 'join the active operations off Trieste'.

So the frigate ran across the sound, passed the channel between Lesina and Brazza, anchored off Spalato and landed a detachment of the 35th Regiment and her own marines. The French troops had departed but there were some officials to be arrested and the city to be occupied until the arrival of the Austrians to whom it would be handed over.

Yonge, with his Classical education, was fascinated by the gigantic ruins of the palace of the Emperor Diocletian, in and around which the city had been built, and mused upon the contrast between the remains of Roman civilization and the 'ferocity and barbarism' of its present surroundings. From the brisk orderliness of the frigate's quarterdeck, the chaplain looked across to the massive ruins and to the great lime-stone mountains beyond and felt the urgings of both curiosity and caution. 'Perhaps no part of the world is less known than the interior of Dalmatia,' he mused in his journal, 'or offers more to gratify the curiosity of travellers, if it were not for the almost impenetrable nature of the country and the barbarism of the natives. In some districts they are so uncivilized as to retain the ceremony of sacrificing animals previous to the commencement of any military expedition.'

On the arrival of the Austrian troops at Spalato, the British force returned to Lissa, where they prepared for an attack on the last of the major islands still occupied by the French, Lesina. This was to be very different from the chaotic rampagings of the irregulars in the Gulf of Cattaro; it was to be conducted entirely by regular British soldiers, sailors and marines. A company of the 35th Regiment was to attack the town while the marines and sailors of the *Bacchante* and the frigate *Mermaid*, under the command of Hoste, would make a night march up the hill behind the town and, at dawn, assault Fort Napoleon on the summit.

The two ships sailed from Port St George at ten o'clock on the night of 8th November with a fair wind and the light of a full moon. At two o'clock next morning, the landing-parties silently clambered into the boats and were pulled ashore. While the infantry deployed to attack the town, Hoste led his marines and sailors up the hill.

From the sea, Lesina and its gently-sloping hills seemed to offer no obstacles beyond the fortifications. When the fugitive frigates from the Battle of Lissa had taken refuge in the harbour, Hoste had often scanned it with his telescope, noting the walls and bastions, the *campanili* and the Venetian theatre and the fort on the summit of the green hill beyond. This hill had seemed to offer easy going; there would certainly be a well-worn track from the town to the fort and its slopes seemed nothing to those who had clambered about the crags of Montenegro.

But distant appearance had been deceptive. The moon threw black shadows to hide rocky crevasses overgrown with brambles; thorns tore at uniforms and equipment and sharp stones cut open shoes; tall grass covered crannies that could break an ankle and the sharp points of cactus stabbed like the Spanish bayonets that gave them their name. Cursing, the column stumbled and struggled through the undergrowth and over the rocks and when the sky above Dalmatia showed its first streaks of grey, it illuminated faces smeared with sweat and blood, gasping with exhaustion, while the outline of Fort Napoleon was thrown into relief against the dawn, still high above them.

At the appointed time, the infantry, far below, rushed the town, taking it by surprise and catching a dozen French officers in their beds. But, long before the sun came up, the garrison of Fort Napoleon were standing-to, amused by the sight of the red coats of the marines floundering in the thickets below the walls and only now coming within musket-range. The commander of the fort had not been among the officers taken in the town and now he contemptuously refused Hoste's summons to surrender, rightly appreciating that there was nothing that a few score men with muskets and cutlasses could achieve against his walls and guns. So, ignominiously, Hoste and his men struggled down the hill again and retreated to their ships.

A few days later, the *Bacchante* suffered another humiliation. Sailing southward again, she had chased a *trabaccolo* to the shelter of a little fort and a landing-party was sent ashore to board the former and destroy the latter. When the charge was laid under the walls, one of Hoste's officers, Lieutenant Gosling, lit the fuse. But instead of lighting the slow-burning port-fire that would give him time to escape before the explosion, he touched off the fast-burning powder-train, and the charges blew up almost instantly, killing him.

Despite such setbacks, Hoste found that he could achieve something on this coast. While the Austrians, supported by Captain Cadogan in the *Havannah*, were slowly working their way down the coast from Spalato, the Ragusans, led by a few of their nobility, had risen against the French and driven most of them within the walls of Ragusa itself. Nothing more could be achieved against the city without the siege-trains that only the British or Austrians could supply and the Ragusans hesitated in pressing either ally for such aid. The Austrians, while exhorting the peasantry to rise against the French, made no mention of restoring the independence of the Ragusan Republic and it was feared that if the British were first to enter the capital they, too, might decide to stay.

However, the Ragusan leader, Count Caboga, raised no objection to a small detachment of the 35th Regiment being put ashore at Ragusa Vecchia [Cavtat], a small but prosperous port to the south of Ragusa itself, in October. The British hoisted their own flag to the *campanile* of the church but proclaimed Caboga as commandant of the town and that the laws of Ragusa, not of France, were again to be enforced. However, the other Ragusan nobles distrusted Caboga's motives, assuming that he would prove to be no more than a British puppet, and hit upon the idea of ceding their little republic to the Ottoman Empire. A move of typically Ragusan subtlety, this might serve to keep the British and Austrians away, while they need pay no more than lip-service to the ramshackle regime that was only nominally controlled from Constantinople.

This diplomatic gambit was, however, forestalled by Hoste himself. Understanding the importance of unquestioning support from whatever forces could be raised ashore, he took it upon himself to win Ragusan opinion and do so by the most drastic means, without reference to Fremantle, who, he rightly suspected, would urge him to await the arrival of the Austrians.

So, on 15th November, the *Bacchante* sailed into the lovely little bay of Ragusa Vecchia and anchored. With some ceremony, Hoste had the British flag on the *campanile* lowered and replaced by the Ragusan standard of St Blaise. Then, as the blue and white flag, emblazoned with the bearded, mitred figure of the patron saint of the republic, flew from the tower, a salute of twenty-one guns from the frigate echoed round the bay and Captain Hoste proclaimed the independence of Ragusa.

Knowing that a British naval officer's word was his bond, Count Caboga determined to press on with the siege of Ragusa itself in the belief that, with British recognition of the Republic's independence, the Austrians would never dare to make any claim of their own. Yet on his return to the insurgents' camps outside the capital, he was disturbed to hear that the Austrian general, who had been advancing down the coast from Spalato, was demanding that the elders of the villages, through which he passed, swear loyalty to the crown of Austria. So Caboga, who now described himself as Commander-in-Chief of the Insurgent Forces besieging Ragusa, asked Hoste's help in taking the city before he was forestalled by the Austrians. The insurgents had no artillery and, without this, the massive ramparts were invulnerable, so he asked for heavy guns to be landed from the ships.

He was asking too much of a frigate captain, whose aim was simply to defeat the French and who only dabbled in local politics to cement relations with potential allies. So before sailing for the Gulf of Cattaro to see whether Harper had been able to achieve anything more, Hoste published a manifesto that dashed Caboga's hopes. 'My sole object is that of aiding and assisting to expel the French from the country,' he announced. 'That being accomplished, I shall have executed my orders . . . With regard to hoisting the Ragusan flag, this is no consideration of mine; it will of course be respected by the English, the same as that of any power acting against the troops of the French government.'

To Fremantle, he confirmed his earlier pessimism: 'I can give you no hopes of Ragusa soon falling . . . I do not possess the means of reducing it.' There were four or five hundred enemy troops manning the fortifications, he reported and, as for the besieging Ragusan irregulars, they were 'like all undisciplined troops . . . sometimes there are two thousand before the place and the next day probably 100'.

With that, he sailed.

On 12th December, the *Bacchante* again entered the Gulf of Cattaro and exchanged salutes with Castello Nuovo and Spanish Fort. Again winds and currents were contrary but now Hoste seemed to be galvanized by a fierce determination, induced, perhaps, by the contrast between his own recent failures and what he found that Harper of the *Saracen* had achieved. Whereas his own first attempts against Cattaro had ended in political confusion and recrimination, Harper, with no more than his sloop and the rabble of Montenegrin hillmen, had actually come close to capturing the city.

After General Gauthier had refused the first summons to surrender on 22nd October, the morale of his garrison began to deteriorate sharply as they realized that a combination of British artillery and Montenegrin infantry might bring the siege to a climax with a bloody assault and massacre. Accordingly some of the Croatian levies planned to kidnap Gauthier and surrender the fortress. Word of this reached Harper and he arranged that, in case the plot miscarried, he would mount a gun to blow in the gates of the city, which would then be rushed by Montenegrins.

But Gauthier also heard of the plan and at once retreated to the fort of San Giovanni on its peak seven hundred feet above the city and warned his officers and gendarmerie to keep careful watch on the mutinous levies. On the afternoon of the 28th, their attempt was made; the Croatians forced the main gates open and scores escaped before loyal soldiers slammed them shut, trapping thirty of the mutineers inside.

Despite the setback, efforts to subvert the garrison continued, large bribes being offered to the commanders of the bastions in the hope that they would not oppose an assault by scaling-ladder. But this was to no avail. At the end of the month Archbishop Petar sent his own summons to surrender and Brunazzi, not to be outdone, followed suit. This, Gauthier contemptuously ignored, remarking only that the mass desertion by his Croatians had rid him of useless soldiers and that his remaining troops would be able to offer a more concentrated and efficient defence.

Even when the Montenegrins dragged some captured guns up to the city and began firing upon it on 12th December it seemed that this would have little effect upon walls so thick. In his attempts to organize the Montenegrins and the Bocchese not only into fighting formations but working-parties, Harper ran into the same difficulties as had Hoste. The Montenegrins squabbled amongst themselves, the men from one village refusing to work with men from another; the Bocchese would promise men and boats to ferry guns and ammunition up to Cattaro but they rarely appeared at the promised time. Matters were made worse by Brunazzi, who, to assert Austrian authority and delay British efforts, issued his own orders and demanded – and occasionally got – his own working-parties.

So when the *Bacchante* arrived off the narrows, Hoste determined to take the strongest action himself and to be deterred neither by enemy nor ally and certainly not by the weather. On the 13th, the frigate began the laborious process of working her way through the channel to the inner basin against north-easterly squalls and a strong current. Alternately sailing under close-reefed top-sails and anchoring, she made slow progress and, as it seemed that the passage of only about a mile might take days or even weeks, Hoste decided to send his ship's boats ahead and accompany them himself.

The first party, commanded by Lieutenant Milbourne, was fifty strong and took with them one of the long eighteen-pounder main-deck guns. The boats made their way between the grey walls of mountains until, round the final bend of the great chasm, they sighted the ramparts and towers of Cattaro, the French tricolour flying from the keep of San Giovanni.

A reconnaissance was the first essential and, for this, Hoste scaled the mountains on the opposite side of the headwaters of the gulf from the city, accompanied by Yonge. The mountains that swept up from the shore stood to heights of between three to four thousand feet and the most prominent peak immediately opposite Cattaro was, Hoste learned, called Mount Theodore. The way to the summit lay first through steep, wooded slopes, then up through gullies that led almost to the bare summits. It was from Mount Theodore that Hoste looked down on the city he must capture and he saw its strength.

The city behind the walls – the stone *palazzi*, the twin towers of the cathedral and the clock-tower in the market-place – were all now visible from the heights. The walls that rose from the water's edge, thirty feet thick, would be able to withstand any bombardment that could be opened. They then ran, zigzag, up the steeps to the fort on the peak of the great fang of rock upon which it had been built; here the walls were less strong than lower down, but they did not need such thickness since it seemed impossible to bring guns to bear on them. Only storming-parties of infantry could get up that mountainside and they, scrambling up cliffs, could easily be outdistanced by the defenders racing up the stone steps behind the battlements.

Thus, it appeared, guns firing from ships, or from the low-lying land on either side of the city, would have little effect upon it. Only mortars, throwing bombs from the shelter of earthworks to plunge into the city, would cause any appreciable damage and this would be limited by the obvious strength of the stone buildings.

Perhaps at this moment, looking down on the impregnable city, Hoste remembered Nelson again and remembered him faced with mountain warfare in Corsica. If he could again emulate his patron there would be a way to take this city. If his guns – the long eighteen-pounders of the *Bacchante* – could be got up these mountains, their shot would clear those thwarting ramparts and smash through the roofs of the city within, reducing it to rubble.

Therefore, Hoste determined, he would lay siege to Cattaro and his batteries would be upon the mountain-tops. Accordingly, next day, his sailors landed the first of the big guns and, in cold clear weather, began to drag it up the mountain. The cannon itself was lashed to a heavy wooden sledge and pulleys rigged to rocks and trees but the power that raised the load of some two tons up the near-vertical mountainside was that of men's muscles.

Watching from the fastness of his fortress on the far side of the valley, Gauthier told his staff that if he need not consider capitulation until a battery had been raised on those summits, he would not worry because a relief force would reach him long before that could be accomplished.

All that first day, the sailors heaved at the ropes – watched, but not helped, by their allies – and the first gun slowly rose. By dusk, it was made fast four hundred yards up the mountainside. At dawn next day work was resumed but with increasing difficulty because, as Yonge wrote, 'the masses of rock proving too loose and unable to support the purchase-strops, which rendered it necessary to cut grooves in the solid rock for that purpose'.

As the sailors strained at the hoisting-tackle, a dozen Montenegrins appeared and, for an hour or two, made themselves useful by carrying sandbags and stores up the mountain, but of the Bocchese there was no sign. Next day there were no visitors at all because it had begun to pour with cold mountain rain. None of the working-parties had a change of clothing and their shoes were soon cut to pieces by sharp stones. There was no possibility of returning to the ship for the night, so that the only defence against torrential rain and cold nights was for them to huddle together beneath a waxed sail that had been rigged across a gully as a tent. However, by the end of the third day, the gun had been raised to eight hundred and forty yards from the foot of the mountain.

Steady rain turned what earth there was to mud and loosened rocks so that not only the men slipped and slithered, despite the emptying of sandbags on the slopes, but the strops holding the gun constantly lost their purchase, threatening to send the gun sliding and crashing down the mountainside. Finally, Hoste ordered that the kedge-anchor should be hauled up the mountain to hold the tackle but even this dragged in the loosening surface and had to be secured by heaping upon it a cairn of rocks. By this means the gun was raised another three hundred yards.

Directed by Hoste himself, who slept on the mountain, soaked to the skin, with his sailors, the gun gradually rose and, on the sixth day, a final heave brought it with a lurch on to the summit of Mount Theodore.

Now other guns could follow and, as nothing seemed impossible at this moment, other batteries could be sited on other mountains to surround the city.

For the first time since early in October, Hoste could settle down to writing a long letter home and in it he described the events of the past week to his mother. 'How you would laugh, were you to see me here,' he wrote. 'I am general, admiral, governor, engineer and complete jack of all trades . . . We have got guns up mountains which were deemed impassable; and the French general said he would give me six months to get one gun up: I have convinced him of the contrary in six days. He says it is a very *unmilitary* proceeding: I tell him English sailors do nothing like anyone else, but they will *astonish* him before they leave him.

'We have torn up trees (in getting the cannon up the mountain) that were *planted by Adam*, I should think, and have upset rocks that *were left there since the Deluge.*'

Even at this moment, exhausted and triumphant, he could not resist a boast that he had wanted to make since hearing of British naval defeats by the United States Navy – defeats of frigates such as his own – on the other side of the world. 'The Yankees may take a frigate or two, with ships twice as big, and double the number of men: but that is not beating us. We have lost three frigates but we did not lose one jot on national honour. When fairly considered, our frigates are by no means a match for them; and yet with fifty more men I should be happy to try *Bacchante.*'

Having delivered this challenge via a Norfolk parsonage, Hoste returned his thoughts to matters more immediate. That first gun was mounted in its battery on 21st December to be saluted by cannon-fire from Cattaro that fell hopelessly short and was greeted by cheers of derision from the sailors who knew that that night they would sleep under blankets for the first time since their labours began. Now this gun was to be joined by another and two eleven-inch mortars on the summit.

On the far side of the valley, immediately behind the city, other guns were being dragged up the mountains. The heights were not so great as those of the Mount Theodore range but it was often more precipitous so that, in places, guns could only be raised by crane. Where enemy fire, or the heights of precipices, made this impossible, lighter weapons could be used. Hoste had already sited two short-range carronades close to the walls so that, by depressing their barrels, their heavy shot

could blow off the roofs of the houses that could then be set on
fire by rockets which, together with mortars, were also brought up.

From the bottom of the deep chasm below the peak upon which
stood the fort of San Giovanni, a narrow path zigzagged up a steep
slope towards a high pass; this was exposed to enemy musketry but
agile marines armed with musketoons – heavy muskets with a long
range – scrambled up to snipe at the French gunners on the ramparts
opposite.

The rain fell heavily and the nights froze as more guns and more
men were brought ashore from the *Bacchante*, which had at last worked
up to an anchorage just below Cattaro. This was a considerable feat
since most of her crew and her captain were now ashore and her first
lieutenant, Silas Hood, had barely enough men to make or take in sail
as squalls struck and abated. Living in comparative comfort on board,
Hood feared for his captain's health which he knew to be far from
robust.

'Frequently for nights would his clothes remain on him, wet as they
were, in a climate either at the freezing point, or drenching us all
with torrents of rain. How the people stood it, God only knows!
and from my heart, I believe, with no other man could they have done
what they did,' he wrote later, 'I was not myself employed on shore;
but when the captain came on board, as he often did during the siege,
he was full of praise for the officers and men, and would frequently
say to me, "This place will kill us all, but go on as you are doing;
let us want for nothing and in a few days I will introduce you to the
French general".'

All that Hood could do to ease the rigours of life ashore, he did, and
the most practical help was the rigging of sails to provide some shelter
from the rain at night. The working-parties on the lower slopes could
and did shelter in houses and a church but on the exposed mountainside, often within range of the guns of Cattaro, the tents had to be
sited in gullies, which were also watercourses after heavy rain and so
would quickly become uninhabitable. Falls of rock, loosened by rain
and landslides, were another danger and, on one occasion, Yonge
noted, 'a large mass of rock detached itself and, bounding down the
mountain, happily cleared the tent in which a wounded man was
lying'.

So far not a man had been killed, despite harassing fire from the
French batteries, as the sailors and marines struggled up the mountainsides, carrying or dragging on sledges cannon-balls, powder, rations
and sandbags, and cut down trees to make platforms for the guns.
By Christmas Eve, batteries had been raised on all sides of the city:
to the north and south, on the lower, cultivated slopes above the water;

to the west and east, the guns on the mountain tops, including another long eighteen-pounder that had been hoisted on to a peak from which it could fire some four hundred yards across the chasm at San Giovanni.

For reasons never explained, Hoste made a decision that was surprising for a parson's son and ordered that the batteries would open fire together at dawn on Christmas Day. Before first light, the gun-crews were closed-up, the mortars at their maximum elevation, the rocket launchers canted on their tripods and the marines settled behind musketoons they had steadied upon rocks. Hoste himself took his station by a battery at the head of the valley, from where he would be able to see the city, the positions of all his batteries and his ship at anchor below Cattaro. So, at about the same time that Dixon Hoste began to read the Prayers for Christmas Day in the cold little church at Tittleshall, his son gave the order to fire, a cannon flashed and instantly gunsmoke stabbed by flame erupted from mountainside and summit as the thunder of the bombardment rolled, thumped and echoed against the rock walls of the Gulf of Cattaro.

Exultantly, Hoste wrote to Fremantle, that this Christmas morning had astonished Gauthier, 'who had said he would give the English Captains 14 months ere they could get a gun up the mountain – we have answered him to the contrary in 14 days'.

The French had also been standing by their guns and now they returned the fire until the city and the mountains were hidden from each other by wind-blown smoke. From dawn until dusk the batteries pounded against one another, day following day until, on the 28th, a British shot – probably an incendiary rocket – struck one of the powder magazines on the ramparts and it blew up with an explosion that silenced the guns, just as the eruption of the magazine of *L'Orient* had brought a stunned lull to the Battle of the Nile.

Next day, the defenders resumed their fire and, although the weather grew even worse, the British brought up more artillery, two eighteen-pounders and a carronade, to complete the batteries by the 31st, ready, as Hoste put it 'to begin the New Year with them'. The French, however, ended the old year by killing their first British sailor, eighteen-year-old Able Seaman William Watkins, with a cannon-shot. He was buried ashore.

The first dawn of 1814 was saluted by all the British batteries firing together with the roar and impact of a line-of-battle's broadside and a launch was pulled towards the watergate to throw mortar-bombs and rockets into the city. Ashore, the wooden mountings of the mortars had been so battered by recoil that the trunnions had to be knocked off and the weapons buried in the ground to maintain their accuracy. Fires now blazed among the shattered houses and Gauthier himself helped carry bags of powder down from the walls to deeper magazines where they were less vulnerable to the fiery rockets.

Deserters, who had escaped over the walls, reported the garrison to be 'in a very wretched state' and prompted by this and the sight of the fires, Hoste sent an Army officer, a Captain Angelo, who had been a passenger in the *Bacchante* and was a linguist, into Cattaro under a flag of truce to demand its surrender. Receiving him, Gauthier refused the terms but complained that the use of rockets was 'a most unmilitary way of proceeding'. 'Why, do you know with whom you are contending?' replied Angelo, quoting Hoste. 'You are not engaged with soldiers, who do all these things in a regular technical manner: you are opposed to sailors; people who do nothing like other men, and they will astonish you when they have done with you.'

When this conversation was repeated to Hoste he remarked that he was not there to be advised by a French general – even by a member of the *Légion d'honneur* – but to give him a lesson.

This would be the storming of the city and, even though enemy fire had appreciably slackened, it was bound to be a costly affair and could not be attempted without the help of the fierce Montenegrins. Hoste's relations with them and the Bocchese had slightly improved. This was partly due to awe at the sight of British batteries on their supposedly inaccessible mountains and partly because Hoste had finally asserted his authority over the Austrian commissioner. When Brunazzi's issuing of proclamations and orders contrary to his own finally became intolerable – and exhaustion had lowered his level of tolerance – Hoste told him that if this continued he would be put under arrest and sent aboard the *Bacchante*.

The Montenegrins had never recognized Brunazzi's authority; neither had they relished the idea of working as porters for the British and few of them had. But now that there was prospect of work fit for warriors, their interest was aroused and Archbishop Petar sent Hoste a storming-party of his best fighting men. Hearing that a general assault on the battered walls was imminent, Gauthier summoned his staff and told them bluntly that he did not think that his men would now face hand-to-hand fighting, particularly in the knowledge that, if defeated, they could not expect gentlemanly treatment by the British but massacre by the Montenegrins. Accordingly, he sent an officer under flag of truce to Hoste, asking that negotiations for surrender might begin.

Conscious that Gauthier had lost all confidence, Hoste maintained the pressure on his defences during the discussions by keeping his gun-crews closed-up at the batteries and the Montenegrin storming-party in view of the defenders and obviously 'ready for the assault at a moment's notice'. So, on 5th January, General Gauthier accepted the terms of surrender. These were that the garrison become prisoners of war but would be sent to Italy on condition that they did not serve against Britain or her allies until formally exchanged for British prisoners. The British would then occupy Cattaro and all its guns and ammunition would become the spoils of war.

Accordingly, on the 8th, the *Bacchante* sailed up to the walls of the city before a light northerly breeze and anchored beneath the muzzles of its silent guns. The marines and landing-parties of sailors were put ashore, or brought down from the batteries, to occupy the fortifications while the formal surrender was made. Gauthier thereupon marched out from the gates at the head of what were now found to be only sixteen officers and two hundred and seventy-nine men of his surviving garrison.

The general himself and thirty-six French officers, gunners and gendarmes were escorted on board the frigate and the rest of the prisoners embarked in *trabaccoli*. Before the French boarded the *Bacchante*, Hoste saw that some troublesome domestic business was out of the way. During the siege there had been no time to conduct disciplinary proceedings and, indeed, little had been needed; but there had been a few cases of men drinking too much to ease the miseries of rain, cold and exhaustion and two of these had been in irons since toasting the New Year to excess. So, before the ship moved close to the city, gratings were rigged, such of the ship's company who were on board mustered and six men flogged.

Meanwhile the sloop *Crocus* had arrived with the news that the Austrians were preparing to send an occupying force up the gulf. Hoste took this ship under command and sent her with his dispatches to Fremantle at Trieste. For himself, he acted immediately upon the news she had brought. He had no wish to become involved in a confrontation between the Austrians and Bocchese on the one hand and the Montenegrins on the other, not only because he felt some admiration for the latter but did not want to betray their confidence by supporting the Austrians, which he would be bound to do. Therefore he hastened the work of embarking his ships' guns and the remaining ammunition and stores together with eighteen cannon, ammunition and hospital stores from Cattaro which, he said, would be needed for operations against Ragusa.

More might have been taken from the city but for the reluctance of the Bocchese to man the small ships necessary for its transportation. Eventually, however, the Croatian and Italian prisoners were embarked in two *trabaccoli* and the French moved into the *Saracen*. Most of the captured guns were embarked in the *Bacchante* and the powder, which could not be stowed in the ship's magazine, went into the pinnace.

Exactly five weeks since Hoste had landed his first gun, the British were all back on board their ships and ready to sail. There was one more formality to complete and that was the delivery of the keys of Cattaro to some established authority. This could only be the Central Commission, although, once the British had gone, the rival factions could hardly be expected to live in peace together before the arrival of the Austrians to impose their rule; or even of the Russians to impose theirs. So Hoste wrote a letter to them in his most dignified style, stating that by expelling the French his task was complete and that the keys of the city would be handed over to the civil magistrate. If 'the Gentlemen of the Central Commission' wished for a copy of the French terms of capitulation they should send a clerk on board for the purpose 'as I have not time sufficient to do it'.

With that, his military triumph complete, Hoste abandoned the political problems of Cattaro, sailed from the city on the 16th and passed the narrows two days later to the welcome of the open sea. Standing north towards Ragusa, he could feel elation at having exceeded his admiral's – and his own – expectations, while escaping the political entanglements that must follow.

He was only just in time. Two days after the surrender, a small Austrian force had arrived at Castello Nuovo under the command of General Theodore Miliutinovich to occupy the shores of the gulf. Their stay had been brief for, almost immediately, they were informed by Archbishop Petar that any further move towards Cattaro would mean fighting his Montenegrins.

Hoste was thankful to have avoided having to support Miliutinovich, whom he regarded as 'a brave man but certainly not a very deep one', and the Austrians, whom he heartily disliked. 'They abuse the English Character behind my back,' he told Fremantle, 'and are the most servile of God's creatures before my face.' On the other hand, he had come to like and admire the wily Archbishop and had more than a grudging regard for his *banditti*, his description of them to the admiral reflecting this: 'The Montenegrins have a great penchant for the good things of this life and are not very nice in their means of getting them.'

Political problems were not all that he left behind. The effort of getting the guns, that had proved so decisive, down from the mountains would be such and the need to evacuate the gulf was so pressing that Hoste feared he might have to abandon those in the high batteries. Harper, who had been in charge of liaison with the Bocchese and had been able to muster some working-parties during the siege by means of good humour, flattery and the spreading of optimistic news about the course of the war beyond the Gulf of Cattaro, was asked to make an attempt to retrieve the eighteen-pounders. As most of the ships' companies were busy on board, embarking other weaponry and ammunition, guarding prisoners and occupying the fortifications of the city, there were not enough men to attempt the re-rigging of the tackle, the securing of the anchors and the fastening of the guns to their heavy wooden sledges. To do this he needed seven hundred Bocchese and tried to entice them, under their own foremen, from the villages with the assurance that to remove the guns would be 'necessary for the good and tranquillity of the province', a clear hint that the weapons, if left where they were, might well be used against the city by the Montenegrins, if they or the Austrians were to occupy it.

But the labour was not forthcoming, there was no time to spare and the main-deck guns were abandoned. This decision moved the chaplain of the *Bacchante* to compose a simple and unselfconscious epitaph to the shared endurance. Since he had looked down on Cattaro from Mount Theodore, Yonge had been away on a visit to Athens, unable to resist a chance of sight-seeing at the source of his Classical education. When, on his return to the ship after the siege, he heard what had been achieved since he had stood at Hoste's side, he confessed that he was 'all astonishment at his success', adding, 'he has been rivalling, since I left him, the actions of Lord Nelson at Bastia and Calvi'. Then he noted, as a clergyman accustomed to solemn commemoration, 'The guns were left in the batteries on the summits as a memorial to the genius and courage of Englishmen.'

X

RAGUSA THE IMPREGNABLE

While his imagination ranged forward to the coming siege of Ragusa, Hoste was to find that he was unable to rid himself of the political entanglements at Cattaro just by making sail. Like Nelson, he believed that a sailor should concentrate upon glory and prize-money and that the only value in politicians was their patronage. But, immediately after Gauthier had surrendered and Hoste had written his official dispatch to Fremantle, he took the unorthodox step of writing a letter to Lord Aberdeen, the British ambassador to Austria.

Vienna was now on the quickest route for mail to England and he was anxious that his own version of recent events should reach the British Government before, or simultaneously with, whatever his admiral and Abbot Brunazzi chose to report. Writing to young Lord Aberdeen that 'I have thought it proper to address myself to your lord-ship direct', he stressed that he had had to act alone against the French and that 'not an Austrian soldier had made his appearance'. Of Brunazzi, he wrote, 'I can assure you I have had more trouble with him than with all the French troops besides. He is a deceitful, intriguing character, but a poor weak wretch, and had employed what little talent he posses-ses in exciting jealousies and sowing dissensions among those who were the friends and allies of his sovereign . . . He has thrown every obstacle in my way to hinder my gaining Cattaro, and at last I told him, if he ever interfered with my arrangements in future, I should order him on board *Bacchante*, and report his conduct accordingly. He will make some representation on this subject, I do not doubt, on his arrival in Vienna, where I hear he is going.'

He then gave the reasons for handing the city to the Central Commis-sion: the rivalries between the local factions and the absence of the Austrians. He concluded with what was intended to be his acceptance of responsibility for such drastic action, which he knew to be contrary to the wishes of both the Austrian Government and of Fremantle, but the wording was tactless. 'In the whole of this affair, I have acted without any precise orders from my admiral . . . Admiral Fremantle cannot be responsible for measures directed by me; but he was too distant to write to for instructions, and I have acted upon motives which at the time I considered as best calculated to avoid giving umbrage either to Russia or Austria, and most for the interest of Great Britain. It is probable that some strong representations will be made to your lordship . . .'

In the event, Hoste's letter reached Lord Aberdeen in France at Chatillon-sur-Seine, where the allies were conducting abortive peace negotiations with Napoleon, by the same post as Fremantle's letter reporting the fall of Cattaro. Replying to the admiral, the ambassador wrote sharply that he was sorry that the capture had 'been attended with some unpleasant circumstances', that 'it was thought necessary to employ the Montenegrins so materially' and that he had always assumed that 'the British force was employed not only to expel the French from the forts on the Adriatic, but to restore them to the Government of His Imperial Majesty'. He then enclosed a copy of his reply to Hoste.

Although Aberdeen was not in the naval or military chain of command he was a man of both influence and self-importance and his letter to Hoste was couched in the terms of a reprimand. After covering the points already made to Fremantle but in stronger language, he concluded, 'I may be permitted to lament the prospect of future dissension which the arrangement as it stands at present affords'. His fears were justified for, when the Austrians arrived, they found Cattaro occupied by the Montenegrins and were only able to drive them out of the city by force three months later.

Hoste replied, again by direct letter, that he had never employed the Montenegrins at the siege, which was largely true, although they had been ready to storm the walls at the climax. He pleaded that the situation at the time had dictated his policy, adding, 'I do say that it is entirely their own fault that the Austrians are not at this moment quiet possessors of the province of Cattaro'.

He heard no more from Lord Aberdeen but the correspondence had displeased Fremantle in several ways. One of his captains had not only acted against his own policy directives but had pleaded his case personally with a major political figure without reference to himself. He was also probably stung by the knowledge that Hoste had been performing feats that he had never thought possible while he was far from the scene of action, living ashore in comfort. Indeed, on the day the *Bacchante* had entered the Gulf of Cattaro for the second time to begin the siege, Fremantle had written to his brother from Trieste; 'I have taken up my Winter Quarters here . . . I have . . . some tolerable Society for the evenings . . . I am settled in a very excellent house.' Certainly Fremantle was busy with diplomatic work and strategic planning and had moved his base from Lissa to Trieste. He was far from idle but for a senior officer, who prided himself on his fighting record, to hear that one of his captains – one for whom he did not particularly care – was reaping the glory, must have been galling.

After sailing from the Gulf of Cattaro, Hoste tried to put political worries out of his mind because, with a fair wind, he expected to be off Ragusa next day and, as some Austrian troops were already before the city, he could demonstrate his willingness to cooperate with them.

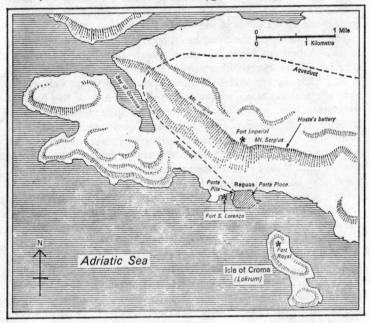

RAGUSA

The first sight of Ragusa from the sea was as impressive as that of Venice, its ancient rival, but in striking contrast. Whereas the latter lay in its lagoon, the distant mountains serving only as a romantic backdrop to its towers and pinnacles, Ragusa seemed to grow out of the rocks on which and from which it had been built. Below the long wall of mountain, some twelve hundred feet high, the city crouched on its headland, only its domes, *campanili* and russet roofs visible above walls rising seventy feet from the crags above the sea.

No force that the Austrians or the Ragusan rebels against French rule could have assembled had any hope of taking so strong a city and, while they waited outside the walls, they quarrelled and intrigued amongst themselves. Indeed, the new political entanglements awaiting Hoste had parallels both with those at Cattaro and those that Nelson had faced in Naples fifteen years earlier. Now that the defeat of France seemed only a matter of time – Wellington had invaded France and the once-formidable Murat had defected to the allies – Ragusa faced the alternatives of exchanging one foreign ruler for another, unless independence could be restored. As at Naples, it was the nobility and the peasantry who hankered after the restoration of the old regime and the middle classes who favoured a wider, more democratic form of government based on the ideals of the French Revolution.

The Austrians, on the other hand, had their own plans for Ragusa as part of their empire and in early January two of their battalions, commanded by General Miliutinovich, arrived before the city. Although he brought flattering letters from his superiors for Count Caboga, the general's first act was to attempt the disbandment of the Ragusan irregulars. This he was unable to do and, instead, found himself recognizing the insurgents as independent belligerents against the French. This, he felt, would placate them while he was away at Cattaro, which he proposed to occupy. But, on arrival in the gulf, he had found the city firmly held by the Montenegrins and had to return to Ragusa. There, the nobility had been far from placid; suspecting Caboga of being a potential traitor to their cause, they formed their own ruling council and on the night of 17th January proclaimed the re-establishment of an independent Republic of Ragusa. There was nothing that Miliutinovich could do but pretend to acquiesce.

The Ragusans had some cause for optimism. Not only had Captain Hoste already recognized the Republic and saluted its flag at Ragusa Vecchia, but the British commandant at Curzola, a Captain Lowen, had told them that British and Austrian forces were advancing on Ragusa 'to give it back its liberty . . . Remember that you bear a glorious name, and fight . . . to restore your independence.'

Using all their traditional diplomatic skills, the Ragusans informed both the Emperor of Austria and the Sultan of Turkey of their declaration of independence, assuring them of the Republic's highest regard for them and hoping for the closest of political and economic relations. It began to look as if Ragusa might possibly return to its old position of influence and power, perhaps even more influential and powerful since Venice was now only a beautiful husk of a merchant-city.

As at Cattaro, Hoste's concern was solely with the defeat of the French. He cared little for the intrigues of the Austrian general and the Ragusan nobles, and concentrated his attention upon his principal enemy, *Général de Division* Joseph Montrichard.

A veteran of Napoleon's early campaigns in Italy, Switzerland and on the Rhine, Montrichard had been in the Illyrian Provinces since 1808, commanding the *Corps du Duc de Raguse*. During Hoste's first year in the Adriatic, he had commanded at Ancona, making himself unpopular by levying heavy taxes to pay for the building of fortifications. Now aged fifty-four, he was an officer of experience, both in siege warfare and the internecine politics of Ragusa.

Montrichard was now behind the walls of one of the most strongly-fortified cities in Europe with a garrison of some five hundred men, provisioned for six weeks and defended by more than one hundred and seventy guns on the ramparts and in four forts that covered the approaches. Ragusa stood on its rocky headland jutting out from a great peninsula of mountains more than a thousand feet high and between five and six miles wide that ran northward for about ten miles, sheltering on its landward side two deep bays. The smaller of these, the Bay of Gravosa, lay four miles from the city, offering a safe anchorage out of range of French guns. It was on the shore here that the Ragusans and Austrians had set up their base and here that the *Bacchante* came to anchor.

Hoste's first action after being told the state of the enemy's defences was to reconnoitre them himself and he found them even more formidable than those of Cattaro. There, daunting as the first sight of ramparts and castle had been, it had been clear that, once he had been able to get his guns up the mountains, it would be possible to batter down the city and the weaker curtain-walls above it and launch an assault. Here the fortifications were infinitely stronger. On the seaward side, the massive walls rose straight from cliffs and salt water. The harbour and the roadstead outside were covered by the eleven guns of Fort Royal, a star-shaped battery which the French had built on the summit of the Island of Croma [Lokrum]. This little island, on which King Richard the First of England was said to have taken refuge from a storm on his return from the Crusades, sheltered the anchorage and scented the city with its wild herbs. But now its highest hill had been shaved of trees and scrub so that its guns could fight off any direct attack on the harbour, or one along the mainland shore from the south.

On its landward side, Ragusa was defended by walls seventy feet high and sixteen feet thick, above a moat and covered by a keep, towers and bastions. The eastern gates of the city were defended by the Revelin fortress and those to the west by the fort of San Lorenzo standing on a crag nearly one hundred and forty feet above the sea. Such defences could only be overcome by a siege train, equipped with the heaviest artillery, and the use of sappers, neither of which were available. Even had they been, their use would have been prevented by the twenty-one guns of Fort Imperial which had been finally completed by the French the year before on the summit of Mount Sergius, twelve hundred feet above the city, from which its landward approaches could be swept by grape-shot.

Hoste immediately wondered whether he could repeat his achievement at Cattaro by mounting guns on this mountain ridge to fire down into Ragusa, but this seemed, at first, impossible. Any attempt to land and drag guns up the steep, sometimes vertical, heights would have to be beyond the range of the guns of Fort Royal and Fort Imperial and that would be on an unsheltered coast, battered by rough seas and winter gales. Another possibility would be to have landed them on the far side of the peninsula, where there were no defences, but the mountains were even more rugged than the hill at Lesina and even if the guns could be dragged to the summit, they would then have to be manhandled across some four miles of rough, thickly-wooded plateau to a point where they could command the city below.

There was other action, less effective but more feasible, that could be taken. On 19th January, a day of squalls, thunder and lightning, the field-guns and mortars from Cattaro were landed from the frigate and hauled to the batteries facing the north walls of the city. Hoste knew the garrison to be well supplied with rations and now asked about their water. He was told that, because of the recent heavy rain, the cisterns of Ragusa must be full, so that there was no point in cutting the flow from the aqueduct that brought fresh water from the mountains since this would only have to be repaired when the city fell.

In Hoste's view, any action that might hinder the garrison should be taken and he directed that the aqueduct be breached just above the town and went to see where this could best be done so that the water would be most easily accessible to the besiegers. The aqueduct that fed the two public fountains within the city had been built during the second quarter of the fifteenth century by the Neapolitan engineer Onofrio di la Cava and, while not so spectacular as those built by the Romans, had been a remarkable undertaking. Water from a spring high in the mountains at the base of the Ragusan peninsula had to be brought six miles down the less vulnerable side of the *massif* and round the tip of the great headland into the city. The gradient therefore had had to be slight so as to induce a steady flow.

The aqueduct, built of limestone, appeared to be no more than a terrace, about ten feet wide, running across the mountainsides, sometimes crossing a gully by high embankment or arch. The water-channel itself – two feet wide and three feet deep – was covered by stone slabs so that, as Hoste first saw it, the whole had the appearance of a narrow, paved road running from close to the Bay of Gravosa to the summits of the mountains, which were where he wanted to go. The aqueduct would be just wide enough to take an eighteen-pounder gun and its carriage, sledge, or rollers, and the men who would drag it to the heights.

On the 21st, Hoste landed one of his main-deck guns and, on the following day, another. Working-parties went ashore and the laborious process of dragging one of them up the long slope of the aqueduct began. This, it was later recalled, 'required some caution' because the aqueduct was so narrow that 'had the gun fallen on either side, nothing could have prevented it from descending into the valley beneath'.

About two miles could be covered in this way before a point was reached immediately across the mountains from the position of the proposed battery. From there the gun had to be dragged up steep tracks, between boulders and over red earth slippery with rain, through oak woods and bramble-thickets. Hoste had himself gone ahead to site the weapon. He had chosen 'dead ground' slightly lower than, and hidden from, Fort Imperial, where an outcrop on the lip of the cliffs could be cleared of rocks to form a rough gun-platform. From this, the gunners would be able to look directly down upon the city and across the sound to Croma.

More men were landed to haul the gun and as they laboured, steady, cold rain began to fall, as it had at Cattaro, and they slept each night on the mountain in sodden clothes. Meanwhile, far below, some activity had started with the arrival of British reinforcements: fifty men of the 35th Regiment. However, their officer, Lieutenant McDonald, found that his party might have to fight alone as the Croatians, whom he had taken under command, would not face the French from whom they had lately deserted. So it was that twice Montrichard was able to launch a successful sortie and send more infantry scrambling up the track to join the garrison of Fort Imperial.

On the 22nd, Hoste's two mortars had opened fire but they seemed ineffectual when the ramparts of Ragusa were engulfed in smoke and flame as its batteries replied. Indeed, as Hoste watched his gun lurching across the mountain tops, the only news of the siege that reached him was that one of his carpenter's crew had been killed by the premature firing of a mortar and that the garrison of Fort Imperial was now so strong that he himself could expect to be attacked.

To reach the site of the battery, the gun had to be heaved over three low, parallel ridges along stony mule-tracks. In spring, these would be herb-scented and bright with rock roses and flowering broom but now the sailors forced their way through dripping branches and tearing thorns. Finally, on the 26th, the exhausted men gave the final heave on the worn ropes and the gun at last rocked to the edge of the cliff. Below was spread an aerial panorama of Ragusa, its roofs now at the mercy of their shot.

Here, as at Cattaro, the gunners above could expect to hit their mark and the gunners below could not hope to hit back. From the crest, Hoste trained his telescope on the city and identified its gates and towers and its principal buildings: the Rector's Palace, the cathedral of St Blaise, the church of San Ignatio and the Orlando column in the main square from which Montrichard flew the tricolor. Out in the sound, at extreme range, lay the green island of Croma.

The gun on the mountain and the batteries below were to begin their bombardment at dawn on the 27th but first Hoste ordered some ranging shots. Taking the piazza as his target, the gunner calculated range and elevation and fired. One shot smashed into the façade of a house in the main street, a few yards from the square, a second struck one of the massive columns of the portico of San Ignatio, inflicting a star-shaped scar. There was no question that, when the bombardment began, every shot would do damage.

The effect of these shots in the city was apocalyptic. For so long Ragusa had seemed vulnerable only to diplomacy and implied threat, never, behind its great walls, to physical destruction by what amounted to aerial bombardment. Now a cannon could fire down into the streets with impunity.

Montrichard had, the day before, summoned his staff to discuss the possibility of capitulation but his three most zealous officers said that as the walls were intact, the garrison manning the defences and the population was not in revolt, there was no excuse for surrender. Then, after the first shots from Mount Sergius, hundreds of Ragusans demonstrated in the streets, jeered the garrison and hoisted the standard of St Blaise on one of the towers. Some said that this had been arranged by Montrichard himself as an excuse to capitulate and certainly he used it as such.

At four o'clock on the afternoon of the 26th, an officer emerged from the city under flag of truce to request a ceasefire until noon next day so that terms of surrender could be discussed. Next morning, while negotiations continued, Hoste was surprised to see another British frigate appear out at sea and concerned to learn that she was the *Elizabeth*, commanded by Captain Edward Leveson-Gower who, being his senior in the Captains' List, would automatically supersede him, so snatching his laurels at the moment of victory.

Leveson-Gower had arrived on the orders of Fremantle to do exactly this. The admiral had already heard with surprise and annoyance of the capture of Cattaro and the circumstances attending it and, while at

Lissa, he received word that Hoste was planning to repeat his exploit at Ragusa. Whether from lack of confidence in Hoste's political judgement, professional jealousy or personal pique, he ordered a more senior officer to take command. He did not like Leveson-Gower and had written from Trieste only a month before that he was 'the only one here who does not do what I wish him, the man growls and is dissatisfied with everything'.

Perhaps Leveson-Gower recognized and returned this antipathy because, on arrival off Ragusa to find Hoste in his hour of triumph, he decided to disregard his orders rather than 'to pluck away a single feather of those glories which he could have no claim to'. So instead of taking command, he remained at anchor well away from the *Bacchante* but sent his boats across with a present of rum, wine and fresh food.

Meanwhile, Montrichard had agreed to the terms offered by Hoste and Miliutinovich. These were that the city would be surrendered and occupied by the allies at midday on the 28th and that the garrison should not be accorded the honours of war but would be shipped without ceremony to Ancona. Both the Austrian and the French generals were adamant that Ragusa should be occupied only by the British and Austrians. But the British had promised Count Caboga that two hundred of his irregulars could march with them, that their flag could fly alongside the other two and that the civil administration of the city would be handed over to himself and the council of nobles.

When he heard the terms of capitulation, Caboga, considering himself betrayed both by Hoste and Miliutinovich, determined upon one last desperate attempt to save the Republic. Secretly he assembled a strong body of insurgents to rush the eastern gates, the Porta Ploce, while the British and Austrians marched through the western, the Porta Pile; then hoist the standard of St Blaise to the Orlando column, which was nearer to the eastern gates than the western, and proclaim the restoration of the Republic.

But the citizens of Ragusa, thoroughly frightened by the bombardment, now feared looting by the irregulars more than occupation by regular foreign troops and warned Miliutinovich of Caboga's plan. So, on the night of the 27th, with Montrichard's connivance, the Porta Pile was cleared of the barricades and bricks that had blocked it throughout the siege and, before dawn, Austrian and Croatian troops with two field-guns quietly entered the city. At midday, Hoste's marines marched smartly through the Porta Pile to take formal possession and, as they did so, Caboga's men stormed through the Porta Ploce. Bursting through the archway, they rushed across the bridge spanning the moat to face a glittering barrier of Austrian bayonets and the muzzles of their guns.

There was nothing to be done but withdraw and this they did; some of them returning later in the day, unarmed and carrying baskets of fresh vegetables to sell in the market.

So fell Ragusa. The last spasm of hope that had been engendered by Hoste ended with a shudder; the Republic to be remembered only in the archives and the architecture of the city, which itself became one more provincial market-town and seaport of the Austrian Empire. Now that Captain Leveson-Gower was ready to supersede him, Hoste had little inclination or time to contemplate the extinction of the city-state. His health was, said Dr Kidd, the *Bacchante*'s surgeon, 'alarmingly bad' yet he drove himself to fresh exertion in re-embarking the artillery and stores and getting down from Mount Sergius the main-deck gun to which victory had been primarily due.

As at Cattaro, there was only time now for the ceremony of punishment. When all the working-parties were back on board, they were mustered to witness the flogging of six men: one for sleeping at his post during the siege, one for drunkenness ashore and four for theft, three of these having spent the past nine days in irons.

On 4th February, he sailed and next day called at Lissa to embark a detachment of the 35th for passage to Trieste. They were to join Nugent's counter-offensive which, by-passing Venice, was attempting, with little success, to rouse the Italians against the French. On the 9th, the *Bacchante* reached Trieste, a haven of peace to her sick and exhausted captain, who now wrote to his father: 'After some fag and trouble we have succeeded in taking Ragusa . . . the fatigue and labour we have all had has almost knocked me up and we are arrived here with a large sick list.

'I am quite delighted at Trieste; after having been near twelve months from any civilized place, this city appears a paradise. It is carnival time and you would suppose all the people were mad: nothing but masked balls every evening, and operas and plays without end.'

Fremantle was there and received him in a cool but not unfriendly manner, Hoste noting with a touch of sarcasm that he had been 'pleased to express his *approbation* of *Bacchante*'s conduct on all occasions'. The admiral had hinted that he might hoist his flag in the frigate for a look into Ancona. Nothing came of this, but Fremantle had shown that he bore no lasting grudge. In any case, it seemed that the war would soon end, Hoste might well have to be sent home to recover his health and the two men shared a feeling of being neglected by their superiors in London. The admiral was hurt that the Admiralty did no more than acknowledge his reports of one victory after another and Hoste remarked, 'I do not know why, but I am in the black book of the Admiralty of late'. Both men were gratified when the Emperor of Austria awarded them, and Captain Harper, the Order of Maria Theresa.

Fremantle performed two more friendly acts while Hoste was at Trieste. First he appointed his brother acting-lieutenant, although his commission had not yet arrived; then he ordered the *Bacchante* to one of the few remaining active stations in his command: the blockade of Corfu. After calling for the last time at Lissa, Hoste made for the island of Paxo, south of Corfu, which was held by the British, and at once found himself caught up in yet another little invasion. The commandant, Major Sir Charles Gordon, wanted the frigate to transport him and some infantry across to Parga, on the mainland, where the French garrison was thought to be ready for surrender. So again, the boats were manned and armed and pulled ashore; the marines formed up with bayonets fixed and advanced into the little port, where a garrison of a hundred and seventy surrendered and the British flag was hoisted over the fort.

It was off Corfu that Hoste's health finally broke. His first lieutenant, Silas Hood, noted; 'Our captain, with a mind stronger than his constitution, kept up, though it was remarked by many of us what havoc Cattaro and Ragusa had made on his health and we much feared losing him; and these fears were soon realized for . . . while cruising off Corfu, [he] was taken ill and lost the use of his legs.' Dr Kidd, diagnosing 'rheumatic fever', ordered him to his cabin but, first, Hoste insisted on taking his ship as close to the harbour of Corfu as possible to see what enemy ships might be there.

As the *Bacchante* stood in towards the shore, he could see a French frigate flying an admiral's flag, protected not only by the expected shore batteries, but by fifteen gun-boats which, on sighting the British, pulled out from their moorings and formed a defensive crescent round the flagship. There was nothing a single frigate could attempt against such a force, so Hoste ordered her helm over and steered out to sea. Knowing these waters to hide shoals, there was not only a pilot to con the ship but also two leadsmen taking soundings, but even so, about five miles off-shore and making eight knots, the ship slithered over one reef into deep water then stuck hard and fast on another.

As the *Bacchante* shuddered to a stop, Hoste was resting on the sofa in his day-cabin. Lieutenant Hood hurried in with his report, saying that he had ordered all sails to be thrown aback. Hoste replied, 'Let there be no confusion; if the ship will not back off, take in all sail together, that the enemy may not suppose us aground but to have only anchored for the night, for coolness must be the order of the day.'

It was a desperate situation, for if the French realized that the frigate was firmly aground, the gun-boats could come out, take up raking positions, which her broadsides could not reach, and pound her to splinters.

She did not back off, so the charade of pretending to anchor in an unhurried, routine manner was performed so that, as Hood put it, 'the ship made to all appearance snug at anchor'. Meanwhile two gigs were hoisted out and sent in search of the frigates *Havannah* and *Cerberus* and the brig *Weazel*, which were known to be somewhere over the horizon. Meanwhile, in Hood's words, 'as a further piece of deception, the telegraph flag, with the distinguishing pendants of these ships, was occasionally hoisted with various numbers, signifying a communication between us and the ships, though not in sight, and occasionally replaced with our answering pendant, making it appear, as it did, to the enemy, that those ships were in sight, exchanging signals with us.'

Attempts were made to warp her off the bank during the night, first with a small anchor that only dragged across the bank; then with a main bower anchor, which was brought by boat under the stern and made fast to its great cable that was passed through the windows of the captain's cabin. But the ship was so firmly aground that, when the capstan was turned, the hull strained and creaked and showed signs of breaking under the strain. So, since the rise and fall of tide was so slight in the Adriatic, the only chance was to lighten the ship and this was first done by pumping out the bilges.

Despite his weakness, Hoste directed this work and cheered on his men until, at about midnight, he told Dr Kidd that he could no longer stand. The surgeon brought him a chair and sat him by the pumps but, even seated, he seemed on the point of collaspe. As the sailors worked, they would call cheerfully to him, as Hood later recalled, 'Never mind, sir, we'll have her off in time'.

Still the *Bacchante* lay trapped on the reef and the ship had to be lightened further. First, provisions – barrels of salt beef and pork and casks of rum and wine – were lowered into the boats or on to rafts, but still she would not move. Then it was the turn of the guns, the main-deck eighteen-pounders, upon which the ship would depend for survival if the gun-boats came out. Six were heaved out through their gun-ports with marker-buoys attached to their breeching-ropes and these were followed by ammunition: shells and boxes of grape-shot and canister-shot. Again the capstan was manned and the sailors strained at its radiating bars; the anchor held, the ship did not move and it was the capstan itself that broke. So eight more guns went over the side and more boxes of shot. At ten to six on the evening of the second day, the repaired capstan was again manned, the anchor-cable tautened and this time the ship began to move.

As she began to swing before the wind, Hood ordered the cable to be cut and the top-sails and top-gallant-sails to be set. At last she floated clear, running through deep water before the breeze and then ran fast aground on another bank. Again, attempts to warp the ship clear failed and this time the only chance seemed to be to get the frigate over this second shoal by lightening her further. Ten more guns splashed into the sea and, as her bows rose slightly, cannon balls were moved forward in an attempt to raise her stern. More heaving on the capstan and the ship shook herself and floated clear.

Soon after, a single gun-boat was sighted approaching from Corfu. Weak as the frigate was without twenty-four of her guns, she was ready for a fight with the whole French force; but it was then seen that the gun-boat flew a flag of truce and one of the *Bacchante*'s boats was sent to meet her. To their surprise she was carrying, as cargo, a present of fruit and vegetables from the Governor of Corfu and, as passengers, a man and a woman, who asked if they might come on board the frigate to meet the captain. So it was that the beautiful Madame Vallié returned to thank Hoste for his gallantry six years earlier, to laugh about her fears of being eaten by his cannibal crew and to introduce him to her husband. While the French gun-boat was taken in tow, the Valliés were given a cabin and were entertained as the captain's guests for three days while the work of re-embarking the jettisoned guns, ammunition and stores went on.

By this time the *Weazel* had arrived and helped with the laborious process of raising the guns from the sea bed. After two days, eleven guns had been salvaged but the remaining thirteen had sunk so deep that they had to be abandoned.

As the *Bacchante* sailed for Zante in company with the *Havannah*, Hoste, unable to stand, lay in his cot. While attending him, Dr Kidd remarked that it had been fortunate that the French frigate – let alone the gun-boats – had not come out because, having so few guns on board and being fast aground, they would have had to surrender.

'I had prepared my mind for that,' Hoste replied. 'I would have sent a few of the worst of the sick and all the youngsters in one of the shore boats' – some Turkish boats had come out to the frigate's assistance – 'to Paxo or Zante. I would have taken every other man with me into the ship's boats, well armed with cutlasses, pistols and tomahawks. I would have laid a train to *Bacchante*'s magazine; have waited the approach of the enemy on the off-side of the ship till they were close to me; then, setting fire to the port-fire of the train, I would have pulled off at once to the Frenchman, and I have not the slightest doubt we should have had her in Malta with us in a very few days.'

On 20th April, the *Bacchante* reached Malta and next day was towed up the Grand Harbour of Valetta to the dockyard, where Hoste went ashore and taken to the Governor's residence where he was put to bed 'more dead than alive'. During the next fortnight, Hood was told that his captain would have to relinquish his command and await the next ship for England.

Before the *Bacchante* sailed, Hoste was allowed to pay her a farewell visit. A boat brought him alongside and he was hoisted in a chair on to his quarterdeck. Recording the scene, Hood wrote, 'Every countenance brighted up with joy at once more seeing him who had so often led them to glory and victory.

'In addressing them, he said he hoped to hear of their success, that he should be happy to serve them should he again be able to go afloat and would not fail to mention their good conduct to the Admiralty. The people being about to cheer him, were stopped by me (in consequence of my perceiving his state of agitation on quitting us) until we had, for the last time, lowered him to his boat, when the ship was instantly manned and I believe no man ever received three more hearty cheers.

'In a moment, as from a sudden impulse, he rose on his legs for the first time for three months and returned the compliment; then dropping into the arms of the surgeon as if in a fit, was rowed on shore regretted by all . . .'

By happy chance the ship that was to carry Hoste home was the frigate *Cerberus*, which had fought at Lissa, and she sailed from Malta on 5th May. Before steering for Gibraltar, she had dispatches for Pellew, who was off Genoa. Sailing these waters, where every landfall brought some reminder of Nelson, it was difficult to recognize that the long wars were over and that the allies had marched into Paris a month before. That this was indeed so was brought home to Hoste as the *Cerberus* passed Elba and he immediately noted the event in a letter to his father.

'We have just spoken by telegraph to an English frigate, the *Undaunted*, lying at Porto Ferrajo,' he wrote. 'She has telegráphed to us, "The Emperor *Bony* is here." Only conceive what ideas such an event must create: that Buonaparte should absolutely be confined as a state prisoner in this horrible island for life, appears almost incredible. The man who, a few months ago, made all Europe tremble is now a prisoner in an almost desolate isle in the Mediterranean. There is nothing like it in history.'

With him in the *Cerberus* was his brother Ned – now known as Teddy – who had been ordered to join the flagship to receive his commission as lieutenant. He could be in constant attendance because Hoste was 'so weak and debilitated as not to be able to move without assistance'. There was now no question of being able to emulate Nelson once again by returning home from his triumphs overland, although Yonge, who was to have travelled with him, was awaiting his arrival at Trieste.

Instead, he had been advised to spend a fortnight resting and taking the medicinal waters at Cheltenham as soon as he landed in England and before facing the journey to Norfolk. But when the frigate reached Spithead in June and ran between the forts at the mouth of Portsmouth harbour, and Hoste disembarked where he had first embarked with Nelson in the *Agamemnon* twenty-one years before, he was too feeble to attempt any journey. Portsmouth itself was thought too noisy and crowded for an invalid, so lodgings were found for him on the far side of the harbour in the relatively quiet little town of Gosport near to Haslar naval hospital.

While he rested there, looking across the water to the ships and the dockyard that had been the fabric of his world, the rulers of the victorious allies came to Portsmouth for a naval review in celebration of their triumph. The gigantic shadows that had been cast across his life and dictated his actions for so many years seemed to assume substance, as he heard the boom of royal salutes, the distant bands and fanfares and saw the bunting flutter. Within a mile of his window, he knew, were now the Tsar of Russia; the King of Prussia; Prince Metternich, the Chancellor of the Austrian Empire, and the Prince Regent of Great Britain. From his open window, the sick man could catch faint echoes of the triumph which he could not share.

XI

WHERE BATTLES RAGE
NO MORE

The recognition that Hoste, like Nelson, so eagerly sought came at last. In July of 1814 he was granted a baronetcy and, at the beginning of the following year, was made a Knight Commander of the new Order of the Bath. Gratifying though this was, he could not forget past neglect and was outraged at the ruling that this second honour would replace all others and that he would have to surrender the medal awarded for his victory at Lissa. This he refused to do and the condition was not pressed. So, now that the Prince Regent allowed him to wear the insignia of the Order of Maria Theresa, he could call himself Captain Sir William Hoste, Bart., RN, KCB, KMT, and augment his family's arms with an arm protruding from a naval crown to grasp a flag enscribed 'Cattaro'.

During the summer, he was strong enough to make the journey to Norfolk and, in September, was invited to Holkham Hall with his father for two days' partridge-shooting. On the first day – when Hoste killed eighteen birds and his father, five – they were accompanied by Lord Anson, whose son had been killed by the gun accident at Lissa, and on the second day by both Anson and Thomas Coke. That Nelson's undoubted successor as the naval hero of Norfolk was not entertained more lavishly was probably due to the chronic extravagance of his father which had now extended to sour even his friendship of forty years with his patron. Dixon Hoste was in debt to Coke, amongst other neighbours, and was not managing his farm to the standards demanded by the great agriculturist from whom it was leased.

A few months later Coke's agent, Francis Blakie, reminded the parson that he owed his patron twelve year's rent and that he must relinquish Godwick Hall and its farm. A new rectory would be built nearer to Tittleshall church and, in the meantime, a house would be found for his family in the neighbouring village of Litcham. So the 'dear old Godwick' of William Hoste's dreams of home lost its emotional, contradictory and affectionate inhabitants and became a farmhouse on land that would be cultivated as Coke expected by Mitchell

Forby, a farmer of known capability.

Dixon Hoste had been ready to move out of the county, exchanging his own living for another, but although Coke wanted no more to do with the old spendthrift, the terms he offered were generous. Until the new rectory was complete, he would pay the parson the rent he would have received for Godwick Hall so that he might occupy suitably modest accommodation and save the balance. This the Hostes did, but the rector was soon complaining of his 'small smoky house' at Litcham, where he brooded upon the loss of Coke's friendship, writing to his agent that, 'I have felt and still feel his late neglect of me most poignantly'.

Sir William's honours enabled him to brush aside such familiar worries and days out shooting or riding to hounds restored his strength so that, when Napoleon escaped from Elba and 'The Hundred Days' of his final grasp at victory began, he at once applied to the Admiralty for an appointment at sea. That this was not forthcoming – while Major George Hoste was able to distinguish himself at Waterloo – was a disappointment but could be put down to the speed of events and the swiftness of their end. He was, in any case, enjoying his new-found status as a country gentleman and a baronet, his field sports and his dutiful attendance at Tittleshall church where he sat beneath a Russian flag that he had brought home to hang as a trophy above the family pew.

To such delights was now added his courtship of a beautiful and intelligent girl, Lady Harriet Walpole, the fourth daughter of Horatio, the second Earl of Orford. The original earldom, conferred upon Sir Robert Walpole, the statesman, having become extinct with the death of the bachelor Horace Walpole, the title was re-created in 1806, being transferred from the Walpoles of Houghton to the Walpoles of Wolterton, to whom Nelson had been related through his mother.

They were married in April, 1817, and shortly afterwards set out on a Grand Tour of Europe that had more to do with seaports and battle-fields than palaces and art galleries. Young Lady Hoste was impressed by her husband's sophistication, writing in awe, 'Intimately acquainted with the details of ancient as well as modern history, minutely informed on every circumstance in the last struggle for independence by the allied powers, each scene was beheld with lively interest from recalling to mind the judgement, the perseverance or heroic acts of the victor or vanquished . . . Arrived at Marseilles . . . in continual conversation with the seamen frequenting that port, he found himself no stranger amongst them by name. When at Leghorn, many were the visits received from those who had known him as a youth under Lord Nelson.' He even wrote a friendly and relaxed letter to Admiral Fremantle, who was now Commander-in-Chief in the Mediterranean, asking if he could arrange a sea-passage for them in one of his ships.

On their travels, a son – to be named William – was born at Rome but their happiness was tempered by some ominous recurrences of Sir William's old ailments: 'fevers' and 'attacks on the lungs'. They returned to England in 1819 and he was gratified at the offer of a sea command. For a Navy that had been run down to peacetime strength it was a satisfactory appointment: he would command the frigate *Creole* when she took Sir Thomas Hardy – Nelson's old flag captain – to South America, where he was to become commodore of a small squadron, then return as captain of the 'seventy-four' *Superb*, which would then become the stationary guardship at Plymouth. Yet Hoste could not bring himself to part from his family and the offer was refused.

Their circumstances were comfortable. Lady Harriet had contributed a dowry of nearly £13,000 to her husband's capital of about £12,000, most of which had been prize-money. But for his father's continued importuning, he would have been a rich man and new grants of prize-money would continue to arrive as some of the more complicated cases before the prize-courts – notably concerning the captures of towns and shipping in the latter stages of the war – dragged on for more than a decade. But the bulk of his fortune – a reputed £50,000 of a total of about £60,000 – was spent by his family, mostly squandered by his father.

In 1822, the Admiralty made him an offer that fitted his domestic responsibilities – he now had another son, Theodore, and two daughters, Caroline and Psyche – and he accepted the command of the seventy-four-gun *Albion*, the guardship at Portsmouth. It could have been a sinecure but he determined that even an old ship, moored permanently off the dockyard with only a token ship's company, should be efficiently manned even if she could not, as he would have liked, be 'ready at a moment's notice to strike the deadly blow that should be expected from the first maritime country in the world'.

This enabled him to keep in touch with naval affairs and he campaigned for the abolition of the Press Gang and the whole system of impressment in wartime. As his wife put it, 'He considered that by offering a fair bounty on entering the service, and that service to be of limited duration, men would be found willing to serve on board men-of-war – would be glad to do so: the heart-rending scenes that continually present themselves along the sea-coast and river banks would be terminated.'

The Admiralty considered him something of an authority on technical matters. When, at the end of 1827, he was crossing the Channel in the Admiralty yacht, he was accompanied by three steam-vessels – the

Lightning, Meteor and *Echo* – and the Board asked him to be 'particularly attentive to the relative properties of the several steam-vessels and report which of them you consider best adapted for sea service to carry a gun in the event of war'. Hoste watched the three little ships wallowing in a gale off the North Foreland then, when the weather moderated, on a trial of speed across to Calais, paddles thrashing. In his view the *Lightning* was 'infinitely preferable . . . both as to stability and speed'.

As, at that time, British naval opinion generally regarded steam-ships as being most valuable as tugs to tow sailing warships into action during adverse wind conditions, Hoste's comment on their properties as warships themselves marked a significant step in naval evolution and helped the beautiful sailing-ships, which he loved so well, towards obsolescence.

The family settled near Southampton – at Itchen Ferry Cottage at Hamble and at Hamble House – and Sir William occupied his free time in sailing, hunting, gardening and reading. His health still gave cause for worry but, in 1825, after the birth of two more children, Priscilla and Wyndham, he was offered an appointment that carried the highest peacetime prestige. This was the command of the royal yacht *Royal Sovereign,* which would involve occasional short voyages in a beautiful little ship and the care of illustrious passengers. After his frigates, she must have seemed almost a plaything. A three-masted ship, launched the year before Trafalgar, she was fitted with every possible comfort, her hull encrusted with gilded carving that included lyre-playing cupids and decorations round her ports fashioned like oval picture-frames.

It was appropriate that Hoste's first employment was to ferry Nelson's old friend the Duke of Clarence from Antwerp to Yarmouth, a gale giving him the chance to demonstrate his seamanship and earn the gratitude of the future King William IV to 'the favourite *élève* of his early and lamented friend Lord Nelson'. There were other royal personages to be carried to and fro across the North Sea and Channel but these duties did not interfere unduly with family life or with jaunts to London. There Hoste joined several of the newly-fashionable gentlemen's clubs including the United Service, Boodle's, the Travellers' and the Thatched House. He kept up with politics, patronized naval charities and the Bible Society and opened an account at Hatchard's bookshop in Piccadilly, where his taste was for the latest history or biography, such as James's Naval History or Medwin's Life of Byron.

There were old friends to see or correspond with, among them three of his first lieutenants: Dunn, whom he met again in one of his clubs; O'Brien, only promoted to post captain in 1821, who had a comfortable house at Hoddesdon in Hertfordshire; Hood, whose legs had become paralysed as result of a spinal injury suffered when boarding an enemy in the Adriatic, and was being cared for in a Devon cottage by his wife.

Not all reminders of the war were so agreeable. While his own attempts to lay hands on all the prize-money to which he felt entitled were enmeshed in interminable legal correspondence – since his share had to be balanced with other claims to shares in the same capture – he often found himself in judgement upon the lesser claims of his former sailors. Letters signed by half-forgotten names from the muster-books of his ships, as far distant in time as the *Mutine*, arrived with humbly-worded requests for his endorsement of a claim to prize-money, pension or a place at the Royal Naval Hospital at Greenwich.

Sometimes these brought back happy memories but occasionally a name rose from the past like a drowned corpse to the surface. One was a plea for help from a man he had saved from hanging for an 'unnatural act' by hurriedly discharging him from the *Mutine*. Another was a veiled attempt at blackmail from a sailor who had been deafened by gunfire at the Battle of Lissa and claimed that he had been discharged for accusing Hoste of cowardice in the action; this he hotly denied but suggested that his old captain could clear his own name of such false accusations by confirming that he had been honourably discharged and was therefore worthy of a pensioner's vacancy at Greenwich.

Such little worries were not exclusive to discontented former ship-mates. His own family was in trouble again. Some had done well: for George there was a lieutenant-colonelcy, a knighthood, a wife and five children and a country house in Norfolk; for Teddy there was a prospering naval career; for Jane there was a successful marriage into a county family. But James seemed to be following his father in more ways than the taking of holy orders.

He, too, regarded William's prize-money as a convenient reserve to meet extravagances, such as a visit to Cheltenham with some friends, ostensibly to relieve biliousness. 'My dear William,' he wrote in 1824, 'A visit to Cheltenham must be attended with some little expense and as I am *hard up* at this moment I should feel for ever grateful if you could supply me with a little of the needful.'

In the same year, James attempted to acquire a living in the nearby parish of Longham by making a small financial offer to the incumbent and threatening that, if he refused to accept, the family's old friend Mr Coke would have him moved without compensation. The rector complained to Coke about such intimidation and was assured that his position was secure. Even so, two years later, James Hoste was enjoying a sinecure as 'perpetual curate' of Longham, although excused pastoral duties on the grounds that there was no residence for him in the parish.

Yet this was trivial in comparison with the troubles of their father. Dixon Hoste was now aged seventy-three, gouty and lonely since his wife had died following a stroke in 1820, but his profligacy was unabated. Coke had absolved him from all his debts but was now well aware of his former friend's failings and there was no more money available from that source, so the old parson turned his attention to another substantial Whig landowner, Colonel Keppel, a member of the family that had long been close friends of the Cokes. Inevitably Keppel found the usual difficulty in retrieving interest, let alone the repayment of his loan.

Dixon Hoste must have known that Keppel, like Coke, would not wish to see an elderly clergyman committed to a debtors' prison – he had even felt confident enough to complain to Coke's agent in what the latter considered 'most insulting' terms about the time it was taking to build his new rectory – but tradesmen were a different matter and held no such scruples.

There were several long-standing tradesmen's bills awaiting payment and finally, early in 1824, one of his creditors, a Norwich grocer, demanded immediate payment, taking the necessary legal action to enforce it or commit the debtor to prison. James Hoste first asked his brother George for support but this was refused unless other members of the family also contributed. So he appealed to William, saying that he was 'dreadfully down in the dumps' at the prospects and that only he and George could save the family's honour.

Soon after, Dixon Hoste left his new rectory prepared for a long absence with, as James put it, 'no other prospect but that of confinement in Norwich Castle'. Next evening he returned with the news that 'in consequence of some irregularity in the proceedings against him, he had been enabled to escape the disgrace of imprisonment!!' When James asked exactly what had happened, his father 'avoided all communication on the subject'.

This financial crisis the old man was able to survive by pledging all his furniture against his debt and in the confidence that neither his sailor nor his soldier son would allow him to go to prison. But his lifelong struggle with his own extravagance had not much longer to run. In the December of 1826, after forty-two years as rector of his parish, Dixon Hoste died. He was buried beside his wife beneath a black marble slab, inscribed with an affectionate epitaph by his children, in the choir of his church, appropriately at the feet of the grandiose monuments to his patrons, the Cokes. His place was taken by Edward Keppel, the parson son of the last of the Norfolk families of whom he had taken advantage.

For Sir William there was compensation for these humiliations in his new connections with royalty and in this he owed much to his wife. While, as captain of the royal yacht, he was a charming host, who always made sure that the ship was well stocked with champagne, and a seaman to inspire confidence on the roughest night afloat, it was Lady Harriet who cemented his popularity by making friends with his regular passenger, the Duchess of Clarence, who would, before long, become Queen Adelaide.

The Hostes had moved to Cobham so as to be nearer to London and the Court and also because most of the *Royal Sovereign*'s voyages were made to or from the Thames. Here, after a spell at sea in bad weather, Sir William could restore his injured health with rest and his passion for riding and gardening. Yet gradually his health deteriorated and, after one uncomfortable voyage with the Clarences, the Duchess wrote to his wife, 'I am truly sorry, my dear Lady Harriet, to learn that Sir William Hoste is so unwell and hope it is not in consequence of our travels by sea . . .'

In the same letter, the future queen demonstrated the degree of intimacy that had developed between her and her new confidante: '. . . I am not well myself. I have suffered horrible pain in my face which is swollen to such a degree that I am more like a *monstre* than a human being; and I own I am vain enough not to show myself to the Public in my present State of ugliness altho' I am perfectly aware that I *never* have been a beauty. If you can call tomorrow I will let you in, my dear Lady Harriet, for you will pity me and not laugh at my present misfortune.'

The consequences of this voyage with the Duchess of Clarence, which was to bring her mother, the Dowager Duchess of Saxe-Meinengen, over from Calais to Dover, were more serious than she realized. Although he was in constant attendance on the royal party, he had had a high fever and, in the privacy of his cabin, had for the first time coughed up blood. On his return home, his condition worsened so drastically that his eldest son was called home from boarding school.

To an old naval friend who called, Hoste confided that he was dying of tuberculosis, which drew a reply that echoed the last wishes of Nelson: 'If it should unhappily prove as you foresee . . . you will feel assured that your children are left a legacy to the country.' Facing his illness with stoicism, he only once allowed himself to speak his thoughts to his family. His wife, who was with him as he rested, described the moment: 'On looking at his children, who were one morning quietly occupied near him, "Had it pleased God," he said, "to spare my life, I should have had great pleasure in seeing them grow up." But no sooner was it said, than the thought had passed; for quietly drawing his hand over the slightly tinged eyelids, the heavenly spirit again beamed on his calm and still brilliant countenance.'

The family had moved to London so as to have the most highly-recommended doctors at hand but, in the spring of 1828, he seemed to make a remarkable recovery and they took a house at Petersham, on the Thames near Richmond, so that he could again go riding in the country. His old vigour seemed to return and he even claimed to be free of disease until a chill October brought a recurrence of the symptoms. They returned to Cobham and depression overcame the invalid, especially at 'the sight of the flower-garden, which he had cultivated with his own hands, and laboured incessantly to adorn in every part, appeared to bring only a sadness of recollection'.

The scenes of his recent, active years were too poignant to bear and they quickly returned to London and Hoste was soon confined to his bed. There was now no hope of recovery but his courage was unbroken. On 6th December, he died at the age of forty-eight years – his years almost matching those of Horatio Nelson.

He was buried in the churchyard of the new and elegant St John's Wood Chapel to the north-west of the Regent's Park and, almost at once, his brother-officers held a meeting to organize a subscription to commission a suitable monument in either Westminster Abbey or St Paul's Cathedral. Suitably, his statue was set up in the latter next to that of Nelson and only a matter of yards from the tomb of his 'second father'.

Grief was expressed with unbridled emotion by Catherine Hood, who was caring for her crippled husband Silas in their cottage at Ivybridge. She wrote and sent to Lady Harriet a funeral ode beginning, 'Where is the spirit of the Hero fled?', a rhetorical question which she answered with:

> *Where battles rage no more, nor cannons roar,*
> *He's safely landed on a peaceful shore,*
> *Removed from mortal fray;*
> *And now promoted to the highest post,*
> *He shines, no earthly, but an heavenly Hoste,*
> *In realms of endless day!*

William Hoste was mourned by those who had known him as a generous and charming friend, a bold commander and a man of deep loyalties. While much was made of his reputation as 'a second Nelson', those who had met both men, or made a study of their professional careers, knew that this was, despite Hoste's achievements, no more than graceful flattery. Nelson had been unique and a genius who could be emulated but never equalled.

While his naval friends may not have realized it at the time, they mourned not a second Nelson but the first of Nelson's professional heirs, the first of thousands to follow in the pattern that he had designed. During the hundred years of peace that followed the Napoleonic Wars, or in the turmoil that came after, naval officers were urged to follow the example of Nelson. But, in the event, the attitudes and ideals that they emulated – the dash, the initiative, the relative humanity and the lack of political motivation – were usually more those of Hoste. There could never be another Nelson but there were – to the abiding benefit of the Royal Navy – many in the pattern of Hoste.

The grief of Lady Harriet Hoste was intense. Although she could continue to enjoy the company of her husband's many admiring friends and her friendship with the Duchess of Clarence would ensure her security and, as it turned out, a grace-and-favour apartment at Hampton Court, a particular anguish was that her six children would grow up without so warm-hearted and exciting a father. Of some consolation to her was the reading of the many hundreds of letters that William had written to his family and which had been preserved so that, at least, she could tell them stories of his adventures.

Perhaps the idea came from Captain O'Brien, the old first lieutenant of the *Amphion*, who, in contented, domestic retirement, was thinking of writing an account of his life: the shipwreck and captivity, the escapes and the battles in the Adriatic. What is certain is that, a year after Sir William's death, his widow determined that his life must be recorded as an inspiration to his children. There would be plenty of material to draw upon: his letters, suitably edited; his dispatches printed in the *London Gazette*; perhaps even the memories of his old shipmates.

The compilation of such a work would be a formidable undertaking, one demanding the services of an experienced historian. Then somebody put forward the name of Colonel William Napier, the most successful historian of the year, the second of whose four projected volumes of *The History of the War in the Peninsula and in the South of France* had just been published. He was, moreover, a Whig, like the Hostes and the Walpoles, and, as a distinguished professional soldier, would handle his precious material with attention to accuracy and taste.

When he received her letter asking for a meeting, Napier found himself in a quandary. The comforting of young women in distress had, in peacetime, become almost as frequent a duty as the acceptance of death in war. To the widows of brother-officers who had died in the breach at Badajoz or the infantry squares at Waterloo, he would not only praise their manly virtues but, as a newly-famous military historian, could put their agony into an historical perspective that might make it appear worthwhile.

This case, however, was different. He had hardly known Captain Hoste, who had, in any case, been a naval officer. Something of his achievements he knew, yet these, coming between Trafalgar and Waterloo, had been over-shadowed by events that could be seen to have had more direct and immediate effect upon the course of the war against Napoleon.

But he had to visit this widow. Lady Harriet had been a Walpole and was therefore from as staunch a Whig background as his own; indeed, her late husband seemed to have contributed generously to the political funds of the cause in their native Norfolk. It was not comfort that she wanted, he knew, but literary advice. A biography of Sir William was to be written and the author she had in mind was himself. While work on his own book would preclude this, he could hardly refuse to look over the material upon which such a book would be based and offer what advice he could.

Whatever reluctance Napier may have felt was dispelled on meeting the young widow and the youngest of her six children, Wyndham. He was a warm-hearted and sentimental man, who had even shaved off the sweeping cavalry whiskers, of which he had been so proud, when they had frightened his own children.

He was moved enough by Lady Harriet ('Poor thing! it was very melancholy to see her . . .') but, as he told his wife, her youngest son quite turned his head. 'He has his father's dark hazel eyes, golden locks and a beautiful, rich, though fair colour in his cheeks; but his face is so oval, his features so beautiful, his look so sweet, so innocent, that I thought it was a girl, and such a girl as was never seen on earth before. He is five years old, large and well made, but scarcely human in grace and loveliness.'

Even so, he was taken aback when shown the papers he had agreed to assess. They proved to be many hundreds of documents, mostly 'an ill-assorted heap of letters', written from the time her husband had gone to sea at the age of twelve. He could only take them home and start to read, having promised to give Lady Harriet his opinion on their literary worth.

As he read letter after letter, the writing changing from a rounded schoolboy hand to an impatient scrawl, the portrait of a man emerged that was far from his own ideal of the intellectual man of action with liberal Whig attitudes. 'He was unquestionably a very able seaman, a very bold man, persevering, full of resources and capable of inspiring his men to undertake anything,' he wrote. 'But then I find no trace of any general views on politics or of war. His speculations on affairs are very few . . . which is quite worthy of Lord Nelson's school.'

That was the trouble. Lady Hoste had told him that, as he already knew, there were those, including the notorious Lady Hamilton, who had described Sir William as 'a second Nelson'. But he could not possibly have explained to the widow that, for him, this was no recommendation. In his view Nelson, a Tory, had held the most simplistic views on world affairs, and this Hoste certainly emulated: 'Everybody opposed to England are always "rascals, damned rascals". Napoleon is a charlatan, until the splendour of his actions at last reluctantly forces from him the confession that his talents are wonderful . . . The world can't be at peace until *"Boney is killed"* and such trash as that.'

Summing up, Napier wrote, 'Still he was a fine fellow and would, under a better master than Lord Nelson, and in a better school than our Navy, have been a *very* fine fellow.'

Returning the papers to Lady Harriet, he enclosed a tactful letter explaining that the pressure of his own work prevented him from writing or editing the book she had in mind. But he had marked some letters as being particularly important, adding that to do more 'would require months of careful examination'. He then suggested that the letters should be published together with 'a short explanatory and introductory sketch of him'. He ended on an encouraging note: 'It must be done with vigour and judgement . . . To do it ill would be a crime against the memory of a great and good man.'

She was disappointed but not downcast and, with a surge of enthusiasm that would have done credit to her husband, decided that she would edit the memorial volume herself for the future inspiration of their children. First, the letters would be arranged in chronological order to be edited individually. Some subjects would not be for public eyes: William's relations with other women could be included only when they illustrated his natural gallantry; the appalling profligacy of his father, the parson, could not be ignored but could be minimized; and William's distressing tendency to use sailormen's oaths and expressions could be omitted, together with other language that was unworthy of his nature. It would be truer to this if he had written to his brother or sister that he longed to see 'your dear countenance' rather than 'your dear old phiz'.

There would be others who could help with reminiscences; middle-aged men who, twenty years ago or more, had trod a deck with him. So letters of enquiry were written to a retired admiral in Kensington and a captain in Hertfordshire; to a doctor, a parson and a Pall Mall clubman; to a member of the House of Lords and a paralysed pensioner in a country cottage; to Cheltenham and to Southend.

Gradually their replies arrived. Most remembered him well but were at a loss for any telling anecdote; one had lost his journal of those days, while another had found his; some wrote with flowery flattery, others with seamanlike practicality. At last she felt ready to write and, her mind ringing with flamboyant phrases, took out a little notebook and, in a bold and aggressive hand, wrote of the youth of her dead hero, 'His mind, while tender in prime op'ning, was bent to strenuous virtue . . .'

NOTES ON SOURCES

Original sources.
The Hoste Papers: recorded on microfilm at the National Maritime Museum, Greenwich; the originals currently in the possession of J. A. L. Franks Ltd; the National Maritime Museum; the Royal Archives, Windsor Castle; and the McCarthy Collection.
Llangattock Papers: Nelson Museum, Monmouth.
Holkham Estate Letter-books and Holkham Hall game-books: Holkham Hall, Norfolk.
Fremantle Papers: Buckinghamshire County Library, Aylesbury, Bucks.
Journal of Captain W. F. J. Matthews, Royal Marines, of HMS Eagle: National Maritime Museum, Greenwich.
Admiralty Letters, ships' logs and muster books: Public Record Office, London.
State Archives at Dubrovnik and Kotor, Yugoslavia.
Archives of the *Musée de la Marine*, Paris.

SHORT BIBLIOGRAPHY

Anderson, R. C. *Naval Wars in the Levant* (1952).

Blomefield, Francis. *History of the County of Norfolk* (1807).

Bruce, H. A. *The Life of General Sir William Napier* (1864).

Dillon, Vice-Admiral Sir William. *Dillon's Narrative* (1956).

Fisković, Cvito. *Viški Spomenici* (1968).

Fothergill, Brian. *Sir William Hamilton* (1969).

Fremantle, Ann (ed.). *The Wynne Diaries* (1935–8).

Hennequin, M. *Biographie Maritime* (3 vols. 1835–7).

Hoste, Lady Harriet. *The Memoirs and Letters of Captain Sir William Hoste* (1833).

Hoste, G. H. *Service Afloat* (1887).

James, William. *The Naval History of Great Britain 1793–1820* (1837).

Jones, Mrs Herbert. *Sandringham Past and Present* (1895).

Ketton-Cremer, R. W. *Norfolk Portraits* (1944).

Ketton-Cremer, R. W. *A Norfolk Gallery* (1958).

Lewis, M. A. *The Social History of the Royal Navy 1793–1815* (1960).

Mahan, Captain A. T. *The Influence of Sea Power upon the French Revolution and Empire* (1892).

Matcham, M. Eyre. *The Nelsons of Burnham Thorpe* (1911).

Milošević, Miloš. *Godišnjak-Pomorskog Muzeja u Koforu*. Nos 14 and 15 (1966–7).

Murray, John (ed.). *Lord Byron's Correspondence* (1922).

Naish, G. P. B. *Nelson's Letters to his Wife* (1958).

Nicolas, Sir Harris. *The Letters and Dispatches of Lord Nelson* (1844–6).

Novak, Grga. *Vis* (1961).

O'Brien, Captain Donat Henchy. *My Adventures during the Late War* (1902).

O'Byrne, William. *Naval Biographical Dictionary* (1849).

Parry, Ann. *The Admirals Fremantle* (1971).

Pemberton, Charles Reece. *The Autobiography of Pel. Verjuice* (1929).

Pocock, Tom. *Nelson and His World* (1968).

Raikes, the Rev. Henry. *Memoir of the Life and Services of Vice-Admiral Sir Jahleel Brenton* (1846).

Stirling, A. M. W. *Coke of Norfolk and His Friends* (1908).

Thursfield, Rear-Admiral H. G. (ed.) *Five Naval Journals 1789–1817* (1951).

Warner, Oliver. *A Portrait of Lord Nelson* (1958).

Warner, Oliver. *The Life and Letters of Vice-Admiral Lord Collingwood* (1965).

Wilkinson, Sir J. Gardner. *Dalmatia and Montenegro* (1848).

Woodward, David. *The Russians at Sea* (1965).

The Dictionary of National Biography.
The Naval Chronicle.
Correspondence de Napoléon Ier.

INDEX